YOUTH AND SUBCULTURE AS CREA
CREATING NEW SPACES FOR RADICAL YOUTH WORK

Hans Arthur Skott-Myhre

Radical youth work is gaining popularity as a means of teaching adults how, in collaboration with youth, they can challenge dominant ways of knowing. This study uses two particular subcultures, skinheads and punks, to explore how constructions of subcultures in time, language, space, body practice, and identity offer alternative ways of understanding youth-adult relationships. In doing so, it investigates youth work as a radical political process and suggests a new approach to current subculture theory.

In *Youth and Subculture as Creative Force*, Hans Arthur Skott-Myhre interviews six youths who identify themselves as members of either punk or traditional skinhead subcultures. He discusses the results of these interviews and demonstrates how youth perspectives have come to inform his understanding of himself as a youth worker and scholar. Youth subcultures, he argues, have considerable potential for improving relations between youths and adults in the postmodern capitalist world. Drawing on Marxist, Foucauldian, and postmodernist theory, Skott-Myhre uses the subjective formations outlined in his study to offer recommendations for constructing legitimate radical youth work that takes into account the perspectives of young people.

HANS ARTHUR SKOTT-MYHRE is an associate professor in the Department of Child and Youth Studies at Brock University.

HANS ARTHUR SKOTT-MYHRE

Youth and Subculture as Creative Force

Creating New Spaces for Radical Youth Work

UNIVERSITY OF TORONTO PRESS
Toronto Buffalo London

© University of Toronto Press Incorporated 2008
Toronto Buffalo London
Printed in Canada

Reprinted in paperback 2009

ISBN 978-0-8020-9164-2 (cloth)
ISBN 978-1-4426-0992-1 (paper)

Printed on acid-free paper

Library and Archives Canada Cataloguing in Publication

Skott-Myhre, Hans Arthur
    Youth and subculture as creative force : creating new spaces for
    radical youth work / Hans Arthur Skott-Myhre.

    Includes bibliographical references (p.[187]-194) and index.
    ISBN 978-0-8020-9164-2 (bound) – ISBN 978-1-4426-0992-1 (pbk.)

    1. Youth.   2. Subculture.   3. Social work with youth.
    4. Youth workers – training of.   I. Title.

HQ796.S517 2007   305.242   C2007-903917-0

The University of Toronto Press acknowledges the financial assistance to its publishing program of the Canada Council for the Arts and the Ontario Arts Council.

University of Toronto Press acknowledges the financial support for its publishing activities of the Government of Canada through the Book Publishing Industry Development Program (BPIDP).

Contents

Acknowledgments

Special thanks to:
  My son, David Skott-Myhre, who was the inspiration for this project.

And to the other skins and punks who contributed their time and expertise. Without them this book would not have been possible:
  Jessica Awes
  Daniel Fala
  Ted Howard
  Michelle Anderson
  Emily Jacobsen

For their conscientious and extremely helpful reading and editing of the text I owe an immense amount of gratitude to Amy Levine, Gauti Sigthorsson, Jaime Nikolau, Meagan Middleton, Nicole Dawson, and Shauna Pomerantz.

For intellectual guidance and inspiration I want to thank Cesare Casarino, Tom Pepper, Rosemarie Park, Michael Baizerman, and Gary Leske.

Further appreciation goes to my wife, Kathleen Skott-Myhre, for all her support and encouragement; and to my parents, Nils and Celinda Skott-Myhre, for instilling in me a tradition of intellectual inquiry and an appreciation for complex ideas.

Preface

In the summer of 1976 I was living and writing as a street poet in Seattle, Washington. I had left the university following the completion of my bachelor's degree, determined that I would not return and be co-opted by the stifling confines of that bourgeois institution. Working in a yarn factory on the overnight shift and writing poetry during the afternoons filled my workdays. Giving readings in coffeehouse bars and on the street comprised my days off. The poetry readings were part of a collective called the Dogtown Poetry Group. As a subculture within subcultures, we had a vision about poetry and poets. We also had an ethos that included at its centre a commitment to breaking the rules and reshaping the game.

One evening we were giving a reading at a local coffeehouse in the university district. As we finished, we were approached by a group of young men. They asked us if we would like to read our poetry in between bands at an upcoming punk rock show. They said that they thought our poetry would mesh well with punk culture.

While none of us were well acquainted with what punk had become in 1976, we were all very familiar with the origins of punk in the work of the Velvet Underground, Television, Iggy Pop, and more recently, the Sex Pistols. We were also aware of the connections between beatniks such as Allen Ginsburg and William Burroughs and the early punk movement. This connection had been overtly made in the work of punk poet and musician Patti Smith. We saw ourselves within this lineage of punk and poetry, and so when the young men who had invited us to their show said our poetry would fit with their music, it made sense to us. The prospect of the show was, for us, exciting in its possibility for new links between punk and poetry.

The show, however, was not at all what we expected. As it turned out there was a great deal we didn't understand about punk culture. Correspondingly, our hosts from within punk culture didn't understand or appreciate what we were trying to do. Whatever it was that they had first heard in our poetry, their companions at the show did not hear it.

The crowd was loud and rowdy and not at all in the mood to hear spoken poetry. They wanted to hear loud, assaultive punk music, not surrealist-dadaist poetry. For our part, we considered our poetry a kind of street fighting. This kind of tough, no-quarter-taken poetry was best read, in our opinion, under the influence of several beers. In such condition we were in a mood to take on anyone, and after about five minutes of loud and rowdy calls for the return of the music, I remember standing and challenging the entire audience to a fist fight if they didn't quiet down. Much to my surprise, they did – a reaction that marked that particular crowd of punks as most likely poseurs. The evening descended from there and ended with one young man telling us that our poetry was not sufficiently violent to sustain the audience's attention. As a response to this critique, one of our members pulled out a large buck knife and asked the critic whether or not he would like to experience real violence first hand. The invitation was declined, and we left the show very shortly afterwards with a bad taste in our mouths about the whole thing.

This clash of subcultures faded over time as I grew older. Faded, that is, until punk re-entered my life in the summer of 1998. Like many people I had assumed the death of punk somewhere around the demise of the Sex Pistols. It was not a death I grieved much, although in the back of my mind, the old connections of early punk and poetry kept a certain part of punk mythical. But punk had died like the other anarchist movements of my youth: the White Panther Party, the Yippies, the Hog Farm, the Diggers, the Merry Pranksters, the Lamar Harrington Collective, Girls Together Outrageously, 62nd Street House, and others. They were gone and while their spirit might continue to inform my private ethos, my days of anarchist companionship and collective action were long since past and gone.

Like the news of Mark Twain's death, however, reports of the death of punk were greatly exaggerated. It was my son who brought punk back and opened that world to me in ways that have both confirmed my connections to punk as well as my critique of it. As I have watched the transformation of my son from David the skater to Dirty Dave the punk to Dirty the grunge punk and to Dave the hardcore punk with the stage name Dirty and then Dave the Trad skin,[1] I have been profoundly altered. As I have watched his band evolve from the first mixed group of punks and non-punks to the current combination of hardcores and Trad skins, I have been informed about how our lives are simultaneously continuous and discontinuous. I have thought a great deal about tradition, lineage, connection, belonging, and pregenerative generations. I have been forced back on my bourgeois self in ways that challenge my comforts and remind me of my younger intentions. In short, his life and culture are transformative for me in important and evocative ways.

It is my relationship with my son and his friends that forms the core of this book. The conversations I have had with them over a number of years about being punk and skin is the ground out of which this writing grows. For this project, I talked in depth with David and five of his friends. These six young people formed a core around a punk band that the three young men had founded in high school and which still exists as of this writing, although with slightly different membership. The young men had all started out as punks in high school but two of the three had become skinheads, moving the style of music gradually away from raw punk towards hard-core street punk with definite Oi influences.[2] In addition to music, clothing style and fashion are essential elements of the scene for punks and skinheads. All six of these six young people had at one time dressed fully punk, with varying arrays of Mohawks, tri-hawks, bi-hawks, body piercings, safety pins, studded leather jackets with stencils and patches, bondage pants with zippers, and Doc Martens. Now, however, the two skinheads wore flight jackets and jeans, Ben Sherman or Fred Perry shirts with traditional cropped hair and tattoos. They had removed their piercings and wore suspenders (braces), pins, and flag patches. The remaining punk now wore more hardcore street attire including the requisite Mohawk, with blue jeans, t-shirts and studded leather jacket over top. Of the two skinheads, one is biracial. For the purposes of this writing I will refer to the biracial skinhead as Gary and the other skin as Frank. The remaining punk I will call Tony.

---

1 Traditional skinheads are non-racist skins who trace their lineage to the original Jamaican-English skins.
2 Oi refers to working-class punk rock associated with skinheads; also called street punk.

The young women I talked with had followed a similar trajectory through high school. All of them starting out as punk, wearing mini-skirts with torn fishnet stockings, Mohawks, studded leather jackets, and body piercings. One of the three had stayed traditionally punk while one went on to become a skin-bird with the Chelsea hairstyle, flight jacket, Doc Martens, flags, and pins. The other young woman vacillated between the styles, sometimes combining elements of punk and skin while at other times going fully punk or just hardcore rock and roll. None of the young women were directly involved with bands, although all of them played a major roll in the scene.

I remember a party held in the basement of my house that was attended by a large number of skinheads. At some point after my wife and I had gone to bed, there was a fight between two quite large skin-head boys, during which they began to break things. One of the young women from this study single-handedly broke up the fight, in spite of the fact that she is quite diminutive in stature. I was later told that she reached up and grabbed the main offender by the ear and dragged him into the next room, where she gave him a stern lecture on how he should respect this house because the house was respectful of skin-heads. The result was that my wife and I were wakened at around 3 a.m. by knocking on our door. When we called out 'Come in,' a very large, sheepish skinhead poked his head in and apologized profusely for causing any disruption to our household. I will refer to the young woman who prompted this apology as Betty, the traditional punk as Alice, and the other young woman as Sue.

In this book, I hope to show that youth subculture is not alien or sep-arate but is integrally involved in the most intimate constitution of the world young people and adults share together,[3] and in the possible worlds they might mutually produce if the space between them was collapsed and their differences turned to productive ends. Perhaps then we could find ways to hear what young people have to tell us. As Frank put it,

Well, you know, there's nobody wants to hear what you have to say. Everybody has their stereotype for us and that's what they want. You know, and the media's been like real nice making good stereotypes for us,

---

3 The terms 'youth' and 'youth subculture' will be used interchangeably to some degree throughout the book. As I hope will become clear, the distinction between 'mainstream youth' and 'subcultural youth' is one that hides more than it reveals.

you know. And you know, everybody really wants to keep their stereotype cause it's a lot easier to have a scapegoat than it is to have a friend.
You know, and, I mean, if people listen to us they'll understand that we're
more there for them than we are for anybody else.

A project such as this, which brings together my world as an academic with the world of young people, inevitably involves a process
of translation. I will endeavor to walk a line between two very different sets of descriptions: those that emerge through the interviews
with the youth identifying as punk or skinhead, and my own personal and academic reflections on those interviews. This book is thus
a kind of auto-ethnography in which I will take the information from
my involvement in the world of the skins and punks I have known
and combine it with what others have written from both inside and
outside that world. I will then reflect on that material in three ways:
first, as an academic reflection on youth and youth subculture to see
if it offers us any insight into our current historical moment; second,
as a theoretical self-reflection on the nature of subculture as a set of
youth-adult relations; and finally, as a self-reflection on the implications of these theories and insights for constituting a new set of
youth-adult relations that collapses the binary categories of youth
versus adult. I will define this new kind of youth-adult relations as
radical youth work.

In order to begin this process of collapsing the separation between
young people and adults in their mutual constitution of present and
future worlds, we need to begin with what it means to be an adult
and to be a young person, both as social categories and as profoundly personal identities. To do that, I will argue that it is necessary to think about youth and adults as both produced by the dominant discourses in society and as capable of producing new
descriptions and possibilities for social forms and identities. In Part
One of the book, I will explore the possibility that youth subcultures
offer us an opportunity to rethink questions of identity, the use of
language, our definitions of the body, the use of time, and the use of
space. I will argue that these possibilities are directly related to, and
in some sense prefigure, significant elements of our current postmodern moment that have implications for both youth and adults in
the world they share. In Part Two, I will investigate the implications
of Part One for youth-adult relationships for practices within the
field of youth work. In addition, I will propose a new model of

youth work that builds on both postmodern theory and on what I have learned from the punks and skins I interviewed. Finally, the question of how to educate youth workers within the world of the postmodern will be explored, and a new pedagogy of youth work will be suggested.

PART ONE

What of Youth and Subculture?

1 The Question of Identity: To Perform Ourselves

To begin to think about the question of identity as both a social problem and a social possibility, we need to begin with that foundational aspect of Western society that underlies both identity and political relations between groups: the subject. In the traditional Western view there are two forms of the subject. The first of these, as outlined by Balibar (1994), is the *subjectus*. *Subjectus* is a term that 'refers to *subjection* or *submission*, i.e. the fact that a (generally) human person (man, woman or child) is *subjected to* the more or less absolute, more or less legitimate authority of a superior power, e.g., a "sovereign." This sovereign being may be another human or supra-human, or an "inner" sovereign or master, or even simply a transcendent (impersonal) *law'* (p. 8).

This is the subject with which we are all most familiar. The traditional relationship upon which many of our ideas about youth-adult relations are premised is that of the sovereign or king.[1] In this set of relations there is always someone who has the ultimate authority. In the Western nuclear family this is generally the parent. In the broader social context the parental authority over youth can be distributed to teachers, adult relatives, coaches, youth workers, religious leaders, police, or other functionaries of the state. Of course, parents and all adults are also subject as citizens to sovereign authority through their submission to a society of law. In this sense, a significant portion of our modern identities are formed and structured according to our relation to sovereign authority.

As Tarulli and Skott-Myhre (2006) have pointed out elsewhere, this subject is like the characters in the type of literature that is driven and

---

1 See Foucault (1976).

controlled by the author's voice. In such writing, the truths of the text are always subordinated to the author's ultimate authority over meaning. Like the characters in such texts, the subject as subjectus is defined in terms of its submission to an overarching authorial vision – its autonomy, creativity, and freedom are essentially closed off by the unitary, monologic voice of an omniscient other/self (Bakhtin, 1984).

The subjectus is a subject whose goal it is to be defined clearly and finally as a coherent set of descriptions and actions without any loose ends or unexplained aspects of character. Unfortunately, as a completed entity enclosed within itself, such a subject enjoys no existential surplus or 'breathing space' from which to undermine, challenge, or simply surprise the author-sovereign (Žižek, 1989).

To rethink the relationship between youth and adults as a field of possibility for worlds to come requires the ability to conceive of a different kind of subject, one that exceeds the traditional definitions of the psychological individual or the political citizen as subjectus. To rethink youth-adult relationships, we need to engage an alternative subject also found in Western thought, although given comparatively little attention: the *subjectum*.

The subjectum is not defined in relation to sovereign authority. Instead, it is defined through its ability to creatively produce itself. We are also all familiar with this subject as the creative personality found in artists, musicians, filmmakers, and children. Unfortunately, in Western society such creative self-production is considered something of a luxury granted to those individuals with extraordinary talent in particular artistic, entertainment, or athletic arenas.[2] The significant exception to this is children, who are allowed a certain latitude to creatively produce themselves, although always within the confines of adult sovereignty.

Subject to Capitalism

Ambivalence towards the creatively produced subject within capitalist society is explained by Marx (1978/1992, pp. 146–201) as the result of two developments within capitalism. The first of these is the need for capital to separate the subject from control over his own

---

2 Although it should be noted that within the regimes of postmodern capitalism such creative latitude is increasingly short-lived and tied to commercial viability rather than simple talent.

creative process. This is necessary because in order to create the conditions in which profit (capital) can be accumulated, the capitalist must own the means of creativity and production. In other words, the creative production of each subject must come under the sovereign control of the capitalist class so it can be turned towards the business of making money.[3] This separation of the subject from the products of her own creativity produces what Marx terms alienation. The subjectus under the sovereign regime of capitalism is precisely such an alienated subject. Indeed, it could be argued that it is just such alienation that underlies the rift between youth and adults, with youth comprising that ambiguous category of social subjects that still maintains some freedom over their own creative production.

Clearly, however, this limited freedom is severely eroded under conditions of late-stage capitalism, wherein all creative production becomes available for sale.[4] This second development, or what Marx (1993) called the moment of total subsumption, is the moment at which all types of production become available for exploitation. In such a moment any alternative to capitalism seems impossible or unlikely. It seems as though capitalism is the only possible system and that all aspects of life operate under its logic. While a full explication of this phenomenon is beyond our scope here, suffice it to say that as capitalism has taken hold globally, it has also deployed the rapid development of technological networks that reach into all aspects of human life. This expansion of technological capital goes beyond the hours we spend working and begins to include the time that we spend outside the workplace. As Hardt and Negri (2004) point out, under such conditions all of our creativity is turned towards profit, including the affective and communication skills used in our relationships; that is, the very ways in which we produce ourselves. Under these conditions, the desire for the freedom to creatively produce ourselves without the constraints of capitalist production makes the exploration of the subjectum, or the subject that is free to creatively act, imperative for any project that proposes youth-adult relations as the ground for producing new worlds.

---

3 See S. Thompson (2004) for a very nice explication of this problem in DIY punk.
4 See Quart (2003), Giroux (2000), and Negri (1996b).

The Subject That Is Not Subject to ...

Since the subjectum is premised in creativity itself, it is not limited by social category or defined by the narrow confines of the subjectus. Indeed, Hardt and Negri (2004) argue (following Spinoza) that the creative force of the subjectum is found outside any restriction placed upon it by the boundaries of the modern individual that demand a private social self separated from community. This is not to say, however, that such a subject is under the rule of the common community either. Indeed, the subjectum deploys both the radical difference found in each expressive capacity of the singular subject and the commonalities found between us in our connections and collisions within one another in the course of daily life.

In fact, I will argue here that the subjectum cannot be found in the singular subject alone as creative genius or child, or in the special circumstance of talent. Rather, the subjectum can only be found in the intersections where we come together to produce the world. Certainly one place where that occurs is in the sets of relations between the social categories called youth and those called adult. In this coming together we amplify the force of each creative singular subject. Such a subject is neither youth nor adult but is made up of the set of relations formed by the collision between both categories of social identity. Such relations are neither stable nor fixed but originate and extend themselves through a movement that is driven both by historical contingency and the contemporary shifts in the ways we now produce the postmodern world.

Subjects of Postmodernity

To speak of identity and subjectivity within the context of postmodernity is both complex and challenging. To do so, we must remember that the postmodern is a space between historical periods. It is neither the full ending of the modern period, with its grand and unifying narratives, nor whatever it is that will come next. It is in this sense a period of radical indeterminacy. To articulate the intersection of youth and adults as productive of new social worlds engages both these categories as definitionally in flux. Indeed, such flux provides more than adequate fuel for the many fields of inquiry, both modern and postmodern, that strive to make sense of adults and youth within the postmodern space.

In keeping with the theme of the subjectum, however, I propose to examine youth-adult relations as a question of creative force. Such force comprises the social categories of youth and adults in the sense of their production as a specific kind of social subjectivity. This is a peculiar kind of subjectivity that is never still. It exists ahead of our perception, like a horizon that recedes as we approach it. As soon as we think we know who we are, we can immediately see the possibility of who we might become. Both the person that we are in any given moment as well as the person we are becoming are products of all the interactions we have had with others. This also includes our own history of struggle, both personal and collective, in our sets of prescribed social roles such as worker, child, adult, youth, male, female, and so on. The question of particular interest here is: does the subjectum, as that subject which is in constant creative becoming, offer a position for rethinking youth-adult relations, one in which the social binary of youth-adult is collapsed into a relation that flees the social containment of both terms?

Put another way, I am proposing that youth and adults within the postmodern world cannot easily be reduced to fixed social categories or psychological constructs but must be seen, instead, as both historically laden and prophetic in their production of whatever it is that will come next. The question then becomes: how might we conceive of the relation between the terms 'adult' and 'youth'?

The Subject and Development

One of the main ways in which we tend to think of youth and adulthood is in terms of development. Certainly one of the defining characteristics of the two terms is premised on the idea that young people are developing into adults and that adults, in rather specific ways, are different from young people. This discourse that arises in modernist psychology produces a relationship of sovereignty and hierarchy between young people and adults that doesn't function particularly well within our definition of the subjectum. Deleuze and Guattari (1987) challenge the modern view when they propose that

> The ... child [does] not become; it is becoming itself that is a child ... The child does not become an adult any more than the girl becomes a woman; the girl is the becoming-woman of each sex, just as the child is the becoming-young of every age. Knowing how to age does not mean

remaining young; it means extracting from one's age the particles, the speeds and slownesses, the flows that constitute the youth of *that* age ... It is age itself that is a becoming-child. (p. 277)

Here, Deleuze and Guattari propose a model of child that is distinct from our more common conception of childhood as a space separate from the adult world, bounded by time and evolutionary development. Instead, they suggest a subject that never becomes adult nor remains young. Child, in their view, is taken out of developmental time or age and no longer refers to a subject that has a certain level of maturation. Indeed, child here refers to the creative expressions of life force, that is, the subjectum, that occur in different ways at different points in time for each subject. In this way we can say that child as a subjectivity never arrives but is constantly renewed as a unique expression of both location and time throughout the lifespan. Put another way, we might say that child as defined by Deleuze and Guattari is an event rather than a subject in the traditional sense.

This view of child exceeds the categories of childhood and threatens the bounded world of adulthood. It proposes that to be child goes beyond the current debates in child rights that argue that the child is a subject on its own without reference to adult status. It goes outside the ideologies of innocent childhood with its nostalgic yearnings for a lost Eden. It claims instead the status of child as a common attribute in all human subjectivity. In other words, child is not a period of time but instead a quality of creative force that is active in different ways at different times in the life of a subject. It is critical to those elements of the social realm that would dominate and appropriate the creative force of life, such as the modes of capitalism discussed above, that such a child be radically excluded from the world defined as adult. In this view, childhood as a space of absolute expressive desire must be produced as an outside or other to adulthood.

We might well say that in order to sustain the alienated subjectivity of late-stage capital, it is essential that child, youth, and adult must be maintained as radically separate subjects defined in time as moments that pass and cannot be regained. The world of the child, with its freedom of time and creativity, must appear radically separate and unobtainable to the 'mature' adult. Similarly, the world of the youth, with its relative creative freedom and capacity for 'resistance' and 'rebellion,' must be created as not only unavailable to the adult but unattractive and unhealthy as well. The adult's 'childish' desire to be fully and playfully creative must always be turned to the benefit of the dominant system. It is important to be constantly productive but not necessarily creative. The desires of the child to fully express herself must be made to seem a lost world to the adult.

The subjectum offers child as an attribute that both youth and adults have in common. It suggests that differences in age are non-hierarchical and that differences can be brought together for mutual creative benefit. The alternate subject implied here allows youth and adults to join together in creative collusion against the forces of containment and discipline that produce adults as 'doomed to dry up and settle down in the face of the reactive demands of the social and familial world ... Isn't childhood the name of vitality itself, of that force, captured at birth, which we continually betray in 'developing' ourselves?' (Zourabichvili, 1996, p. 211).

This is not to romanticize childhood or youth. As I have pointed out above, such subjects are equally imbricated in the social system of familial and social sovereignty described as the subjectus. Instead, the point is to reject the categorization of adolescence and childhood and recuperate youth and child as attributes of political force common to all human subjects rather than as binary, rigidly defined categories contrasted to adulthood. In short, I propose that we begin to conceptualize youth as subjectum, or what Deleuze and Guattari (1987) refer to as a becoming-child.

What of Youth?

Youth as a becoming-child holds an ambivalent position within the context of postmodern capitalist production. Indeed, youth is peculiarly apt as an example of becoming-child because of its status as the subject between. Youth as a social category is in constant mutation, both definitionally and temporally. Its boundaries have been notoriously malleable, ranging from the advent of puberty (a shifting target in a world in which young women of some countries enter puberty at age eight or younger) to the entry into adulthood (a similarly mutating target that ranges from ages eighteen to thirty).[5] One might well say that youth is a social category that neither fully arrives at its

5 This latter category has been dubbed the adultescent or adultolescent, which seems particularly apt for my argument here. The term began as a marketing strategy (see D. Reed, 'Hey Big Spender,' *Precision Marketing*, 17 June 1996) but entered the popular press with P. Tyre, K. Springen, and J. Scelfo, 'Bringing up Adultolescents,' *Newsweek*, 25 March 2002.

inception (it always holds traces of childhood) nor fully arrives into adulthood. This positioning of a subject that never fully arrives and cannot be digested or assimilated into the patterns of domination operates within the logic of Nietzsche's notion of the untimely. By the untimely, we are referring here to the production of a thoroughly postmodern subject that constantly creates an exception to the rules of domination through the expression of its own idiosyncratic force. Such a subject produces itself without ever making any effort to engage a transcendent outside to the mode of production within which it is situated.

Such a subject, who never arrives and never leaves, might well presage the advent of what Deleuze (1995) describes as a social subject inhered fully within a system of infinite deferral. Such a system of infinite deferral holds an ambivalent function for the subjectivities operating within its regime. For example, a system of infinite deferral can serve as a mode of domination through its denial of entry into any form of security or final fiscal or social stability, but as Hardt and Negri (2000) point out, such a system also produces new formations of the proletariat who through their exclusion from security or stability form new political forces. In this sense, the category of youth as becoming-subject holds the capacity of maintaining its status of in-between as a certain kind creative horizon of future possibility; a subjectum.

Youth as subjectum is premised in the moment of action. The possibility inherent in creative force is brought into being in the moment of the act. In this sense we might say that youth as subjectum is composed of things done rather than comprising any set of attributes associated with a category or set of taxonomic definitions. Youth, then, is constantly being brought into being at the edge of what has been called an event horizon.[6] This horizon, which we have already gestured towards, is made up of what is done in any moment. However, what is done is already over in the moment of instantiation, and so the horizon is always moving away from what has been done through the force of what has not been done yet. In this, youth never fully consists of the actions that we see but also includes all the creative force of acts which could have happened but haven't happened yet. The result is youth as the subject that never arrives, because it is always producing itself through the surplus of events not yet brought into being. In other words, youth as subjectum is not a particular age range or set of bio-

---

6 See Deleuze and Guattari (1994) and Bergson (1997).

logical criterion but instead a range of performances that never repeat themselves. By contrast, the mature adult, regardless of age, comprises nothing but repeat performances.

Youth as performative might well be seen as a series of acts;[7] each act fleeing the one that precedes it. In producing youth in this way, the subject as subjectum creates itself in the moment of the act. In Deleuzio-Guattarian terms, each act creates the boundaries of certain territory or territorializes the subject. That is to say, each act creates a possible set of definitions of the subject as a social or psychological category. This is not to leave out biology. The body acts as well, and in acting creates itself as also available to sets of categories and definitions. It is important to note, however, that no set of categories or definitions can fully capture the complex dynamism of creative force in any given action. Indeed, in this case the language of description falls short each and every time.

This shortfall, however, leaves a surplus not bounded by either definition or the act itself. This surplus escapes the territorializing effect of the initial act and its attendant definitions and again, in Deleuzio-Guattarian terms, deterritorializes the subject through the creative force of the next act. Youth, as a subjectum that comprises territorializing and deterritorializing performances, creates itself as series of events. These events are in constant productive interaction with other events and subjects. Each of these encounters produces new possibilities for exceeding the boundaries of definition prescribed by the limited view of the individual. In this sense, youth as subjectum in collision with others produces a space of unstable encounter, within which performances of time, language, space, body practice, and identification create what Deleuze and Guattari (1987) refer to as lines of flight. Lines of flight, for our purposes here, refer to escape routes from the structuring effects of dominant social forms. They are like a complex array of tunnels under and through society that split off in a multitude of new directions whenever they encounter a limit or obstacle. In this sense, the tunnels have no predetermined direction or end point but extend infinitely into the event horizon described above. Such tunnels, or lines of flight, are composed of creative force and provide avenues for movement across and within even the most repressive or oppressive societies.

---

7 The concept of the performative subject owes much to Judith Butler, whose ideas I will take up in some detail in the next chapter.

Youth as subjectum travels on such lines of flight in fleeing the constraints of definition or the social demand for repetitive acts and generate the lines through creative action. Such lines of flight contest the dominant modes of subjectivity through radical performances of alterity that both challenge definitions of youth produced by societal disciplines such as traditional psychology and biology, as well as provide new possibilities of intergenerational alliance. These new possibilities of creative alliance stem from our argument above that youth belongs to no age group or generational category but is a moment of creative action that can occur at any point within the life continuum.

This, of course, runs directly counter to the ways in which Western science and the disciplinary practices of schools and families have delineated young people. Under the regimes of capitalism and liberal democratic state forms, there has been considerable effort to control and mediate the creative force of the subjectum across the lifespan. Indeed, much of the discourse surrounding 'healthy' development has focused on the notion that young people should seek to become coherent, singular identities with a unitary psychological core self rooted in Western psychological notions of individuation, esteem, purpose, boundary, and assertion. Deviance from these normative formations is both an expected part of the disintegration and reintegration process predicted in the Western cultural formation of adolescence, and corrected as part of the transition to the privileges of a 'mature' adult. This construction of adolescence within Western capitalist culture serves multiple purposes and holds distinct political agendas, both culturally and economically. The political formation of subjectivity, developed through the disciplinary apparatus surrounding adolescence, has significant implications for new productions of subjectivity within the space of youth-adult relations. As Butler (1990) points out in relation to gender, 'If the "cause" of desire, gesture, act can be localized with the "self" of the actor, then the political regulations and disciplinary practices which produced that ostensibly coherent gender are effectively displaced from view. The displacement of a political and discursive origin of gender identity onto a psychological "core" precludes an analysis of the political constitution of the gendered subject and its fabricated notions about the ineffable interiority of its sex or its true identity' (p. 174).

Similarly, if one can make the claim, as we have, that the capacity to freely produce oneself through acts of creative force is inherently transgressive under capitalism, then those young people and adults engaged in performing themselves creatively become a marginalized population. If such a population can be localized within the psychological confines of the core self, then the political and cultural constructions of youth as subjectum are obscured from view. The creative force of youth becomes subject to the definitions of psychological development and emotional health within the taxonomic descriptions of adolescence, with its focus on deviance and pathology, risk and resilience. This shift attempts to appropriate the creative force of the subjectum within the constraints of the subjectus by constructing youth as a 'colonial subject ... constructed within "an apparatus of power which contains, in both senses of the word, an other knowledge: a knowledge that is arrested and fetishistic and circulates through colonial discourses that limited form of otherness, that fixed form of difference, that I have called the stereotype"' (Bhabha, as cited in Chambers, 1990, p. 27).

This stereotype of youth as core identity fixes the multiple possibilities of subjectivity, as created through an infinite variety of acts, within the rather narrow confines of an identity comprised of qualities, habitual responses, and predictable psychic structures. Such a core identity can only repeat its production within the limits of bounded knowledge and experience. All variance must be appropriated to this end and brought into circulation as a part of this repetitive circuit.

This is amplified when we take into consideration the fact that core identities, although comprised of idiosyncratic combinations of certain qualities and psychic capacities, are generally constellated around certain clusters of repeatable personality types, such as the type A personality, the artistic temperament, the obsessive compulsive, the compliant child, and so on. For young people, this categorizing is further intensified by descriptions of age-derived pathologies, such as attention deficit disorder or oppositional defiant disorder. Finally, young people in Western societies are defined by developmental psychology as incapable of fully producing a core self capable of full rationality, and as a result, lack the maturity necessary to make reasonable decisions about their lives.

Hence, constructions of youth that suggest they are capable of offering viable alternative constructions of society or subjectivity are discounted as not meaningful on the basis of the idealism, lack of maturity, or emotional instability attributed to youth. In addition, transience of purpose, focus, ideal, or identity is seen to confirm this construction of youth as a stereotyped transition to an idealized utopian maturity that is stable, continuous, and responsible to a core identity and function. To rethink this formulation requires an alternative construction of subjectivity that steps away from psychological subjective essentialism and constructs a different mapping of the self.

The traditional map of the self in the Western tradition includes the descriptive elements we have suggested thus far in terms of a core identity that entails a degree of coherence and stability, as well as an interior aspect bounded by the outlines of the body and the Freudian mechanisms of the psyche, with its unconscious and preconscious structures. Such a topography of surface and depth produces a subject that is contained and bounded. Healthy development, in fact, includes the development of 'ego boundaries' and the development of good social boundaries as well. Youth are considered to be in the process of developing such a bounded sense of self and, we are told, are in need of role modelling and instruction on the proper development and maintenance of a private interior space. Such a self, however, is a certain kind of incarceration, with all the limitations that this implies. It is the production of a social and personal self premised in the same process of territorialization we have associated with the subjectus.

Towards a New Map of the Subject

To challenge such a model, I propose a new mapping of the subjective that entertains the concept of the self not as a bounded interior but as a surface or plane. Such a shift means a move away from a geography of the self based on surface and depth similar to the commonly used psychoanalytic metaphor of the iceberg. In this traditional map the self consists of a structure in which the conscious mind is a small portion showing above the surface and the rest of the unconscious lies deep below the surface. Such a model splits the self between its desires, which arise from below, and the mediation of desires through the filter of the preconscious, which allows a small percentage of them into conscious awareness on the surface. This model of the self, based on the works of Freud (1963), constructs the self as always subject to the preconscious filters of social constraint. Interestingly, it is the full expression of life force which is mediated and constrained in its relation to the demands of any given historical social form.

If we expand this psychological explanation of the self by placing it within the context of the Marxist economic analysis of capitalism, we find a similarity in the role of mediation. In Marxist analysis, the life force of the subject as manifested in the creative activities of daily labour also comes from below. The force that builds the social realm is crafted through the self-production of life in concert with others. For capitalism to gain force, it must separate the conscious connection between an individual's activity and the production of society. To do this, capitalism must produce labour as though it were a product of capital itself. In other words, the actual source of social production that resides in the activities of each person must be relegated to a social unconscious that resides below the surface of social consensus. This social unconscious is then mediated by the ideological machinery of the social forms of capital: the state, the educational system, the nuclear family, the media, and so on. The conscious awareness of society must only accept the creative desires of its members as mediated through the lens of profit and appropriation.

The imbrication of the Freudian psychoanalytic model into the ideological apparatus of capital provides a powerful social construction of the self as fully mediated by the needs and demands of the dominant social system. The model of an interiorized, alienated, and mediated self produces a form of identity well suited to that of the subjectus.

An alternative approach might well be found in the philosophy of immanence, in which there is no interiority. For an immanent philosopher, the idea of depth or interiority has particular problems associated with the need to separate the world into binary categories such as inside and outside, depth and surface, and ideal and actual. Such categories immediately produce a distance between the material world and a world that is representative of the material world. All mediation is comprised of some set of binary categories which require negotiation. For example, in the Marxist analysis cited above, the material world of actual labour produces the relational and material conditions of the social world. The division of that world into the material world of labour and the symbolic world of value (money) creates a need for mediation between the two and obscures the actual nature of production. This obfuscation of the actual material source of what produces the world allows for the abstraction of such force to a symbolic level. By then defining the terms of the abstract symbolic ideal to its own advantage, capitalism can turn the creative force of the subjectum to its ends by recasting it as the subjectus.

For immanentists, the key is in conceptualizing life as a plane of force that has neither depth nor ideal outside. In such a conceptual framework the immanent plane of life produces itself through lines of force that criss-cross its surface, simultaneously composing and fleeing their own composition. In short, we have arrived again at a map that is highly suggestive of the subjectum. On this surface of immanent construction the self produces itself not as a fixed object but as a line of infinite extension. However, as Foucault (1975) points out, such a line is in constant collision with all the other lines running in all directions at once. At each point of collision something is produced that is composed of unpredictable elements of the lines involved.

The self produces itself out of all of the elements of a particular moment in time, including specific aspects such as new technology, new conceptual frameworks, historical developments, new encounters with other bodies, biochemical interactions, fragments of history and struggle, art, politics, the sciences (human and otherwise), and culture, to name but a few among many. This self-produced self is therefore made up of a heterogeneous array of mobile assemblages, an interplay of space and intersection. Such a 'perspective suggests an overlapping network of histories and traditions, a heterogeneous complexity in which positions and identities ... cannot be taken for granted, and are not interminably fixed but tend towards flux' (Chambers, 1990, p. 27).

Within the world of postmodern capital our concept of youth-self as self-producing is played out on planes of cultural pastiche and collage across the lifespan. Youth is constructed not as essential or core identity formation but as fractured and discontinuous lines of improvisational performance. Perhaps this can be seen most clearly in the identity formation we think of as youth subculture,[8] which is characterized not only by literal performances such as hip hop freestyling, punk/skin slam-dancing, mosh pit dynamics, and the constant recycled agglomerations of punk fashion, but also by the multitudinous splintering of subcultural trends, such as skinheads into old school, new school, SHARPs, street punks, crustys, mobs, and so on.

Youth and Subculture: Resistance and Flight

This shattering and dispersion of youth subcultural identity is not accomplished through self-conscious processes of analysis, categoriza-

---

8 It should be noted that the term 'youth subculture' is a contested one, particularly in the critiques of post-subculture literature. I will address this in some detail later.

tion, review, and reflection. Rather, it is an effect of radical performances of self.

> Well, punk comes from a billion different subcultures. Punk was about
> poor kids being fed up with shit. And just saying fuck everything. We're
> going to do it our way and we're going to have fun about it too. You
> know, it was, really punk was a bunch of kids who lost hope and decided
> to do their own thing. And when they decided to do their own thing I
> guess they sort of decided on some crazy dressing and just went their
> own way and it's been around ever since because ... Originally it [the
> music] was a lot like rock and roll. And it got a lot harder and faster and
> angrier as time went on and then it sort of came back now with I guess
> the scene is ... more the whole country is more right now is more on a
> street punk kind of track. (Gary)

The becoming selves of youth subculture are produced as call and
response – not as a response that reacts to the call, but as in musical
improvisation, where the call opens a space for an array of responses,
each situated within the specific circumstance of that particular
moment. The call and response of youth subculture illustrated in the
above quote is produced in the relational dynamism of the social
subject of the adolescent being called into being.

Althusser (2001) describes a similar notion of being called into a
subject position by the ideological force of the social embodied in a
functionary of the state. Althusser states that when our name is called
by the policeman, we are immediately produced as a subjectus. Foucault (1975), however, points out that each instance of becoming
subject to the forces of domination produces a simultaneous moment
of resistance. In other words, when the subjectum of youth is called
into the subjectus position of adolescence there is, according to Foucault, an immediate resistance to such calling. However, Negri (2003)
suggests that Foucault has the sequence reversed. He notes that resistance precedes domination because the creative life force precedes any
attempt to dominate it. Put another way, Negri proposes that there is
nothing to dominate or appropriate if there is no creative life prior to
domination.

In this sense, then, the social call and response of adolescence allows
the proliferation of multiple improvisatory responses to being called
into that specific social identity by parents, teachers, peers, or others.
Each of these moments comprises, as noted above, all of the elements
of the moment assembled into dance, fashion, music, speech, along

with any other performative platforms available to the self in the moment of production.

> I mean, it's just like saying fuck you, fuck your conventions, and fuck whatever you want to think if you want to look at me and not like me for it, well, I don't care. You know, because we don't need you. You know? Most people aren't worth your time anyway and it's like, me personally, I thought it was one of the greatest ways to root people out anyway on who I really gave a fuck about anyway. Because I mean, if somebody's not going to give you the time of day because of the way you look? Then fuck them. (Tony)

While Foucault (1975) and Hebdige (1979) – each from very different perspectives – describe these moments as resistance,[9] I would suggest, following Deleuze and Guattari (1987) and Negri (2003), that such performances do not operate in reaction but through the surplus of life force that exceeds the territorialized identity called into being by the dominant ideological social structure. Such a surplus, which resides in the subjectum, exceeds the limited parameters of adolescence and creates youth subcultural formations as lines of flight that cut across dominant cultural constructions.

Indeed, one might argue that the concept of adolescence itself slices open fissures and produces cracks within the edifices of the psychological and rational self that if not dismissed as transitional or immature might open avenues to the concept of youth as subjectum we are proposing here. In this regard, youth subcultural formations of self are performative in the sense Bordo (1993) describes in delineating the work of Judith Butler and of Irving Goffman: 'For Butler, as for Goffman, our identities ... do not express some authentic "core" self but are the dramatic effect (rather than the cause) of our performances' (p. 289).

Such effects exist within the grids of Foucauldian power and along the lines of Deleuzian desire we have been discussing. They become visible in the intersecting points, knots, and nodes outlined by Foucault, but they also exist in full force along the lines in between. We have already discussed lines of flight, but St Pierre (1997), following

---

9 See the introduction in Weinzierl and Muggleton (2003) on post-subculture theory for a nice overview of the critiques and complications of the notion of subculture as resistance.

Deleuze and Guattari, expands that map to include three types of lines: 'Individuals ... are made up of a tangle of three kinds of lines: (a) lines of rigid segmentarity (sedentary lines like family, school, profession, etc.); (b) more supple lines of molecular segmentarity (migrant lines that operate at the same time as rigid lines but confound their rigidity, e.g., the hidden or mad things that happen within families or schools, or professions, etc.); and (c) lines of flight (nomadic lines of creativity, lines that are always in the middle, lines of flux – not synthesis – that disrupt dualisms with complementarity)' (p. 370). The performative subjectivities of youth and youth subculture are certainly made up of these lines in complicated tangles of families, schools, professionals, and the 'mad things that happen' within them. But they are also made up by lines of flight produced by the creative force of the subjectum, which exceeds the rigid and semi-rigid confines of social structures with their activities and moments of resistance. In other words, the rigid molar line of the nuclear family creates fixed and bounded identities with prescribed social roles for each of its members, such as father, mother, child, and so on. The molecular lines can break up some of the rigidity of these roles by allowing flexibility to their function that might well include resistance to the full acceptance of the functions of family identity. A good example of this is the ways in which gender-stereotyped domestic tasks have been redistributed between family roles of mother and father without actually challenging the gendered nature of father as male or mother as female. The molecular line allows some degree of modification to what happens in the family but cannot alter the fundamental structure and social function of the family.

Lines of flight, on the other hand, violate and exceed both molar and molecular constraints. Such lines cut across structures and events. It would be a mistake, however, to imagine such lines as separate from or not influenced by the social structures they cross; indeed, they traverse such structures and events, picking up the flotsam and jetsam of cultural debris and rending them loose from their moorings along the lines of rigid or molecular segmentarity. Such material collides, slams, melds, and dances forward along a hybridized line of becoming that only momentarily solidifies into a coherent form and points of intersection with other lines, as we have discussed regarding Foucault. These momentary points of instantiation produce a continuous multi-sited tension along the full length of the line of flight. This tension in the skinhead and punk community generates continuums that encompass such politically polar opposites as Nazis, anti-racists, communists, anarchists, isolationists, and communitarians, all within and along the same line of subcultural subjectivity.

> The hammer skins being nazi skin and straight nazi, complete racism. And the national front still being anti-immigration. Around that time, the same time came sharp skinheads. Sharp skinheads is skinheads against racial prejudice. Originally sharp was not a kind of skinhead. It was not a political movement. It was anything, it wasn't anything like that. It was a patch that said skinheads against racial prejudice. And originally it was just meant to say I'm not racist. And those are your four, oh, and you've got rash, which is red and anarchist skinheads, which are communist and anarchist skinheads. (Frank)

This effect of producing diverse and divergent continuums becomes visible at points of intersection, where certain schools, mobs, or musical forms become identifiable. The tension of these productions exists in an ongoing dynamism as an impetus towards release that drives the line continually forward. What is notable for our purposes here is that the line of flight is composed of two aspects. In the first aspect are pre-subjective moments, when no identifiable subject has been formed yet. Such pre-subjectivities are like strange attractors that cross the social realm, gathering up bits and pieces of cultural material on their way without fully forming into any particular identity. In the second aspect are moments of instantiation, when an identity comes together into performative being. It is, however, the pre-subjective nomadic moment that constantly rearticulates the spaces within which new forms of youth-adult relations might be formed.

For this reason, in examining modes of alternate subjectivity as produced within youth subculture, it is a dangerous seduction to conflate the visible and the actual. In fact, the contrary is true. As in any performance, the effect is antecedent to the act while perception occurs later. Youth and youth subculture as a line of flight cannot be discovered through visible formations. The point of coalescence or visible performance is already finished and exists only as a dead form.[10] To attempt to know the subjectum through its products is to discover only its ossified droppings. The quarry has long moved on.

---

10 This is the reason that subcultural 'scenes' so often appear to lose their coherence or 'authenticity,' a phenomenon that I will discuss in the next chapter.

In this respect, the effort to utilize anti-hegemonic constructions of identity rooted in race, sexuality, or gender in order to understand or engage youth subculture is both misleading and irrelevant. As Nealon (1998) points out, 'Being-black is finally no guarantee of being outside the mainstream, posing a question to dominant racist codes, just as being-white or -Asian is certainly no guarantee of anti-black racism; it is rather, in *becoming* that deterritorialized lines of flight might appear' (p. 122).

Youth subculture, outside its points of visible capture in identifiable forms and modes, is absolute affirmation through movement. It is not a reaction but an effect. As noted above, it is an improvisatory singularity of call and response – a constant anticipatory emptiness of listening to respond. In this call and response there is a gap between the known moment of the performed event and its effect, and the mobile subjectivity of the performer. This gap occurs because the performance is always slightly ahead of perception and hence capture. This gap between what can be performed, perceived, and known creates a subjective nomadic becoming; that is to say, a subject always in motion through its creative productions.

Such a moment always stands in danger along the edge of the outside. It is important to note here that alternate subjectivity is positioned at the edge of the outside and not within the realm of the outside itself. The outside, following Deleuze (1993), is entirely virtual, existing as pure possibility unconstrained by form. In another term, it is the event horizon discussed previously. This is not the domain of alternate subjectivity. There is no transcendent self, no Platonic ideal represented in or through alternate subjectivities performed by youth or youth subcultures. The space, through which lines of subjective flight move, is a space of immanent materiality. Lines of subjectivity move deeply within the inside of the material world while constantly traversing the edge of the outside as absolute potential.

Youth Subculture: Affirmation, Anger, and Resentment

This corridor of flight, or what Nealon (1998) refers to as 'hazardous performance,' exists as affirmation. It is not a reaction, nor an act of resistance, but is rather subjective power in the Foucauldian sense of the purely creative. Reactions of anger and resentment within the context of the line of flight as pure creativity become quite complicated. Resentment and anger have been separated as quite distinct phenomenon. Resentment, as Nietzsche points out, is a regressive affect – or what the seventeenth-century philosopher Spinoza (2000) would call a sad passion. Such passions reduce or eliminate the capacity for creative force, because in Spinozist terms they reduce our capacity to act. In the case of resentment this loss of power occurs because it is always a reaction to something that no longer exists. Therefore any action premised on resentment is action in response to false perception of the actual conditions of lived experience. To attempt to act in response to a mythical set of conditions reduces the pragmatic effect of one's actions, reducing their creative force. This is not to say that actions premised in resistance do not have impact. It is simply to say that the impact is either negligible or destructive and as such, reduces the capacity of creative life force.

If we were to describe this within our mapping of the line of flight we would say that resentment is a product of a certain deceleration of velocity along the line. In other words, in order to produce passion out of the past, one must slow the creative impetus driving forward into the constantly becoming present. When the line of flight is slowed in this way it bends back on itself, crossing its own meridian and constructing a point of subjectification well behind its turning. Put in another way, when we remember an event in order to produce the sad passion of resentment, we must bend back into the past and revisit or cross over the line that has already been traced. When we do this, we reconstruct our already finished moments of subjectivity that lie behind us as dead remnants that bear little relation to our current becoming selves. This has a regressive effect on our line of flight as a hazardous performance.

> As long as identity is not thematized as a hazardous performative act – a verb rather than a noun, a multiple becoming rather than a monological symptom, a deployment of force rather than an assured process of mourning, a subjection that calls for(th) response rather than the revelation of an assured lack of wholeness – it seems destined to remain a locus for resentment, naming itself always in terms of its expropriation from an ideal that it can't ever hope, and doesn't even wish to attain ... ethics like cultural and sexual difference must be reinscribed outside the realm of loss, lack or failure. (Nealon, 1998, pp. 12–13)

The locus of resentment to be found in loss, lack, and failure, however, needs to be separated from the cultural fetishizing of 'adolescent anger' as regressive and negative. In fact, I would argue in this context that it is the inherent instability and unpredictability of anger that has the capacity to deterritorialize the static subjectivity of the Western 'adolescent' as a constant return to a mode of shaped and predicable development. This is not to say that the anger of youth as an oppressed or marginalized group deterritorializes youth-adult relations. It may well, in fact, accelerate or amplify efforts at control and discipline. As a result, anger within certain sites, such as subcultural affiliations, will have markedly different subjective effects than anger within a molar or molecular site of production, such as a school or family setting. 'Anger ... can be deterritorializing at certain sites; it can produce something other, a line of flight. Anger does not accrue quite so easily to an assured movement of subjective appropriation and control ... anger can produce a response that is more than a repetition of the same: anger is perhaps another of the myriad names for a movement outside the self that does not merely return to the self' (Nealon, 1998, p. 142).

This self that constantly flees itself operates in an arena of positive absence or emptiness. While the notion of a positive absence may seem paradoxical at first glance, this is absence as absolute affirmation of life as velocity. This is to say that when we attempt to describe the subjectum or youth as event, we need to move away from descriptors of static space towards a more dynamic description of identity as an event of performance that takes place in an empty space. This empty space is filled with movement defined by its speed. Some performances are very fast, some are slow, and some are of mixed velocity.[11]

Perhaps an even better example is the blank screen of a computer, where graphic images can fill the screen in an infinite variety of ways, each with its own velocity that varies with the program application. Each requires a space in which to become, and the intensity of the experience is determined often by the velocity of the image production on the screen as it comes into being and disappears.

The subjectum creates itself in a similarly empty but potent space. It is the line not yet drawn that defines its self-creation. It is not a repetition of what is but arises as life in the space between what already exists. The self that produces itself outside its own previous lineal manifestation is always a space between things, always a crack, a gap, an emptiness. (Bhabha, as cited in Nealon, 1998, p. 10) This site of

---

11 See Deleuze and Guattari (1987).

difference that exists as a highly diffuse, mobile, multiplicity of no-where and no-thing yet, is critical in the formation of new types of sub-jectivity. Such subjectivity exists in an infinitude of becoming actuali-ties; that is to say, it brings into the empty space a moving line of production that fills the space moment to moment with material that constantly creates itself as difference. Even when patterns repeat there are minute differences in each repetition, so that the eternal return is always one of difference.[12] This means that as the lines of the subjec-tum produce themselves across the plane of immanence, they split in many directions at once. Instead of the two-pronged split of 'either/or' so common to modernist philosophy and psychology, we have what Deleuze and Guattari (1987), following Jung, call a rhizome. A rhizome extends in a network of lines moving in all directions simultaneously. As they split, these lines tangle and cross in different and mutating combinations of found and unfound identity, constantly opening shift-ing sites of new identity performance.

Each crossing produces identities whose circulation and return gen-erate both core and remainder. It is the tension between centralization of identity as known and its escape through remaindered fragments that constitute 'the violent exclusions that secure normative identities' (Nealon, 1998, p. 28). Such violent exclusions constitute the dy-namism of the 'other' against which the 'normative' self is posited with such force. It is in the relationship of the core and its remainder that the performative act of self-flight into self is performed. 'The subject comes about through a performative response to the call of the other, through the bodily taking up of a "position," "the irruption in anonymous being of localization itself." Here the subject is brought into being through a radically specific performative event' (Nealon, 1998, p. 58).

Such an event occurs on the horizon of history, seldom in the centre of its known and explored domains. For the world of youth subculture as subjective field, that historical horizon is always the edge of colonial modernism. As Chambers (1990) points out, 'On the other side of [modernism's] constructed order lies the unordered discontents of civ-ilization – the extremes of artistic expression, the urban masses, the colonial subject, the subaltern cultures and individuals it does not rep-resent, its unconscious, an excess – which threatens its stability with dissidence and decadence, nonsense and nihilism' (p. 32).

---

12 See Deleuze (2006).

Youth Subculture and Cultural Collisions

The specific subjectivities of flight erupting as punk or skin take as their historical horizon the hybridized world of the postcolonial British Empire, as reflected in the experience of Jamaican and English working class youth (Hebdige, 1979; Hamm, 1993; Moore, 1993).[13] For our purposes here we should note that it is in the ways that the boundaries of the British Empire begin to erode as it fails that produce the opportunities for peoples and cultures to come into contact with one another in unexpected and unanticipated combinations. It is in this flux and flow of boundary, horizon, and frontier that the elements of colliding and eliding peoples, manners, modes, and patterns slip away from themselves and adhere to each other. These moments in which cultures and peoples brush by one another in moments of lived mundane contact elicit sparks of creativity that hybridize the empire from the inside out. As Chambers (1990) notes, 'It was through the appropriation of distinctive foreign cultures and tastes drawn from the cinema, dances and leisure styles ... from the fragmented inheritance of an imperial past brought home ... by postcolonial migration that a different sense ... has managed to both historically and aesthetically establish itself' (p. 32).

The selection and apportioning of performative identity is random in the specific lines of flight that were rhizomatically produced as eruptions of subculture with initially great force and speed in the late 1960s up through the early 1980s. The effects, however, begin much more slowly in the moments that challenge cultural continuity at the deep centre of the old empire. The ambivalent positioning of 'working class youth,' with all of its attendant edges of 'whiteness' and 'barbarism,' holds in tension the frontier of new postcolonial identities within the centre of the 'mapped' world of the old colonial culture. It is a space both determinate in its historical coordinates of class and yet indeterminate in the ways it shifts and evolves within the modes of globalized capital.[14]

The subjectivity called 'working class youth' in the postcolonial context is a space shot through with contradiction and uncertainty. At each level of historical constitution, whether gender, class, race, func-

---

13 I will have more to say about this later.
14 See Muggleton and Weinzierl (2003) for a series of essays that explore subcultures in this context.

tion, or politics, the sedentary and migrant lines that criss-cross the space of who and what is to be are, through the incursions of global capital, invaded, splintered, abandoned, and exploded. The lines of flight founded in the skinhead and punk subcultures 'represented a chosen cultural "exile" in their conscious and unconscious attempts to go beyond the immediacy of class and community referents ... [to] temporarily extract yourself from the weight of a local past; it was to conquer the limits of your own history and confidently, if only temporarily, manipulate a language; a code of desire and imaginary identification' (Chambers, 1990, p. 68).

These efforts to 'extract,' 'conquer,' and 'manipulate' the coding of desire and identification can only occur in the visible and nameable spaces of exile, in which the binaries of exclusion and otherness come clearly into view. This space of exile delineates the boundaries of the known, the seen, the spoken, and the excluded. To manipulate this language of the existent other is a project of critique and reaction, in and of itself incomplete and insufficient, both to the full becoming of subculture and to the interests of this book. To engage the relationship of language to youth-adult relations outside the modes of manipulation requires an alternate analytic premised on a fragmented and mobile remainder. Such a remainder operates from within the instrumental colonialism of language while simultaneously maintaining a position outside its influence.

2 Language, or Can the Subculture Speak?

Most part it is angry. It's trying to call out for a brave new world a better world. The language is trying to say we want something different we want something better. (Tony)

In her essay 'Can the Subaltern Speak?' Spivak (1988) proposes that in fact, she cannot. Obviously, Spivak does not mean to say that articulation for those groups subject to colonial domination and outside the networks of privilege becomes impossible. Rather, the capacity for speech as that act which conveys meaning becomes impossible for those subject to the effects of colonial rule. Meaning in this sense is dependent upon acts of translation and consensus between the subaltern and the dominant group, as well as within the subaltern class itself and within the subaltern subject's internal discourse of identity and worldview. Under the complex system of domination within the colonial and postcolonial regimes of power this becomes exceedingly difficult, due in no small part to the imposition of educational and linguistic imperatives upon colonized populations. That is to say, that when the colonial system is imposed it brings with it its own system of codes and meanings embedded within the language of the colonizer. Part of the system of control and domination is the privileging of this language system over indigenous linguistic codes and practices. Local populations are forced to engage with the dominant system of descriptive codes in order to get access to any aspect of privilege associated with colonial rule.

What makes this particularly insidious is that the privileging of a given set of linguistic codes has the effect of producing all other language systems as secondary to this privileged code. Under these terms all knowledge must be filtered through the dominant system of codes to have any sense of legitimate meaning. Even if a member of the dominant colonial group were to learn the language of the local population, he would translate all speech into the coding system of the colonial regime of power.

This becomes particularly difficult for those colonial subjects situated as mediators between the dominant group and the subaltern group, as they must negotiate between these language codes a sense of identity that sustains their affiliation to the subaltern class while serving the interests of the dominant class. This constant process of translation can have a devastating effect on the capacity of subjects to express themselves. Lindsay Aegerter (1997) points out in relation to the Jamaican writer Michelle Cliff that 'her British Education, culminating in a London University dissertation on the Italian Renaissance, had severed her from her linguistic and cultural heritage. She could "speak fluently," but she "could not reveal." Her education gave her an "intellectual belief in myself" while at the same time "distancing me from who I am, almost rendering me speechless about who I am"' (p. 898).

This inability to reveal oneself through language presents a problem worthy of attention for projects interested in resistance to or flight from domination. This problem centres on the inability to adequately express or reveal the lived experience of the subaltern group independent of the overarching system of codes that cover over and mask the actual antagonisms and struggles they experience. For example, this issue is endemic in the field of cross-cultural psychology when examining the struggles of immigrant families immersed within the colonial centres of North America or Europe. The lived expression of the struggle in which these families are engaged is investigated by psychologists through extensive interviews, observations, and surveys. Indeed, one could argue that the subaltern group's voice is more than adequately represented, often in their first language. However, in the process of translating the speech of the subaltern group into language suitable for the discipline of psychology, the information is processed into already existing social codes developed by Western science to explain and categorize human behaviour. This process can obscure the actual struggles for postcolonial identity existing within the lives of these families. This is the problem that Rabinow (1986) points to in his essay 'Representations are Social Facts,' where he argues that the anthropologist in the field creates a system of representation that translates the world observed into a world represented, which then gains a reality all its own.

In the case of the families we are discussing, the explanations created by the translation of lived experience into psychological expertise can create a system of truth that constructs a social reality to which these families must respond. The psychological framework that explains, for example, different parenting styles as being culturally based is often placed against normative structures of parenting that have powerful political and social implications. What constitutes good parenting is often conflated with which parenting style allows for the greatest degree of successful assimilation into the dominant social norm. Parents seeking acceptance within a new social environment find that they are subject to these new parenting codes developed, ironically, out of data provided by their own community.

The serious complication introduced by the need to learn and be inducted into the language codes of the dominant society causes real problems for expressing the lived experience or creative force of the subaltern. It is in this sense that Spivak is suggesting that speaking becomes impossible. Indeed, she is certainly not alone in expressing this conclusion. Audrey Lorde (1984) also expresses this problem in her essay 'The Master's Tools Will Never Dismantle the Master's House,' where she suggests that one cannot use the language and theories of the dominant society to dismantle that society; the subaltern must find her own modes of expression. Spivak (1988) critiques theorists such Deleuze and Foucault on the grounds that their theories of resistance and flight are premised in the capacity of the subaltern to express or speak an alternative narrative that can provide grounds for insurrection, and that such capacity is undercut by the colonial dynamic we have been discussing. Spivak maintains that the notion of alternative discourse does not adequately account for the fact that the subaltern subject cannot be heard without a translation that renders their speech inarticulate, often even to themselves.

Should the Subaltern Speak?

This is the problem that we are faced with in our exploration of youth as subject in relation to performing language within the worlds of youth and adult as subjectus and subjectum. Clearly the colonial distribution of language codes creates linguistic subjectivities that are governed by the overarching codes of the dominant linguistic system.

The descriptions of ourselves as categorized by age, gender, sexuality, nationality, class, and so forth are representations of the world produced by the ongoing colonial project of global capitalism. Indeed, the various categories and problematics of the adult-child distinction we outlined in the previous chapter are premised on just such coding. In Spivak's terms, the child or youth must always express themselves with the codes of the adult world. The child or youth is always produced as a comparative category to the adult. Indeed, one of the primary frustrations of childhood and youth is the frustration of not being able to adequately express the experience of being child or youth to the adults in one's life.

This raises an issue that haunts the Spivakian discourse, which is the question of the possibility or even the desirability of seeing speech as a way of directly expressing the lived experience of the subject. It would seem that in Spivak's view, speech must be able, in some way, to express the antagonisms and desires of the subaltern in order to mount a viable political project. There appears to be a need to reveal or uncover the mechanisms of domination inherent in class struggle through the spoken expressions of the subaltern. Indeed, as I have noted, she takes Foucault and Deleuze to task for not paying adequate attention to this inability to speak on the part of subaltern groups.

But for Deleuze and Foucault, speech holds a different function, and I would argue that Spivak's critique misconstrues their meaning. On the question of the capacity of speech to reveal the actual conditions of antagonism, Foucault holds serious reservations. Indeed, it is precisely Foucault's point in his discussion of the confessional in *Discipline and Punish* (1975) that one of the central mechanisms of disciplinary power in the early development of industrial capital was the demand to constantly reveal oneself. For Foucault, the confessional is the model that will develop into psychoanalysis and into what Debord described in *The Society of the Spectacle* (1967/1994). This model, according to Foucault, is a mode of social discipline where one is compelled to reveal oneself; to confess to society or the church on an ongoing basis one's sins or repressed desires. This process of revealing oneself subjects one to the gaze of society, with its political and social agendas. To use a term we have been exploring, it is a direct avenue to the subjectus.

In a broader sense, though, there is a larger problem with language as a system for representing the actual conditions of antagonism between classes. If the subjectus, as we have suggested in the previous chapter, is produced through an alienation from the creative perform-ances and acts of lived experience, then representation in language becomes problematic precisely because it is neither the act nor the per-formance, but a representation of that act or performance. In this sense, language is highly susceptible to the productions of regimes of domi-nation because signifiers, or those terms we use to point at something, are inherently empty of intrinsic meaning. They are just symbols or sounds that don't necessarily mean anything until we decide that they do. As such, they can be made to mean anything within society, pro-vided people can be convinced of the proposed meaning. For example, multiculturalism is often put forward as an advance in a given society's ability to combat racism and overcome bigotry. However, as the term has gained force it has been developed and expanded into a contested set of contradictory definitions that are often used to obscure actual antagonisms and historical inequities. The debates in the United States and elsewhere over the linguistic terms that signify racial dif-ference are examples of this process of re-signification of common terminology.

Resistance and Subjugated Knowledge

Foucault (1976) argues that it is just such struggles over disputed meaning that dominant language structures endeavor to hide from view. In other words, dominant systems of language seek to appear as though the meanings they assign have always been true and that any adjustments must be justified within the logic of the prevailing system of power.[1] Resistance, or what Foucault calls the insurrection of subju-gated knowledge, occurs when alternate meanings contest the domi-nant hegemonic effect of colonial linguistics. This resistance through alternative narrative produces cracks in the solid construction of meaning proposed by the current regimes of power.

The question remains, however, whether such resistance is premised in a 'truer' accounting of the conditions of subjugation. To answer this

---

1 This is also, of course, another way of making Spivak's point about how dominant language systems deny subaltern groups the ability to speak, in that their meanings and even the actual words of their language are subject to the dominant system's codes and rules of meaning.

question, we need to return to the concepts of the event horizon and the line of flight. As discussed in the last chapter, the event horizon is composed of the actual events occurring at any moment. It is also, however, composed of all the events that could occur at that moment. The representation of all possible events in language therefore constitutes an infinite pool of description. In other words, no one set of meanings can answer to all the possible descriptions of any event in both its actual occurrence and all the possible occurrences existing in the moment at the same time. Therefore no one set of meanings can be absolutely true; there are an infinite number of meanings to any given event, all of which hold some truth value. As such, it becomes less important whether a representation is fully accurate. More important, perhaps, is the political and creative potential of the description provided. It is the creative force of language rather than its ability to represent that begins to hold interest for our project here. If we are to reconceive the relation between youth and adults along the lines of the subjectum, or creative force, then the question of accurate representation of antagonism becomes less interesting than that of which description offers a new vision of relations.

In this light, as we examine the area of language within and about youth as subjectum, we become interested in engaging a movement away from language as a given ground for the description of 'reality.' Indeed, in order to take seriously the performative subjectivity outlined in the previous chapter, we must begin to address the unique terrain of a performative linguistic frontier; that is to say, language as performance or act rather than language as representation of reality. This is important because descriptions of reality are not reality itself, but always an account of something that has already passed and is now being described.

Our descriptions of reality are always memories of something we have already witnessed and are now reporting. Such a use of language as a depicter of realism can only reinforce what has already been. It is like looking at a photograph only as a direct representation of a past event. If we do not inscribe upon it our own current experience and affect, it holds very limited relevance to any kind of creative response on our part. For language to enter the realm of the subjectum, it must move out of the already mapped world of the past and enter into a frontier zone on the boundary with future – the moment of the act which is always and eternally the present.

Language Is Not Life, It Gives Life Orders

Language as act is also a complicated proposition. In their discussion of linguistics in *A Thousand Plateaus* (1987), Deleuze and Guattari propose that language operates not as a set of signifiers that are used to pass information about the world between people, but rather as a system of signifiers that passes information between signifiers.[2] That is to say that language communicates information about language. Language is not answerable to the needs of the subjects attempting to use it to understand one another. It only functions within its own logic, separate from the realm of the living subjects that articulate it. Deleuze and Guattari argue that language 'is not life; it gives life orders' (p. 76). They argue that under these conditions, the understanding of language as a code that can explain everything if used properly breaks down, and the notion that speech can be used to communicate accurate information about the world no longer functions either. What language does is to order the world rather than describe it accurately in a way that can be communicated between subjects.

What Deleuze and Guatarri (1987) refer to as order-words, or those bits of language that tell us how we are to conceive the world, are inherent in the very structure of language itself. Every phrase is composed of order-words that hold within them instructions about what we are to think and how we are to think it. This order is embedded in the rules of how language must be used and what constitutes the moment when language makes sense. Clarity of meaning is always based on such order, and such order is premised in our collective recycling of words and phrases over and over in various combinations of sense. It is on this basis that we imagine that we know what a child or an adult is, or what youth is. As Deleuze and Guattari (1987) point out, 'Bodies have an age, they mature and grow old; but majority, retirement, any given age category, are incorporeal transformations that are immediately attributed to bodies in particular societies. "You are no longer a child": this statement concerns an incorporeal transformation, even if it applies to bodies and inserts itself into their acts and passions. The incorporeal transformation is recognizable by its instantaneousness, its immediacy, by the simultaneity of the statement

---

2 In this, they seem very close to Luhmann's (1995) theory that society is produced by language as a self-producing system of binary codes.

expressing the transformation and the effect the transformation produces' (p. 81).

The ordering of the world is through such proclamations. Today you
are an adolescent, an adult, a woman, a man. Of course, as the needs
of societies change, these proclamations about who we are becoming
and when often mutate and redistribute themselves across the social
realm. This historical process of redefinition can create moments
within the development of a society of profound uncertainty and
anxiety about who is supposed to fit into which categories, and based
on that, who holds which responsibilities and privileges within the
social world.

In our current postmodern condition there is considerable anxiety
about the increasing indeterminacy of the age at which childhood ends
and adolescence begins. The boundaries of both the biological and
social child or youth are being challenged by shifts in the body's rates
of maturation and by the shifting expectations of such bodies in the
world of capitalist labour relations. This uncertainty about the boundary between childhood and adolescence is reflected in the ongoing
modification of discourse at the scientific, psychological, legislative,
and juridical levels. Such shifts constitute an ongoing re-coding of the
order of language surrounding the subject constituted as child/youth.
These margins and definitions are prescribed by the order-words
assigned to bodies by the social collective through indirect discourse;
that is, a specific body is not ordered into becoming an adolescent, but
a collective of bodies are ordered into being by collective social fiat.
This is the subjectus at work.

The effects of such ordering, however, also hold within them a possible avenue of alternative response. Because the group social cannot
specify the conditions of development for each individual subject, they
produce effects of a general nature that can only be responded to on an
individual basis. This produces the idiosyncratic creation of individual
bodies who must respond to such orders, and it is in this relation of the
order-word to the body that Deleuze and Guattari offer a glimpse of
the possibility of flight. They argue that the content of language upon
which the order is fully dependent is produced out of the intermingling and productive capacities of life itself. Such life is made up of all
bodies in combinations across the social realm. This life, made up of
billions of bodies, constitutes an infinite variability in both act and
interaction. The interactions, or what Deleuze and Guattari term 'intermingling' between bodies, exceed the 'power of sentencing or judge-

ment' (1987, p. 108). That is to say, they go beyond any power of the order-word to contain or restrict one's capacity for self-definition. The force of bodies together simply can never be fully contained by language. In other words, the creative force of life itself – what we have called the subjectum – allows for an excess of force that 'pushes language to its limits, while bodies are simultaneously caught up in a movement of metamorphosis of their contents or of exhaustion causing them to reach or overstep the limit of their figures' (p. 108). This implies that the lived experience of bodies intermingling with one another changes and shifts in ways that cannot be fully accounted for by the ordering structures of language regimes.

Beyond Language

The body of an individual youth will always exceed any capacity to be fully described in its movement through time and space. Such movement cannot be communicated through language but must be understood at a different level. This is why no description of youth or youth subcultures can adequately encompass the creative intermingling of the bodies involved. In fact, our best descriptions simply serve as order-words that attempt to recycle bits and pieces of description that fix the acts of subcultures and transform them into incorporeal judgments and instructions on how we are to think of them. What is particularly important to note here is that the bodies themselves become subject to just such an ordering until either metamorphosis or exhaustion causes them to overstep the limits of description. That is to say that it is either the force of morphogenesis or entropy – the drive to mutate or the drive to devolve into chaos – that carries life beyond the limits of language.

In a short essay, Deleuze (1995) defines a new set of power relations he terms the 'Society of Control.' He states that within the postmodern world of global capital we must produce 'vacuoles of non-communication' if we are to create the spaces necessary for the production of new worlds. We can see from our earlier discussion of Deleuze and Guattari that communication itself constitutes a set of power relations with the arena of the subjectus. In the moment of postmodern capitalist development, this aspect of domination extends itself in such a way that the order-word becomes not just a vehicle that produces ideological linguistic constructions useful to the dominating system of control, but becomes a mechanism whereby the lived social (the spaces where bodies mingle) becomes a site of capitalist production in its own right.

To be more specific, within late-stage capitalist society the realm of what is appropriable to capitalist production has expanded beyond the realm of goods and services to the very realm of human interaction. As Hardt and Negri (2004) point out, this extends into the commodification of communication and other skills previously deemed to be outside the areas of sale and profit. It is in this context that Deleuze proposes his move towards spaces free of communication and designed to frustrate the constantly mutating machines of capture and appropriation of meaning that are the hallmarks of late-stage capitalist society.

What would such spaces look like? In an article on postmodern ethnography, Tyler (1986) argues that there is a system of relations premised in expression that is neither 'presentation nor representation' and calls this evocation. Under the terms of evocation, what we know is cooperatively produced, not as a repeating whole of order-words but as bits and pieces of text and discourse intended to suggest new possibilities of the world(s): 'It is, in a word, poetry – not in its textual form, but in its return to the original context and function of poetry, which, by means of its performative break with everyday speech evoked memories of the community' (p. 124).

Tyler goes on to argue that postmodern ethnography as an instance of evocative work breaks up the coded world of language inherent in the language of the subjectus and instead evokes a fragmented world where 'fragments of the fantastic whirl about in the vortex of the quester's disoriented consciousness' (p. 126). In other words, evocation is the point at which we stop making sense through ordering the world and begin to create the world in motion, as fragments of perception organized in the moment of the acts between bodies.

In a concrete sense, this way of speaking the world into being produces the terrain of youth subculture as unavailable to coherent explanation or interpretation. This formulation stands in radical disjunction from the traditional frameworks for subculture theory that propose interpretations or explanations of subculture as an object of study or observation.[3] Subculture within the terrain of the subjectum as poetry

---

3 See introduction in Weinzierl and Muggleton (2003) for a related critique in the post-subculture literature.

cannot inform from the outside but must operate out of what is evoked for each subject as it intermingles with other subjects or the creative productions of other subjects. Evocation is a calling forth of a unique response premised in the radically distinct configuration of each singular body.

This echoes arguments made in the last chapter about the nature of call and response as integral aspect of performative subjectivity. This process of producing the world through idiosyncratic and momentary productions of meaning originates out of the response of each body. Each body produces and then produces again the mingling of bodies that produce a scene or subcultural formation. This goes beyond the notion of the neo-tribe,[4] because the tribal still maintains within it elements of the order-word in its descriptive containment. Nevertheless, as Tyler suggests, the language formations have echoes to earlier formations and ways of knowing the world that we will consider later when exploring the world of skinheads. In the evocative production of the scene or tribe, however, the formation must be finished at the moment of its creation, or it will become a code itself that can be appropriated to the ends of global capitalism.

The language of subculture as evocation thus becomes a performative description: that act of speech which both articulates and acts, such as the violent language of the skins or punks that is both violent in its expression and in its action.

> Oi is skinhead punk rock. It's a little bit slower, usually has no political messages to it. Most songs about drinking beer, getting laid, and getting in fights. It's sort of like, it's just music to be, to drink to, to fight to, to do whatever you want, you know. It's like, it's us, only in music form. And punk's sort of gone a lot towards that. Street punk, the music is just Oi with punks in it. (Gary)

Such speech acts do not communicate and as such, become unavailable for translation into dominant language codes. Indeed, one might say that they bring into actuality Deleuze and Guattari's (1987) assertion that 'the order-word is always something else, inseparably connected; it is like a warning cry or message to flee' (p. 109). Youth subcultures in their eruption as creative alternative may well be one of those social forms that both speaks and acts out the warning cry of the

---

4 See Maffesoli (1996).

order-word as performative description. This kind of speech performance then sets aside interpretation, explanation, or understanding, and
in its evocatory capacity operates as absolute act. Such acting has no
inherent central organizing feature. By definition it flees appropriation
through observation, categorization, or structural analysis. The linguistic domain of the performative speech act as evocation exists as a
kind of constant becoming that resists the redundancy of fixed definition and whose mobility is premised in a pragmatics of action.

This resistance to being fixed is to be distinguished from a utilitar-
ian pragmatics in which there is a confusion between the act, its effect,
and its usefulness to a particular framework of effect. The pragmatics
of the evocatory does not rely on whether or not the actions are useful
to a particular end. Its pragmatic effect is not necessarily of use to any
social effort to organize and structure creativity to a specific purpose.
The pragmatics of an evocatory performative linguistics is utility separated from a particular framework of effect and released into the full
desires of creativity itself. This is articulation, not as language in the
sense of the order-word, but instead as absolute creativity; a poetics of
action not reliant on outside definition. This is not to say an ignorant
or unknowledgeable sphere, but rather a sphere of what is always
purely imminent knowledge, or knowledge that produces itself free
from outside restraint.

Passages of Life through Language

An evocatory performative linguistics is one that functions within the
logic of immanence that was discussed in the previous chapter. Within
the field of immanence, as we noted, everything produces itself. In this
sense, the evocatory performance of language produces further evocatory performances of language. The creative actions of the subject do
not lend themselves to separation into hierarchies of difference or type.
So, for example, there is no ability to separate the act from its structure.
Nor is it possible to cleanly delineate an individual as a user of speech
or language. Individuals do not use speech or language, they are productions of speech and language who then produce more speech and
language that produces more social subjects, and on and on. For
example, the youth subculture that produces a musical form or a style
of dress is also produced by that musical form or style of dress. This
mutual production holds two distinct responses. One is the response
of the order-word, which seeks immediately to structure the musical

form or style into a redundant series of repetitions such as a mythical 'scene' or fashion style. The alternative is the evocatory response to the order-word's other capacity, which is to induce flight. This flight of creative articulation produces passages across the social world that exceed the capacities of order. As Deleuze and Guattari (1987) point out, 'In the order-word, life must answer the answer of death, not by fleeing, but by making flight act and create. There are pass-words beneath the order-words. Words that pass, words that are components of passage, whereas order-words mark stoppages or organized, stratified compositions. A single thing or word undoubtedly has this twofold nature; it is necessary to extract one from the other – to transform the compositions of order into components of passage' (p. 110).

To turn language, speech, and subjectivity towards the production of such passages is to begin to answer Spivak's question of whether the subaltern can speak. In the case of youth subculture I would argue that youth-adult relations must be reconstituted outside the domain of the order-word. The intermingling of bodies of different ages and compositions constitute themselves through collisions with other bodies. These intersections produce words, fashion, music, and art.[5]

However, to fully understand how such collisions can produce passages that allow for movement underneath the regimes of the order-word, we must remember that the productions themselves are finished as soon as they are produced. All of the elements that go into the productions of a single moment, such as the collision between two bodies of different ages, one ordered into adulthood and the other into youth, cannot be extracted into an abstract order outside of the actual collision itself. The elements of that collision are composed of both virtual and actual elements. For example, within the realm of the actual are differences in bodily composition produced as the body ages; differences and commonalities of style and taste; differences of history produced through experience; affectual responses to the other including components such as anger, love, resentment, grief, affiliation, and alienation; and differentiated responses to the environment, such as who is more comfortable in the space where the collision occurs, among other kinds of responses. In the virtual range are all of the possibilities evoked by the collision, such as things hoped for, fear of things unknown, memories of things, events and selves past, projections of previous collisions

---

5 See the earlier discussion of Foucault in chapter 1 on power as a set of intersections that produce everything.

with other bodies among an infinitude of echoes and resonances. This combination of the virtual and the actual, which was described above as the event horizon, produces a micro-political site of struggle in which all the elements vie with varying force for inclusion into the production of the moment. The irony is that the production of the moment only holds its immanent force in that moment of its production. Once it is produced it ceases to exist in actuality and instantly becomes an event of the past, a memory. It is out of such memories that the order-word produces reality. Such reality can never be spoken by the subaltern. It is fully the province of the colonial or dominant class, which must rely on the control of memory to sustain its pre-eminent position. Put in another way, colonial power must always be sustained through the control of history as a finished project, whereas the force of the subaltern is produced through those projects that haven't happened yet.

The language of the subaltern then must arise out of the alternative that we are proposing: the evocative imminent performance of articulation as a passage beneath the realm of order and control. Such linguistic production relies on shattering the points of production while constantly re-composing them into new creative configurations.

Poetic Relations

> Because, back in the day, back in the 70s and early 80s there used to be skinhead poets. What they would do is they would stand in front of a crowd, a skinhead audience, a skinhead show, before they would stand up and read their poems. It's a different kind of poetry. It's street poetry; street poetry out of necessity. I think it's not just that we speak it, you have to live it. You have to live it because if you're skinhead you're poor. There you go, there you go, you're poor you have to live it. You have to live your life before you do. (Frank)

Youth-adult relations as a liberatory project cannot be found in the productions of relationships as they have been constructed thus far, but must be found in the set of relations not yet produced. That is not to say, however, that new relations are to be built without regard to memory or previous history. Indeed, they are to be found precisely in such history as the order-word. However, these new relations are what Deleuze and Guattari have reminded us are inherent in the second implication of the order-word; that is, the words of passage hidden within each word. We must discover what words of passage are obscured from view by our current understanding of the terms youth and adult. In this process of discovery, the evocative performance of language is driven by constantly resurrecting the remainders of any given description or what is left over when we think we know something or someone.

How do we discover such remainders, such pass-words to new worlds? Perhaps, as Tyler suggests, the vehicle lies in the poetic. Indeed, 'poetic language, [Kristeva] claims, is the linguistic occasion on which drives break apart the usual, univocal terms of language and reveal an irrepressible heterogeneity of multiple sounds and meanings' (Butler, 1990, p. 104). This is not a proposition to reduce the world to nonsense or to a field of language incomprehensible within its own articulation. Instead, it is a move towards what Derrida (1980) would term deconstruction, or the process of revealing what is obscured within each word – its history of struggle. This history of struggle or contestation over meaning is released through any form of utterance that allows the unique creative expression of bodies intermingling across space and time. Poetry is one such form that allows for the expression of the unique utterance that is fully available to an infinitude of evocatory response. Perhaps this is why the lyric or poetic form can be found across youth subcultures in the words of songs, the articulations of rap and hip hop, the patois of world beat, the cries and whimpers of emo,[6] and the infinite expressive capacities of slang. These are linguistic forms that have limited stability. They flee the order-word by using the pass-words hidden within it. In doing so they create a world in which youth subculture can indeed speak fully within and through the world of postcolonial global capital.

---

6 Emo refers to softcore punk that emphasizes romantic or depressive emotional content.

3 Time Has Come Today

If language and identity hold a set of relations in which the praxis of domination and liberation, or subjectus and subjectum, operate through a complex array of antagonisms, the concept of time brings these antagonisms into an even clearer focus. Like the order-word in language and the notion of a fixed and articulated identity, time brings the world into a certain kind of order that can be deployed both to the ends of dominant regimes of power and in resistance and flight from those regimes. In the arena of youth-adult relations it is a certain concept of time that marks the boundaries of age, dividing the years into stages and the stages into progressions. Indeed, it is only with the concepts of evolutionary and teleological time that the categories of adolescence and adulthood hold their particular social force.

In dividing the world into moments that progress towards an ideal future, Hegel unwittingly set the stage for all manner of distinction premised on what might be called normative time. The Western scientific notion of biological development, with its neat series of stages and normative benchmarks, forces the world of growth and change into a predictable linear progression of limited alternatives. According to this model all bodies will progress through time in a certain order that can be projected into the future if one allows for certain margins of variance, or what are known in psychology as exceptionalities to 'normal' development. This version of time is so deeply rooted in Western consciousness that we seldom question whether this is the pattern of our lives. We simply know that we will develop from infants to children to adolescents to young adults to mature adults to older adults and finally, to death. This kind of time is verified through the science of the body, which claims that variations in bodily form, function, and composition signal discrete trajectories of evolution. This body, we are told, has a normative trajectory that if violated can retard or pervert the normal progression of the body, including the brain and mind. These deviations create exceptions to the 'normal' course of development and can fix a body at a particular stage, such as child or adolescent. According to this model, delays in development can restrict a person to a limited cycle of behavioural options within which the capacity to function and grow becomes significantly constrained. Such bodies are considered to be in need of social intervention to assist them in attaining as much 'normal' development as possible.

These 'struggles' for normative development are not just limited to those considered to have bodies or minds that don't 'develop' within the time frames specified by Western science. Those with exceptional development that exceeds the margins of normative growth, such as the artistically, musically, or intellectually gifted, are also often considered developmentally challenged to the degree that their emotional or social behaviour doesn't conform to what is considered maturity. The portrait drawn in the popular imagination of the absent-minded genius is someone with no practical ability to function in the 'real' world, often characterized as childlike and in need of parental supervision by someone more mature and practical. Similarly, the gifted musician or artist is often portrayed as emotionally immature and lacking social inhibition, a characterization resonant of cultural concepts of the immature adolescent.

It is not, in fact, too difficult to classify any deviation from bourgeois values as fitting into some form of developmental deviance. In particular, any behaviour that holds what is considered to be an excess of emotion or sexuality is often characterized as immature and in need of remediation. For example, the unfiltered expression of anger at unjust working conditions or the unwillingness to submit to the restraints and requirements of the workplace can be categorized as an anger management issue or an issue with authority. The free expression of sexuality without the structures of monogamy or heterosexuality can be characterized as an unwillingness to 'grow up' or an unwillingness to assimilate into the dominant regimes of social authority.

Hence, the legitimization of homosexuality within the North American context rests on the question of gay marriage. With gay marriage comes the possibility of 'mature' behaviour modelled on hetero-normative patterns of development that include a progression from 'playing the field' to the eventual maturation into a monogamous relationship with one partner for life. This developmental model, of course, leaves aside the fact that monogamy is not an actual portrait of heterosexual relations, since a significant percentage of marriages end in divorce, and serial monogamy punctuated by affairs with multiple sexual partners over a lifetime typifies what might be called the heterosexual lifestyle.

To say that what troubles Western society about homosexuality is a perception of the 'lifestyle' as a perpetual adolescence without the proper restraints of 'mature' sexual behaviour is to point to the role that developmental concepts play in the political realities of the postmodern world. One can see this quite clearly in the efforts to quiet the anxieties of the hetero-normative body politic by presenting media portrayals of monogamous gay couples who desire nothing more than marriage and the rights and benefits of the 'mature' adult. Such portrayals convey these couples as older, securely employed, levelheaded and reasonable. This is not accidental, but an overt political strategy developed by a certain sector of gay rights advocates who propose to move away from the public portrayal of the flamboyant drag queen as the spectre of anxiety that haunts the hetero-normative body politic.[1]

Time Is Political

For our purposes, what is compelling in this portrait of gay politics is the political deployment of the categories of maturity and adulthood versus adolescence in the advancement of social inclusion of a subaltern group. Certainly, one could point to similar political projects relating to the inclusion of women and people of colour. For these populations, the ideological shift towards inclusion in the political process in Western societies necessitated a campaign to portray them as mature and responsible social actors. To accomplish this, any trace of what would be considered adolescent behaviour, such as high degrees of emotion or unrestricted sexuality in particular, must be eradicated.

Indeed, even in the political development of child rights, adolescence is largely omitted as a political category in favour of the more sympathetic developmental stage of childhood, or more specifically, the period of latency. In this regard, the ideal political portrayal of a child who deserves rights is a young person six to twelve years of

---

1 See Brewster (1994).

age. Such a child is past the difficulties of infancy and early child-hood and not yet into the difficulties of adolescence. Children are considered innocent subjects, or in Western discourse – laden with the legacy of Christian ideology – sexually pure and unsullied. Indeed, one might argue that the ideal candidate for child rights is always a virgin.[2] Such a child can still be protected from the sins of a fallen world and at the same time might well be considered to have a higher degree of social malleability. Again, what is of note here is how certain social concepts of developmental time hold considerable political force within the juridical field of law as well as in the arena of political economy.

Adolescence and Time

Clearly, the singular figure that most troubles the regimes of power and order produced by developmental discourse is the adolescent, or what we have been calling youth. Perhaps what is most troubling about the figure of the adolescent is its status as a space between things. Produced by psychology at the beginning of the last century, the concept of adolescence has always held a peculiar social function as a moment of entropy within an overall evolutionary process.

Adolescence is a period designated as either time reversed or time paused. In its instantiation as time reversed, the adolescent is seen to be repeating the developmental battle for the right to refuse that was first mounted in the stage between infancy and childhood, at around two years of age. This battle for the right to refuse is seen as the first step in the development of the individuated self. That is to say, the infant is perceived as needing to separate itself from identification with its mother in order to form a healthy and separate identity. As noted in chapter 1, this production of the separated self holds an ambivalent relation to the form of identity we have been referring to as the subjectus. To frame the right of refusal as a normative develop-mental process that produces the beginnings of what Freud referred to as the ego is to significantly mute the political possibilities of radical negation.

---

2 And often valorized as female. Thanks to Shauna Pomerantz for noting that the word 'virgin' conjures femininity.

Radical Negation and Refusal

> Basically punks have a negative outlook a negative outlook on every-
> thing, but who's to say it's negative? I mean it isn't positive but we kinda
> look at it with a sceptic's eye. (Tony)

The term radical negation needs to be separated from the idea of the
negative. The concept of the negative in human development is built
on a theory of lack. In the case of time as development, the concept of
lack implies that what drives development forward is an absence of
something at each stage that will be at least partially fulfilled at the
next. In the case of the two-year-old, what is lacking is an identity
capable of autonomous functioning separate from the mother. This
lack drives the two-year-old into a refusal of the commands of the
mother or parental authority, which then produces a new lack: that of
order or authority itself. The solution to this new lack is an internalized
parent, which Freud called the superego. The superego allows for
autonomy from the parent but lacks the ability for autonomy of the
self. In other words, the superego can only repeat the codes of the
dominant society as initially inculcated by the parents or other social
intermediaries. As such, the child with only a superego is pure subjectus. This constitutes another new lack that must be mediated by the
production of what Freud called the ego, which attempts to balance
the desires of the child against the commands of the social. All of this
is premised on the concept that each stage is missing something that
the next stage will fulfill. In this dialectical model of development, the
infant's refusal is simply a function that allows for the mediation of
lack. That is to say, the refusal has no function in and of itself. Its only
purpose is to set the conditions for the move to the next stage.

Radical negation, on the other hand, posits that refusal is not a mediation between stages of development, but is an act of resistance to
domination premised in an increasing capacity to creatively act. That
is to say that the infant's act of refusal is not based on a lack of individuated self that requires a separation from the parent figure, but on
a surplus of creative self-constitution that forces a radical break from
previous modes of relationship. In the mode of radical negation,
refusal clears a space by negating any obstacles to creative assertion.
This shifts the mode of refusal from an act of the negative to an act of
affirmation. For the category of adolescence, in its instantiation as time
reversed to the previous stage between infancy and childhood, this

mode of refusal echoes the role of anger discussed in chapter 1 as that function which takes the world apart.

These two modes of the act of refusal open very different types of time for the adolescent. In the first mode of the negative, time is driven forward towards an unrealized future consisting of ideal forms that the body brings closer in each moment through its failure to achieve them in any particular moment of the present. In the second articulation of refusal in the act of radical negation, time opens constantly onto what we have called the event horizon through an absolute negation of any obstacle to the assertion of creative force. This is what Deleuze (1997b) refers to when he states that

> babies display a vitality, an obstinate, stubborn, untamable will-to-live, different from all organic life. With a young child there is already a personal, organic relationship, but not with a baby that, for all its smallness, concentrates the energy that shatters paving stones ... With the baby there is only an affective, athletic, impersonal vital relationship. It is certain that the will to power appeared in the baby in an infinitely more precise manner than in the man of war. For the baby is combat and the small is the irreducible site of forces. (p. 167)

This is the moment of return for the adolescent body:[3] to be returned to that site of contestation that opens the event horizon otherwise foreclosed by the sets of constraining relationships developed during childhood with teachers, clergy, parents, and peers; each in their turn proscribing and inscribing the rules and regulations of the social; each inscription producing time in a predictable progression of developmental tasks to be fulfilled in turn as the body moves from birthday to birthday, grade to grade, and skill to skill. In adolescence this orderly progression is disrupted and there is the reassertion of what Deleuze calls the 'affective, athletic, impersonal vital relationship.'

A Different Kind of Time

This reassertion of force through return opens a Nietzschean alternative temporality different from that of the linear progression proposed in the teleological model of time as progress. This kind of time evokes

---

3 See Deleuze (2006) for the way in which I am using Nietzsche's notion of the eternal return here.

an earlier mode of temporality found in pre-modern cultures: that of cyclical time. This is time that moves in circles or spirals rather than in straight lines. It is the time of seasons which repeat in an infinite cycle; an endless resurgence of the same elements but always in an unending combination of difference. That is to say, each season is always different from the same season in the previous cycle, and each difference has a radical impact on the life, geography, and geology that respond to climatic changes of seasonal change.

This is another possibility of reading youth as subjectum. If adolescence is the return of a certain season of life, then such return holds the creative force of infinite difference in each return. Youth in this sense is the creative force of assertion through refusal that cycles across all ages of the body, like the return of the seasons across all ages of the planet Earth. Just as such seasonal returns are responsive to each shift of planetary composition,[4] resulting in vastly different environments over millions of years, so the seasons of refusal are responsive within their return to shifts in the lived body of the subject that produce vastly different identities. Each of these identities holds a new combination of creative refusals depending on the age, composition, and circumstances of that body. This is youth as subjectum in every age.

The second reading of adolescence we referred to above is the moment of adolescence not as return but rather as pause between childhood and adulthood. In this sense, being adolescent marks a break, a space between things. This is a deeply problematic reading within the conceptual framework of developmental or evolutionary time. How are we to account for a break in the steady advance of progressive temporality? We have already noted how cyclical time, or that time that returns, marks a radical break with developmental time. This break, we have argued, allows for the creative assertion of the subjectum. Now we need to account for the production of a subject that pauses between stages in what might be called an indeterminate status of deferral.

Without a doubt, when the concept of adolescence was introduced by G. Stanley Hall at the turn of the last century, it served an important social function for the development of early industrial capitalism. The notion of adolescence solved a number of problems relating to shifts in society that were the result of industrial development. Perhaps most significantly, it deferred the entry of a large number of young people

---

4 An example is global warming.

into a labour market that desired to regulate and control the flow of workers into the arenas of production.[5] This deferral was based on the fact that early capitalists needed to control the movement of workers as part of a larger effort to assert control over the entire productive capacity of society.

The logic behind this is premised in the logic of capital itself, which proposes that the primary function of the social is the process of creating surplus capital or profit for a small group of people who control the means of production. If the workers control their own modes of labour and benefit fully from the result, there is no profit to be accrued by the capitalist. One way to assure that this does not happen is to regulate the number of workers who have access to the means of production, so that the ability to produce things and benefit from what is produced becomes a social privilege bestowed by the capitalist class. If everyone can work whenever and wherever they wish, doing whatever creative activity suits their temperament or talent, then capitalism can no longer function. The ability to produce and create the elements of society, including material goods and social relations, must be regulated for capitalism to succeed.[6] The introduction of the concept of adolescence served just such as a regulatory function by deferring the entry of a previously productive group of young people into the world of work.

Capitalism's production of a certain group of bodies as a social space between has immense implications for the production and understanding of time within capitalism. To suggest that progressive time can be manipulated to the particular ends of an emerging social process is a radical proposition, to say the least. In this instance, what was being proposed was that a group of people previously deemed mature at a certain point and capable of entering into the tasks and responsibilities of adulthood must now be deferred from such entry. In order for this to be accomplished, the notion of developmental time as moving resolutely forward into the future had to be modified. Somehow the notion of time must come to be understood as a series of variable dependents premised on the discovery of new factors related to the status of particular bodies. In other words, the deferral of young people in time that holds them back from progressing to the next stage of development must be premised in the discovery of previously

---

5 See Perrot (1997).
6 See Gray (2000) and Marx (1978/1992, pp. 146–201).

misunderstood or unknown characteristics of these bodies that pre-
clude their entry into the social apparatus of production. What must
not become obvious is the role of the dominating social system of capitalism's need to produce these bodies to its own ends. The cause of
deferral must be located in the bodies themselves.

This requires that the adolescent body be produced fully within the
time of lack or the negative. The body must be seen to be missing key
elements of what is necessary to function in society as an adult. What
marks this as radically different from the notion of developmental lack
described above is the fact that this lack indicates a space rather than
a drive. In other words, to produce the adolescent as lacking various
elements of biological and emotional maturity does not so much signal
a drive to achieve such maturity, as it does with the infant, but a space
in which such maturity is resisted. This is a particularly complicated
bit of social machinery. While it is not unusual for the body to be seen
as lacking the biological and emotional prerequisites necessary to complete a given task, such lack is generally seen to be resolved within a
relatively fixed time frame, during which progress towards that task
can be marked by outside observation. Infant development, for
example, is easily marked for parents by the family doctor with charts
and graphs revisited at regular intervals. Any deviation from this set
pattern of growth and development can mark the kinds of exceptionalities we referred to earlier.

For the adolescent, this predictable linear progression of developmental tasks has largely vanished into a description of pure lack that
prescribes an indefinite withholding of the space of maturity. The adolescent is seen as incapable of completing designated developmental
tasks not only on the basis of such biological factors as brain function
and hormonal instability, but also on the basis of a lack of specific
markers of skill development that might indicate passage into maturity. Indeed, the passage into maturity is now an extended period of
time described as extending anywhere from age eighteen to thirty. This
range has a remarkable elasticity that can shift developmental task
completion and entry into what are considered adult behaviours
across the age range with remarkable speed. The age at which a body
can consent to have sex, use tobacco or alcohol, fight in wars, get
married, have children, enter the workplace, leave school, or enter university varies immensely in both common practice and legal statute.
This creates adolescence as a time of radical indeterminacy dependent
upon an increasingly random but not irrational set of social and scientific determinates.

Time and Capitalism

The definition of adolescence as thoroughly historically and socially contingent is, as we have noted above, a hallmark of the relationship of the very development of the term with capitalism. As Negri (1996b) notes, time is the heartbeat of capital (p. 154). Without the capacity to divide the world into moments that can be apportioned to tasks, the world of industry would simply decompress into forms of creative desire freed from the logic of capitalist exchange. The time of the task, however, begins to take new forms and purposes as capital has developed.

In his essay 'Time Matters,' Casarino (2003) traces the thinking of Negri in relation to this development of time. He argues that time has traditionally been seen in the West as that mechanism by which the world can be divided 'into discrete units.' This model, which produces time as a certain kind of measure, brings the world of time and space together. Put in the simplest terms, in order to divide the world by time, time must have a spatial aspect because division requires the dimension of space. This, according to Casarino 'subordinates and enslaves time to space' (p. 189). It takes what might be called free time or immanent time and produces stoppages and limitations to its function. To make this a bit clearer, we can refer back to our earlier reading of Deleuze and Guattari's discussion of the order-word as that element that structures language by producing limits on its ability to act as pure creative force. To force time into space accomplishes a similar function. While it is hard for us to imagine free time, or time that produces itself independent of space, each of us has had a hint of such time in our dreams, daydreams, and other states of altered consciousness in which time operates according to a different logic than that of the boundaries premised in minutes, hours, days, or years.

This enslavement of time to space has had tremendous utility for industrial capitalism, which used it to move agricultural bodies embedded in the time of agriculture, or the cyclical time referred to above, into the segmented time of the factory with its many divisions of the day according to function.[7] Casarino, following Negri, notes that the time of industrial capitalism shifts into a new kind of time with the development of postmodern capital. Under postmodern capital, time is produced under the conditions of what were referred to in chapter 1

---

7 An excellent example of this is the first few minutes of the film *Modern Times* by Charlie Chaplin (Warner Bros., 2003).

as total subsumption, or that moment in which all social relations fall within the regimes of global capitalism.

Within the postmodern period of capitalist development, time becomes something different, in keeping with the new demands that global forms of capitalism place upon it. Instead of time as component measure, we get 'a decidedly non-quantifiable and non-measurable time' (Casarino, 2003, p. 189). This shift in time is the result of a complex array of factors involved in the new modes of productivity and distribution that have become dominant within the global economy. These include the deindustrialization of labour in North America and Europe and the redistribution of factory-type labour to other parts of the world. In this shifting of the industrial function, its form and use of time also changes. Instead of factory time built around discreet units of production driven by the clock, we enter a period where all time is available for appropriation. In other words, not only does the workday extend its time by reversing the gains of labour that limit the number of hours a worker can be held at work, but the time outside work is invaded by work through pagers, cellular phones, laptop computers, answering machines, and other devices that make the worker available to capital twenty-four hours a day. Time becomes a commodity and is endlessly for sale, both in the workplace and in the extension of capital into both leisure for purchase and the infinite workday. Capitalist time and its moments construct a way of making meaning out of our lived experience that melds the human rhythm of our own creativity with the rhythm of the global machine of capital production.

Obviously, we are once again entering time within the domain of the subjectus. Interestingly enough, however, this kind of time without limit mimics the kind of time we find ourselves engaging when we are taken up with our own creative passions. The kind of creativity we engage in during our free time often opens up our limited concept of time, so that we lose any sense of time passing when we are being creative for ourselves by painting, writing, creating music, writing computer code, or playing games. This is also 'a decidedly non-quantifiable and non-measurable time.'

Casarino makes the point that this similarity between these kinds of time creates a problem for capital. On the one hand, we have free time as the 'time most expressive of our productive and creative energies' (p. 189), time that belongs to our own life and experience; on the other hand, we have capital's desire, perhaps even its requirement, that such time become available to its uses. Under these circumstances, capital must simultaneously control and manipulate such time through producing it as measurable so that it can be used to generate profit, as well as keep it incommensurable to maximize its creative force. In other words, it is under the rule of capital that time gains the same duality we have noted above in relation to subjectus and subjectum in identity and language. 'It is also in this sense that postmodernity can be said to constitute the full fruition of the projects of modernity: if the real subsumption of society by capital has entailed that there is no longer virtually any aspect and indeed any time of our lives that is not productive for capital, time then – Negri seems to suggest – is that which capital needs now more than ever and yet that which capital always hopes against all hope to reduce to zero' (Casarino, 2003, p. 190).

Adolescence, as constituted as a space between, becomes for capitalism one of the prime social categories for experimenting with 'zero' time. In producing adolescence as a space within which developmental time comes to an indeterminate pause, capitalist society can produce a subject whose time is simultaneously rigorously controlled and at the same time constituted as an open field of free time in which youth can create music, style, language, art, writing, scenes, subcultures, and neo-tribes.[8] These creations come into being alongside forms of bourgeois identity simultaneously being produced within the regimes of control and discipline that also operate in this 'free' zone.

In this sense, for youth produced at the centre of the postcolonial machinery of global capital, the moment in and of itself carries immense significance. Such significance is sketched upon the lives of youth in the double articulation of the subjectus and subjectum. In this case, however, capital more than ever needs to produce spaces that both open time and foreclose time. The foreclosure of time can be seen easily in barcodes and timecards, school bells and bus schedules, paycheck dates and bar times. These timelines outline the shape of the other that is appropriable to capital.

Free Time

We centre our time around what we actually need to do. Like say you've got a doctor's appointment you've gotta to go to, you've gotta to go to

---

8 Graham St John (2003) makes this point when he notes that Maffesoli proposes a different kind of time for the neo-tribes of postmodern capital who oppose the time of capitalist production and its dominating effects.

that. If there's a supermarket you've gotta to get food, you've gotta get your food. But, in terms of hanging out time, it's really ... how we spend our time is different. 'Cause us punks on Friday nights it's really the time to figure out who you are. If you've got a regular five-day-a-week job, like from eight to five, you don't do anything on the weekend, weekdays. But us punks, on the weekends what we do is we call people and find something to do and find a party. (Tony)

The alternate form of the subjectum occurs in the re-appropriation of moments outside capital that operate without reference to a designated moment to follow. This is what might be called 'free time.' Not free in the sense that time is volitionally controlled by the 'free will' of the subject in time, but rather time as free in the immanence of its becoming without capture – that is to say, capture through the production of life defined through the moment before or the moment after. Living within the temporal space of free time engages youth as subjectum along a terrain that is produced by an immanent desire for pure subjective production. As Marx would have it, this is lived time in which the performative identity we have been tracing here as youth constructs the subject in time where 'nobody has one exclusive sphere of activity but each can become accomplished in any branch he wishes ... to hunt in the morning, fish in the afternoon, rear cattle in the evening, criticize after dinner ... without ever becoming hunter, fisherman, shepherd or critic' (Marx 1978/1992, p. 160).

This tension between the two modes of time – free time and captured time – is immensely productive within postmodern capitalism. For example, the use of time and its constant redefinition under different modes and regimes of capital constantly seeks to subject the creative force of youth to developmental time. However, as we have been arguing, the kind of time in which capital has encased adolescence is a negation of developmental time. Because adolescence is created as a space in which 'free time' or the time of creative force is allowed to operate, it must be held radically separate from the other kind of 'free time' the global adult is subject to in the world of work. There are thus two kinds of free time: the time of creative force in which the subjectum operates, and the time of free capital in which time can be used to capture labour in every moment without relief. This latter time is thoroughly dependent on the creative productivity of the free time of the subjectum because it has no creative force of its own.

Capturing and Controlling Free Time

Capital can only produce capital. It cannot produce anything else. Since it needs other productions in order to create profit, it requires spaces of free creativity. However, it must both contain and release such creative force in order to keep it alive while controlling it. In this sense, we can begin to see adolescence as a colonial situation in which the free colony of youth is allowed to operate within boundaries prescribed by the worlds of childhood and adulthood. Such boundaries must remain flexible so that shifting needs of capital can be accommodated as they develop. Incursions into the free colony of youth must be mounted on an ongoing basis to extract the material necessary for capital to produce capital. These incursions are in the form of the marketing and packaging of 'youth culture.'

These assaults into the territory of free creative time are not attacks to destroy but attacks to define and appropriate – in a word, to capture. It is within the frontier of free temporality that youth subcultures produce themselves. However, those subject to colonial rule but not of the colonial class are produced as perpetually visible on the surface of a society. This is because youth as creative force violates both the disciplined time of industrial capital, still extant in the postmodern world, and the free time conditions of postmodern capital. Such violations of the rules of capitalist time produce subjects which can be spotted outside of their assigned temporal role in the grids of age, gender, class, and location. It is precisely in this formulation that the categories of youth and adult begin to collapse, producing subjects of free time regardless of chronological age.[9] If one's movement through space, at any age, is not plotted by the progressive directionalities of school, profession, acquisition, and accumulation within capital, one is quickly visible as delinquent and guilty of the misuse of time. As Fabian (1983) points out, 'Time being an essential condition for "goal attainment," misallocation of time is at the bottom of most deviant behavior' (p. 40).

---

9 Gabriele Klein (2003, p. 41) makes a similar point when she states that pop culture 'has become a phenomenon that overlaps generations; it can therefore be characterized as a cultural practice that seems to dissolve the borders between youth and youthfulness.' She goes on in a footnote to cite the Rolling Stones and Eric Clapton as instances of this collapsing of traditional age-defined time.

To become what one will at any moment of the day is to radically re-conceive time outside of capital. It is a margin lived at the edge of the current mode of production, shot through with desire for a certain kind of liberation. This desire exists in constant tension between the productive contradictions of capture and liberatory impetus. Desire as the engine of production in this thoroughly material sense of struggle is rooted in the body. In this sense, it is the body in the end that sets our measure of time. All of the forms of time we have been exploring are fixed in the intensities, speeds, and slownesses of the body. It is the body that develops, that creates, that lives and produces. As Casarino points out, 'At the end of time there stands the body and its demands forever waiting to be attended to' (2003, p. 194).

Time and the Body

It is the body that produces history but not, as Casarino points out, through the subjectus that lives in developmental linear time. The history of the body is not a long line of progressive development to which the corporeal must subject itself. Instead, Casarino argues that history is precisely the liberation from such servitude to unbroken linear time. The moment of the body is a disruption in the temporality of development because the body lives only in the moment of its own becoming. That is to say, the body can only produce itself in a particular moment of contingent time. The body assembles itself in every moment out of selected components of all of the available elements of that moment, as we have already discussed in the definition of the event horizon. Those components are selected on the basis of their affinity to the composition of that particular body in that particular moment. In each of these contingent selections of composition, the body stops time. Casarino, following Benjamin, suggests that such a stoppage constitutes the time of authentic revolution. In such a 'halting of time and an interruption of chronology ... there springs not a new chronology but a qualitative alteration of time' (2003, p. 194).

This new time is premised on the pleasures of the body experienced in the assemblage of elements to which the body holds an affinity. To compose the body out of such elements increases the ability of the body to act. This notion that the body's capacities are composed from its ability to assemble itself out of elements with which it shares com-monalities comes from the philosophy of Spinoza. Indeed, Spinoza (2000) suggests that it is just such an assemblage of the body that produces the body's capacity to act, and it is in such capacity that Spinoza roots his definition of power: power is the capacity to act. Such capacity produces pleasure for the body, and it is the intensity of such pleasure that holds time in abeyance.

For our purposes here at the end of our discussion of time, youth as subjectum is composed of both the lines of desire and the experience of pleasure. The lines of desire are those elements of pure force we have delineated above using Deleuze's description of the infant as that subject in whom the affirmation of creative life force exceeds the capacity of the negative and breaks the bounds of developmental time. The experience of pleasure is the expansion of the body's capacity to act. Youth as subjectum in relation to time always stops time through the intensity of the experience of pleasure. Conversely, the agony of the subjectus is the pain of being caught in a time in which pleasure is but a fleeting moment.

In this regard adolescence, as that space between, is constituted as a realm of great pleasure and immeasurable agony. Youth as subjectum breaks that space open and stops time in its brutal progression towards entropy. As creative force rooted in the realm of affect, it collapses the developmental distinctions rooted in time as interval and opens youth as the force of pleasure to be experienced in radically different ways based on the different compositions of the body as it assembles itself out of the becoming world that surrounds it.

4 Bodily Powers

That one can liberate and recompose one's own body, formerly fragmented and dead in the servitude of an imaginary and, therefore, slavelike subjectivity, and take from this the means to think liberation freely and strongly, therefore, to think properly with one's own body, in one's own body, by one's own body, better: that to live within the thought of the conatus of one's own body was quite simply to think within the freedom and the power of thought.

Althusser[1]

It is to the composition of the body that we now turn our attention. The body is, finally, the site where all that we have been discussing thus far takes place. The creation of the worlds of identity, language, and time as we live them are located within the realm of the corporeal. It is through the body that we come to know the world. All that we can know must in some way be perceived, and that perception occurs through the body's sensory apparatus. Yet if the history of philosophy and science teaches us anything, it is that such perception is inevitably distorted. We do not know the world as it is, but only the world as we perceive it. These two kinds of knowledge, the world itself and the world we know, remain perpetually separated in the ways they are composed in the interaction between the body and the world. In sum, our senses deceive us. For example, as Spinoza (2000) points out, our perception of the size and distance of the sun comes nowhere close to its actual distance and dimension. We do not perceive it in its actuality.

---

1 Quoted in Caroline Williams (2005).

The discussions and debates on the role of the body in perception and reality are vast and complex. They are most certainly beyond the scope of our undertaking here. However, there is a small corner of this discourse in post-subculture literature that might well assist our exploration of youth as a new category of the political. This discussion centres around the theoretical work of Bourdieu and Butler that describes the body as a site of cultural production. In her essay on the performative body and pop culture, Klein (2003, pp. 44–5) traces the differences between Butler's and Bourdieu's work in terms that echo the distinctions we have been sketching throughout our discussion of the subjectus and the subjectum. The two central theoretical elements common to both theorists, as they consider the body in the context of pop culture, are the body as a performative space and the body as constituted through historical processes. Obviously these are themes we have encountered before in our discussion of identity, language, and time.

The Culturally Inscribed Body

In the work of Bourdieu, the body is produced as a container for what is learned over the course of lived human history. It is an expression of pragmatic learning garnered over centuries of experience. This field of knowledge interacts with the current lived experience of the body in performing what has been learned in an ever-shifting historical environment. In this interaction between what has been historically lived experience and what constitutes the current conditions of the social, structures and norms are confirmed and replicated. In this sense, the body is subject to the social history it has inherited and is the site in which the social norms and structures of the society are performed and confirmed.

For example, people in different parts of the world have culturally derived differences about the appropriate distance between bodies when speaking to one another. In North America, the cultural norm is to stand at a respectful distance and not 'get in their face.' However, in Central and South America the distance is much smaller and conversation can be comfortably held in much closer proximity. These habits of speech and the bodily performance of space are inherited by each of us and replicated in our daily lives without much reflection. If we are from North America and someone stands too close to us when speaking we become uncomfortable. Similarly, if someone from Central or

South America talks with a North American who stands at a distance, the North American can be perceived as cold or 'distant.' Bourdieu refers to these rules of corporeal engagement as the social codex of the body.

The Historically Inscribed Body

For Butler, the force of history in producing the body holds similar value. Following Foucault, Butler argues that the body is the site on which history inscribes its norms and habits. Like Bourdieu, she sees the body as the site through which the normative and disciplinary discourses of society are performed. However, as we have discussed previously, such discourses are not constituted only by their dominant forms, such as the normative structures described by Bourdieu. Instead, for Butler (1990), as for Deleuze and Guattari with respect to language, each discourse holds within it the possibility of resistance through the reassertion of alternate discourses or the discourses of those histories pushed aside in the rush to a common dominant discourse. It is the performances of these alternate discourses that also inscribe the body, in combination and contestation with the normative structural aspects of the social.

The Body as Alternative Discourse

To continue with the example introduced above, there are groups whose habits of body space stand outside the cultural norms of their society, whose inclination is to violate the social codex. An instance of this is the fact that girls and adolescent women in North America have a very different orientation to body space than the rest of the population does. Their sense of distance is much more intimate. If one watches a group of girls or young women, they often touch one another, stand close together in small groups to talk, or even comb each other's hair and adjust each other's clothing. Boys in a similar context do much less touching and hold considerably more distance in their interactions. One would very seldom find a teenage boy combing another boy's hair or adjusting his clothing. As the dominant mode of North American society remains predominantly patriarchal and heterosexist, this male habitus or codex constitutes the dominant discourse. The subjugated discourse of same-sex body proximity and intimacy both inscribes the body with a desire for intimate contact and prohibits such contact as individuals 'mature.' In other words, it inscribes the body with an alternative discourse that provides a mode of resistance to the dominant codex.

However, as Klein wisely points out, there is a significant 'difficulty [in] breaking a codex of norms in social practice precisely because the habitus inscribes itself in the body in such a subtle way that the body reproduces the codex of norms' (2003, p. 45). In other words, the body both produces and reproduces the norms and disciplines of the social, while the norms and disciplines of the social also produce the behavioural patterns of the body. This double inscription of norms that reproduce themselves between the body and its social environment makes it very difficult for the body to break free of old patterning. Once again, we have clearly found ourselves back in the arena of the subjectus.

The Biological Body

In order to move from this realm of the historically inscribed body that operates within the regimes of social discourse, either as an extension of normative practices, as Bourdieu describes, or as a site of resistance to such practices, as Butler proposes, we need to consider Klein's comment that 'both authors [Bourdieu and Butler] ... term the cultural constitution of certain phenomena "performative" to emphasize that they are not determined ontologically or biologically but produced by cultural processes' (2003, p. 44). This constitution of the performative sphere as outside biology and ontology is a laudable effort to bypass the essentialized aspects of both the philosophical and scientific discourses on the body. However, it does not provide the tools necessary to mount the new politics for youth-adult relations we have been constructing over the past few chapters. Nonetheless, the argument is worthy of examination on the way to seeking an alternative description of the body as subjectum.

Western scientific discourse has traditionally produced the body as limited to its physicality as a composite of flesh, bones, organs, electrical impulses, and chemical interactions. The focus has been thoroughly pragmatic and functional; that is, constrained to mapping the topography and function of the body and its component elements. Such a body is composed of normative functions that either work in predictable ways or break down and must be repaired. If the body cannot be fixed then mechanisms must be produced to compensate for the deviation.

Such compensatory mechanisms range from pacemakers for the heart, artificial limbs, and wheelchairs, to chemical compounds such as medications. The goal, however, is to restore the body to a normative baseline of function premised on an essentialized 'normal' body.

In the case of the physical body and its extended function through its limbs and organs, such remediation to functionality has been largely uncontested. The ability to have a heart that beats in a strong and regular fashion or legs that can convey the body with little or no trouble seems like a reasonable set of ambitions. The problem at the level of organs and limbs has been the cultural inscription of the non-normative body – the body without sight, hearing, mobility, or stamina. These bodies have, within the history of Western modernity, been read as holding inherent limitations. The description of these limitations by the dominant society has led to a range of disciplinary responses and mechanisms, including institutionalization, restricted access to work, school, or housing, exclusion and discrimination in the realm of social interaction, and the proclamation of these bodies as radically distinct and inferior to the normative body.

Terms such as able bodies and disabled bodies carry the stigma of such difference. In this sense, the ability to augment sight, hearing, or mobility in a way that does not signal a broken body any more than the use of a car indicates a disability for the normative body is certainly a boon. The use of computerized wheelchairs, speech enablers, advanced hearing aids, prosthetic limbs, and computer-aided virtual sight create whole new possibilities for the differently-abled body.

These are cyborg formations of flesh and machine that recompose the body within the postmodern moment as being able to exceed the limited categories of abled and disabled. Through cyborg technology, both normative bodies and bodies constructed as outside the norm begin to lose their functional distinction through cyborg technology. They introduce whole new discourses of the body that shift the normative codexes of society and produce new modes of resistance to the description of the 'broken' body. These cyborg forms bring a new cachet to Spinoza's (2000) famous assertion that no one knows what a body can do. In this sense, we can begin to see how reading the body according to its evolving historical and cultural descriptions, as Bourdieu and Butler propose, allows us to make sense of the body outside of the limited frameworks of essentialized biological medicine and imagine new horizons for the body's capacity to act.

In the realm of the chemical body, things become considerably more contested. In this arena, the chemistry of the brain is similarly essentialized by Western medicine and biology as a series of cause-and-effect relations between chemical levels and behaviours. The dominant discourses on brain science assert clearly that depression, schizophrenia, mania, learning disabilities, and attention deficit disorders stem from a chemical imbalance in the body. Such an imbalance is considered to be a disease process and like the physical body, the chemical body requires remediation through the introduction of other chemicals designed to bring it back into normative balance.

Certainly, this discourse has had a huge impact on the field of adolescent science, where the adolescent body has been essentialized as inherently out of balance chemically, due to the hormonal changes of the maturation process. In addition, youth as developmentally defined bodies are subject to chemical intervention at an increasing rate of frequency for behaviours the dominant society finds troubling, such as not paying attention in school, being sad and withdrawn, or being defiant. The fact that an increasing number of researchers have questioned the validity of chemical explanations and pointed to dangerous side effects of chemical intervention has only minimally slowed the distribution of the medical discourse of chemical imbalance as an explanation for what the dominant social perceives as troublesome behaviour.[2]

The notion of the adolescent body as a body inherently out of balance has tremendous force in contemporary society. It produces an immense array of social discourses about how the adolescent body should be managed, including the production of laws regarding drug and alcohol use; the age at which one should be allowed to operate a car; the age at which one should graduate from secondary school; the age of consent for sex; the sentencing options for crimes committed. All of these laws incorporate the essentialized discourse of the chemical composition of the adolescent body. In addition, parenting strategies, counselling and therapy techniques, educational approaches, and other forms of social interaction or intervention are riddled with the discourse of the chemical body.

Lost in this essentialism is any alternative discourse on the body that might view its chemical composition outside of the normative codex that constructs the adolescent body as an essentialized biological reality. Also missing here is any analysis of the historical struggles in psychiatry and biology that have contested the idea that chemicals can

2 See Garland (2004).

be directly linked to behaviour or their presence generalized beyond a specific body at a specific point in time.[3]

Problems with Bypassing the Biological Body

Although Bourdieu's and Butler's strategy of bypassing the biological body in favour of the culturally or discursively constructed body is valuable, it also runs the risk of producing an alternative transcendent description. That is to say, it generates a description that stands aside from the body-as-body in order to produce an explanation of the body from the outside. By transcendent, I am referring to a system of belief or knowledge that stands separate from and hierarchically superior to that which is being described or known. In privileging the discursive or the cultural, descriptions of the body transcend the body itself. The body is seen to be produced as an effect of the social through its performances of historical struggles over knowledge and power. Thus the body's performances do not arise from within the body but are the result of the struggle for meaning and structure in society. As Foucault states, 'The body is the inscribed surface of events (traced by language and dissolved by ideas), the locus of a dissociated self (adopting the illusion of a substantial unity), and a mass in perpetual disintegration. Genealogy, as the analysis of provenance, returns us to the articulation of the body and history: it exposes a body invested by history and history ravaging the body' (Foucault, quoted in Chambers, 1990, p. 67).

I am not arguing here that the discursive or cultural proposals about the body should be dismissed. Without question, there is a complex relationship between the discursive and cultural realm and the behaviours of the body. The insight, even more pronounced in the writings of Marx, that the body is both a product and a repository of historical struggle is crucial to our discussions of youth-adult relations. In the company of other subaltern bodies such as the female body, the working class body, the racialized body, and the gay body, the adolescent body is clearly a performative instance of exactly such struggles. The adolescent body that is habitually disciplined into the stereotyped postures and walks of the rebellious youth provides a more than ample example of both Bourdieu's and Butler's positions.

I guess you kinda see ... I see everybody with tattoos and I guess with the

---

3 See the anti-psychiatric writings of Guattari (Genosko, 1996; 2002), Laing (Burston, 1998; Miller, 2005), Szasz (1984), and Basaglia (1987).

movement, the movements the body, I would say that a lot of like punk-like guys, especially like kinda slouchy sorta, you know, not really ... don't really sit up straight ever, kinda sit back cool in the chair with a cigarette or something and I guess you know, most people have pretty decent posture and you know sit with their hands in their lap or crossed or something like that and I guess I can't really describe the movements of like a skin but punk rockers definitely have kind of a definition. You know they kind of look like ... the way I describe it isn't the best but, kind of dangly or somethin'. Like Gumby, I don't know. (Tony)

As we noted above, however, the culturally constructed body is largely a description of the subjectus. Even in Butler's argument (following Foucault) that there are performances of alternative knowledge that dissemble and resist the force of dominant description, the body still holds no force of its own but remains the vehicle for discursive expression. If we are to think the body-as-youth in its aspect as subjectum, such a body must hold an immanent relation to its own productions; it must be a body that creatively produces itself.

Towards an Immanent Biology of the Body

In order to articulate an imminent biology of the body, we need to return to the seventeenth century and the philosophy of Spinoza. In his classic and highly controversial text *Ethics*, Spinoza (2000) offers a definition of the body that might be useful here. He proposes that the body is not a single entity made up of component parts, each of which is subordinate to the body as a whole. Rather, he suggests that the human body is a composite of many bodies. These bodies include everything from atoms and molecules to organs and the brain; in short, every kind and combination of living matter. Instead of being just one body made up of parts, bodies are instead composite organisms of living matter.[4]

---

4 In a recent article in the *New York Times*, Robin Marantz Henig reports, 'Of the trillions and trillions of cells in a typical human body – at least 10 times as many cells in a single individual as there are stars in the Milky Way – only about 1 in 10 is human. The other 90 percent are microbial. These microbes – a term that encompasses all forms of microscopic organisms, including bacteria, fungi, protozoa and a form of life called archaea – exist everywhere. They are found in the ears, nose, mouth, vagina, anus, as well as every inch of skin, especially the armpits, the groin and between the toes. The vast majority are in the gut, which harbors 10 trillion to 100 trillion of them. "Microbes colonize our body surfaces from the moment of our birth," Gordon said. "They are with us throughout our lives, and at the moment of our death they consume us."' *New York Times*, 13 August 2006.

Spinoza is arguing here against the idea that the human body is a singular mass that can be understood as a totality. Instead, all living matter, including what we call the body, is made of many bodies all operating in common purpose. He goes on to argue that each body has structural similarities but radically different expressive capacities. That is to say, each body is a unique and idiosyncratic expression of the life force that comprises it. And every body is made up of many bodies, each of which expresses a unique aspect of life force.

According to Spinoza, the force of each body resides in what he calls its conatus, or its desire to persist in its unique expression of life. This desire to persist is amplified or given more force by its collision with other bodies. Conversely, its conatus can also be restrained by such collisions. Each of the bodies that make up the human body is colliding with the other bodies that make up the organism. To the degree that these collisions amplify the ability of each body to persist in its expression, that body has more power and its expression is extended and given more force. Spinoza goes on to suggest that what determines the quality of the collision is whether or not the bodies in question have the capacity to recognize the life force they hold in common. If this is the case, then the bodies together each amplify each other's unique idiosyncratic expression. To the degree they do not hold commonality, they are toxic to one another and decrease each other's the life force.

In concrete terms, each of our organs is comprised of composites of atoms, molecules, and cells arranged in a unique configuration based on certain commonalities and differences. To the degree that these composites are sympathetic to the common purposes of the organ, that organ gains force in its unique function within the body. To the degree that a cell or chemical is introduced that holds no sympathetic correspondence, the ability of the organ to function is decreased or even eliminated. A concrete example of this is the process of cancer, which can be initiated through the introduction of chemicals, cells, and genes that hold no sympathetic correspondence to the existing composite body or organ.

This model extends throughout the body in the sense that each organ has a unique and idiosyncratic function that either holds a sympathetic correspondence of purpose to the other organs or does not. If the heart and liver operate well to common but distinctly different purposes, the composite human body functions well. If they operate without correspondence, through the introduction of bodies with which they hold no commonality, they lose capacity or force to express their function.

What is of interest to us is that this is a biological explanation of the body that is non-essentialized.[5] There is no normative biological body in Spinoza's philosophy. Each biological structure is made up of radically idiosyncratic expressions of life in combination for a common purpose. Obviously I am not suggesting, nor would Spinoza, that this is a conscious process in which atoms and cells make decisions about what they hold in common. Rather, this is a thoroughly immanent biology in which combinations are made through random collisions that create the body as a dynamic ongoing process of living matter. What makes Spinoza's notion of the body additionally interesting is the fact that this living matter is expressive of an infinitude of different capacities. This is why Spinoza says that no one knows what a body can do.

Seeing the body as a fully expressive organism means it cannot be essentialized or reduced to any set of structures or relations. To say that the body is limited by a particular set of chemical interactions based on an analysis of observed behaviour, as the most reductionist psychiatry attempts to do, is to miss the fact that each body holds the capacity to form itself into new configurations of expression and force based in new collisions with other bodies it has not encountered yet. With this, we are returned to Deleuze and Guattari's definition of the child, which states that the child is the becoming aspect in every age. That is to say that the body over its lifespan will encounter many, many bodies, and that each body will either amplify or decrease its creative expression of a particular and unrepeatable singularity of life force. Clearly, here we are in the arena of the body as subjectum, or the body in its full creative expression of life force. This is the body as fully biological in its expressive capacities of performance. Indeed, Spinoza would say that the field of the discursive, as described by Bourdieu and Butler, constitutes inadequate knowledge – knowledge that is not necessarily wrong, but not fully able to describe what a body can do.

The Ontological Body

In attempting to describe the body as an immanent rather than an essentialized biological organism, we have come to the second half of Klein's argument about the performative body, which is that it is not

---

5 For a current scientific utilization of Spinoza in neurology, see Damasio (2003).

ontological. In saying that the performative escapes the field of ontology, Klein suggests that ontology implies a certain essentiality of being-ness. That is to say that the body, in being described as an entity that exists, runs the risk of becoming fixed in time and space within the categories and taxonomies of scientific and social description.

However, I would argue that Klein offers a limited reading of the ontological body. Ontology, or the study of what exists, often comprises an inquiry into the essence of the body. This kind of examination tries to determine the actual core nature of the body and how we might discover its essential qualities. In this sort of a discourse, there is a notion that bodies can be defined by a careful taxonomy of their essential components. The distinction here is between the real body that exists and perceived bodies that we believe exist but do not. In this distinction, the essential body is that body which best manifests all of the component essences of the complete body.

In the arenas of childhood, adolescence, and adulthood, the discussion has focused on whether child and adolescent bodies can be seen to have ontological reality, as they are described as incomplete bodies in comparison to the adult body. In other words, the ontological investigation of what constitutes the essential human body is based on the adult body as having the greatest degree of reality, because it is considered to be the completed body. Child and adolescent bodies are considered merely transitional stages on the way to this adult body.[6] In debates over child rights, this point begins to have serious political consequences when we are trying to decide which bodies are allowed to have rights within society.

The issue of contention centres on whether the child body exists as a separate ontological being or whether it only exists in relation to becoming an adult. If it exists as a state of being with its own ontological integrity, then it can claim legal status or rights as a political subject. If it is only seen as a becoming adult, then the argument is that it must always be subject to the greater realities of adult bodies. In other words, the child or adolescent body is not as real as the adult body and therefore cannot claim as great a degree of political right. This argument is often tied to the question of whether a child is being or becoming. Becoming in this sense is seen as less real, because it is a

---

6 My thanks to Shauna Pomerantz, who points out that the young female body is seen as even less complete than that of the male adolescent: she needs more care, takes more worry, and in Freudian terms is experienced as a 'lack.'

transitional stage on the way to the essential body. Here the essence of the body is seen to be best expressed in the body as a finished developmental being which has ceased to transform and is now perceived to be biologically mature. It is this kind of essentialism that Bourdieu and Butler are trying to leave behind in stepping aside from the ontological body.

Towards a New Ontology of the Body

Leaving aside the dubious nature of the claim that the adult body is biologically complete, I want to engage a different form of ontology premised in an immanent description of bodies. In his book on Spinoza, *Expressionism in Philosophy*, Deleuze (1992) makes a complex and challenging explication of Spinoza's ontology. While the full implications of Deleuze's challenge cannot be addressed here, his main points suggest a different usage of the terms being and becoming in describing the body.

According to Deleuze, Spinoza states that what we know as physical being comes into existence as when 'an infinity of simple bodies, corresponding to its essence, actually belong to it ... in a certain relation of movement and rest' (1992, p. 208). This should be somewhat familiar from our previous discussion of the body in Spinoza; this description adds the idea of an essence and a certain set of relations. Let's turn to the question of the essence first.

For Spinoza, the essence of a body always involves its expression of a particular and idiosyncratic aspect of what he called God or substance, and what we have been calling life force. In this sense, the existence of a body is premised not in any sense of an essence that can be distilled through a taxonomic examination of its mature form; rather, the being-ness of a body is premised on its unique expression of life force. In other words, the essence of all bodies is premised in their common relation as expressions of life. However, each body's essence in this sense is always radically different. It is always a composite of other bodies, as described above, in 'a certain relation of movement and rest.'

That is to say that the body is both collective and dynamic. Its essence is no particular thing or state; rather, the essence of the body is always made of a set of relations that constantly express a particular set of living capacities. In this sense, the distinction noted in our brief discussion of child rights between being and becoming collapses, because being and becoming are the same in Spinozist ontology. Being and becoming are simply different moments of movement and rest within the larger set of relations that define the idiosyncratic logic of each body's constitution by the collectivity of bodies that comprise it. This set of relations, according to Deleuze, consists of 'three components: a singular essence, which is a degree of power or intensity; a particular existence, always composed of an infinity of extensive parts; and an individual form that is the characteristic or expressive relation' (1992, p. 209).

In this definition of the ontological status of the body or its existence, the state of being that comprises the body is always a relation between a) intensity/power; b) an infinite and contingent set of relations with other bodies; and c) an individual or singular expression of the previous two states. This three-way relationship should look somewhat familiar as the same set of relations that comprises the subjectum. If we recall, the subjectum is comprised of a certain kind of power which we have described as the power to act. In an ontological definition, this power is augmented by another element discussed briefly in our description of youth as subjectum: the intensity of such power. In examining the becoming youth or child, we quoted Deleuze and Guattari (1987) as describing the force of the child as being able to 'shatter paving stones.' Power, for our purposes here, is the intensity with which life force can be expressed through the acts of the body.

The second term of existence is the infinity of extensive parts, which we can read here as the connection all bodies have to all other bodies. One of the reasons that Spinozist ontology allows us to escape the essentialist ontologies that pit adolescence and childhood against the mature adult is that there is no body separable from other bodies. All bodies, as Deleuze (1992) points out, are 'grouped in constantly changing infinite wholes.' Therefore, there is no opportunity to essentialize a particular body as ideal, because it is always in a set of relations with other bodies that determine its composition and decomposition according to mechanical laws that no body can control. These mechanical laws are the laws of sympathetic or unsympathetic relations, which either amplify conatus or decompose the body. Therefore, the body is a dynamic and constantly shifting form which cannot be essentialized as separable from the web of living bodies that produce, sustain, and decompose it.

Finally, there is the individual body that has the primary function of expressing a particular aspect of the web of life we have been discussing. This is not an expression of an individual essence but the individual expression of a common essence shared by all bodies. Things become complex here, however, because according to Spinoza this essence that is common to all life, which he calls substance or God, is not an ideal pre-existing form. It is instead a form that can only know itself at the moment it expresses its essence in an infinitude of ever-shifting new thought and physical expression.

There is no essential form to life in Spinoza's philosophy. The body as an expression of life expresses an essence through the manifestations of the body. In a word, it is a thoroughly immanent system, or something that produces itself. The Spinozist ontology is an immanent ontology that describes the process by which life produces itself through the infinitude of expressive capacities found in both the individual body and the infinite collective of bodies that is life at any given moment. Clearly, here we can see the subjectum as the force of creative expression at work once again.

The Body as Subjectum

We can see that the body as performative can be read at the level of historical discourse, as with Bourdieu and Butler, but that this reading has limitations because of the problems of language outlined previously. However, we have also seen how the performative body holds what Deleuze and Guattari (1987) refer to as 'pass-words' beneath the 'order-words'; in other words, there are lines of flight from the historical transcription of norms onto the body. These lines of flight are to be found in the creative performance of the body by the body. In this sense, the body as subjectum-youth is performatively both communal and individual space. It is biologically and ontologically multiple and contingent, dependent on the field of life that surrounds it and simultaneously the very ground out of which that field comes into being.

We can see this in the manner in which subjectum youth within subcultures produce the body in an ongoing proliferation of creative performance. It is tattooed, dyed, stretched, pierced, dressed, cut, and shaped.

> Punks are sort of crazy about their bodies. I mean, the crazy coloured hair, the Mohawks, the I don't give a fuck attitude. I mean, it's just like saying fuck you, fuck your conventions, and fuck whatever you want to

think if you want to look at me and not like me for it, well, I don't care. (Tony)

For all of this, though, the body does not simply comprise an inside and outside space upon which the codex of society can be produced and resisted. The body offers us a mode of performance that produces itself in a manner that exceeds the trap of speaking and the ritual of subsequent interrogation. The body cannot be questioned. The body in producing itself precedes the conditions of its own awareness as thought through the mind. As Spinoza observes about life per se, the body cannot know itself until it has expressed itself through all of the bodies involved in its expression. Similarly, the body cannot be aware of itself until it collides with all of the other bodies in the moment of the act.

However, the acts of the body have no meaning and can give no explanation within the realm of communication. They are absolute performativity, which can be read but does not speak. This sounds like a solipsism until we realize that a body cannot read another body. Each collision between bodies only allows each body to know its own state of being, not the state of the other body. Youth as the subjectum of any age can allow each body to amplify its conatus or power to act to the degree that each body comes to know its own idiosyncratic state at any given moment of its production. In other words, the individual body can only come to awareness of itself through other bodies, but it cannot know other bodies through such an awareness.

In our exploration of youth-adult relations, this takes us back to the Spivakian problem of speech and communication. The question is, can the body of youth as subjectum speak? Can we interpret the creative acts of the body through reading the tattoos, piercings, dyeing, walking, dancing, and fighting? I would argue here that we cannot. The body of youth as subjectum is an impenetrable surface which does not speak of itself. In this sense we cannot know it. That said, the body can speak to us of our own potential creative force. The creative acts of another body hold the force of the truly political; that is, the capacity to inspire our own body to act and create itself in its own idiosyncratic form. The body in collision allows for the proliferation of creative force. To the degree that this force produces copies or mimetic repro-ductions, we can see the world of the subjectus in operation with all its attendant communication and coding. The subjectum, on the other hand, is pure performativity of a unique unrepeatable expression of the body in the differences produced through elision and collision. This body is the workhorse of desire, whose lines and movements operate in contradistinction to the order-words of language. As Butler points out, 'the body is always under siege, suffering destruction by the very terms of history. And history is the very creation of values and meanings by a signifying practice that requires the subjection of the body. This corporeal destruction is necessary to produce the speaking subject and its significations' (1990, p. 165).

The body, as the productive space in which desire is expressed through the acts and labour of living beings, both creates the history to which it becomes subject and eludes that history to produce a new history; that is to say, the future. In this process, youth and adult bodies operate in tandem and the developmental distinctions between them break down. We do not produce history according to our age, but through the acts of all bodies at all ages. Both our memories and our future are produced by the acts of the body in a perpetual state of the present. The body as subjectum is not a being subject to the forces of history limited to the realm of signification, but a moment-to-moment becoming; a constantly produced Foucauldian point of intersection between lines of history, politics, discourse, technology, and geography, to name but a few of the productions, elisions, and collisions of bodies in flight through time. If, however, the body is not subject to the realm of communication and language in its signifying manifestation as the order-word, 'then what language is left for understanding [its] corporeal enactment ... that constitutes its interior signification on the surface?' (Butler, 1990, p. 117).

Such a language can only follow the logic of poetry and evocation outlined in chapter 1 – a logic of performance that explodes from the inside of an idea, a structure, a pattern, a life. The language of evocation breaks apart the logic of the socially constructed body, not through making sense of it but by challenging the logic of physical sense through re-combinatory pastiches of performance out of time and context. In the postmodern world of youth subculture we can see examples of how the body is performed in this way as a combination of expressions from different geographies, historical periods, and cultural contexts. Hence the logic of the Mohawk, the tribal piercings, the work boots and sweater vests, the suspenders and t-shirts. It is the African-American skinhead with the 'Made in America' tattoo, the English boots, the Irish cap, and the love of American muscle cars. Here we can refer back to Butler (1990), who sees this performative pastiche as a way of subverting the codes inscribed on the body through the very deployment of such codes. 'If subversion is possible, it will be a subversion from within the terms of the law, through the possibilities that emerge when the law turns against itself and spawns unexpected permutations of itself. The culturally constructed body will then be liberated, neither to its "natural" past, nor to its original pleasures, but to an open future of cultural possibilities' (p. 9)

Returning to Butler Anew

With this reading, we come full circle in our examination of the body. The circle, however, arrives at our point of origin and finds that it is new. For here we find Butler describing the same immanent process Deleuze and Guattari have been tracing. This is the moment in which the order betrays itself, or as Butler puts it, the moment in which the law turns against itself. It is in this moment that the subjectum gains full force. In our own historical moment, it is when the logic of capital opens the colonial regimes of control and domination into the new regimes of global control. This shift breaks apart the hybridized constructions of postcoloniality through the collisions of millions of bodies previously held apart. These new and unpredictable collisions open the possibilities for an infinitude of subversions and insurrections of the body as a new collective force without limit. This new world of the global produces new bodies that flee in all directions in massive flows across borders and identities. This body as rhizomatic flight, or flight in all directions at once, extends and amplifies the creative force of the body in ways we cannot yet imagine.[7]

Of course, these new possibilities also increase the efforts of those whose interest is in domination to re-inscribe the old codes into the new world through war, terror, and economic subjugation. Nonetheless, the body as productive of the force of desire that drives history forward continually exceeds any capacity of the subjectus to fully contain or capture it. Such a new body is not, as Butler asserts, the 'interior signification on the surface,' but the extension of the surface in infinite multitudinous lines of flight operating within and against the new modes of control; the new codes and laws of culture and language. It is, in short, the body as space – as frontier.

---

7 See Hardt and Negri (2000).

5 Space:
Of Burrows and Mirrors

> How can we escape the 'politics of space,' the inevitable striation of mapping? As Deleuze and Guattari remind us, liberation is impossible even in smooth space, but within it we might at least find different fluxes and trajectories and the possibility of further deterritorialization. (St Pierre, 1997, p. 371)

We have already begun our entry into the relationship of space to youth-adult relations in describing adolescence as a 'space between.' Now we need to seriously engage this phrase in its concrete implications for a material mapping of youth and adults in the literal distribution of bodies across space. We have discussed in the past few chapters the ways in which time and identity provide both liberatory possibilities and disciplinary structures for the body. We have also reviewed how the body itself is a certain kind of space of both social and self production. Of course, all of this occurs not just within the domains of thought and concept, but also within the material world of the landscapes and geographies of schools, homes, cities, fields, jails, streets, highways, and towns. The question we must ask here is a variation of the same one we have been pursuing throughout our discussion so far: is space simply a given reality which we all share, or is it – like language, identity, and time – a contested arena in which youth and adults struggle to create a place and a space of mutual self-production?

In the quote that opens this chapter, St Pierre suggests that space is political. Of course we know this, at one level, from our own experience of nation states, cities, and even schools as geographical entities that have boundaries established by political processes such as treaties, constitutions, laws, and/or revolutions and armed struggle. Such spaces require entry and exit documents that provide proof of membership in the body politic. Indeed, a significant aspect of our identity is tied up in our affiliations with various political geographies, including neighborhoods, schools, cities, or towns, and of course the nation state. Many people feel such a strong affinity to national identity that they would even fight and die for their country.

> Like, I'm Norwegian and Swedish I put on my flag because I'm really proud of that. I'm really proud of where I came from. I'm not so much proud of what my race is but where I came from. I think it's really cool, like, I don't identify myself racially. I identify myself as country, like where I'm from. (Frank)

Geographies of Bare Life

The constitution of national geography is space as the macro-political or space writ large as a dominant construction to which each body must acquiesce or face sanction. To be without national identity is to place oneself in a very dangerous situation. Indeed, it is to become what Agamben (1995) refers to as 'bare life,' or life that can be killed, imprisoned, or enslaved without legal sanction. We can see this in the ways in which undocumented immigrant populations, refugees, and non-state-affiliated combatants are dealt with by powerful nation states such as the United States. For example, undocumented youth who travel across the national boundary of the nation state to either seek work or to re-unite with family members residing there illegally can be incarcerated without trial or right to legal counsel until the state sees fit to release them. Even at the point of release, such young people do not have any right to decide where they are sent but are at the mercy of the state, which can send them anywhere it chooses without any responsibility for their welfare. Similarly, refugees who have fled war or genocide to live in other nation states have little or no legal rights within the host country. Any humanitarian aid is contingent on the benevolence of the nation state and the non-governmental organizations that work between and across nations to provide for basic needs such as food, medicine, housing, and even water. Such populations of young people and adults hold no legal right to self-determination or even rudimentary defence. Indeed, any armed response on their part to military incursions into refugee camps or to denial of basic human needs is often classified as terrorism.

This takes us to our final example of bare life, the terrorist, who is defined here as a non-state-affiliated combatant. Such combatants become, by virtue of their armed resistance to the nation state, a stateless subject. Leaving aside the particular agendas and tactics of non-state combatants, the issue here is the consequence of their status as stateless. In particular, within what the United States has called the 'war on terror,' such subjects lose all legal rights, either national or international, and are subject to the particularities of bureaucratic policy. Through this they can be incarcerated, tortured, moved from state to state, and kept incommunicado with the outside world. It is not insignificant that many of these subjects are young people.

Of course, for centuries totalitarian regimes centred in individual states have used this practice of designating certain people who oppose state power as having no legal status. In this case, however, while the war on terror is centred in an individual state (the United States), its practices are distributed among many nation states that cooperate in incarceration, torture, and transport. The ability to engage in this international effort is premised on the status of the terrorist subject as having no national status as a combatant.

Obviously, then, we have a significant number of people who are, as Luhmann (1995) would term it, radically excluded from the realm of citizenship and its benefits.[1] Such subjects are clearly 'bare life,' without any legal status or rights under national statute. The United Nations has attempted to provide international protections for these subjects, but such instruments as the Convention on the Rights of the Child have proven woefully inadequate in the face of genocidal national policies in places like the Darfur region of Sudan, the Middle East, Somalia, Brazil, Chile, Nepal, the suburbs of Paris, and the inner cities of the United States. In addition, such international law holds very little force against the economic policies of entities such as the International Monetary Fund and the World Bank, which structure the economics of nation states through loans and economic disciplinary mechanisms so that even citizens are denied such necessities as free schooling for young people.[2]

---

1 See also Hardt and Negri (2004).
2 See Lewis (2005).

Geographies of Citizenship

Indeed, the politics of space, as articulated within the formations of the nation state, offer only slightly more protection for the loyal citizen subject than they do for the 'bare life' subject, and such protections always come at the price of acquiescent discipline. As Foucault (1975) has so eloquently argued, it is specifically within the productions and discoveries of how certain spaces function that the disciplinary mechanisms of modernity came into full force. In modernity it is the deployment of what Foucault calls social diagrams that structure social space to the ends of dominant power structures. Such a diagram is defined as a mapping of space that is initially rather specific, such as the panopticon that was designed as a mechanism for disciplining prison populations through twenty-four-hour surveillance.[3] According to Foucault, this purely physical mechanism expanded into a much broader social diagram of surveillance that held both physical and psychological properties, allowing the church and state to use it to produce self-observing and self-disciplining subjects. A similar diagram was constituted in the assembly line of the Fordist factory, which extended itself from disciplining workers so they would efficiently produce goods into a deployment within the practices of education that disciplined child bodies into the habits of good factory workers. Such social diagrams use space as the vehicle for producing a micropolitics of the body that is then internalized within the psychic structures of self-discipline.

Geographies of the Subjectus

We can see that space is not at all a neutral arena of passive landscapes and structures, but a dynamic and contested geography that can be used to the benefit of dominant power. By now we recognize such a formulation as the domain of the subjectus. Space as the domain of the subjectus constitutes what St Pierre refers to as 'the inevitable striation of mapping.' By this she means the ability to divide space according to diagrams such as a certain description of the body, a certain designation of living beings as belonging to a certain geography, or a certain

---

3 The panoptocon consisted of a tower from which guards could monitor inmates at all times, but inmates could not see the guards and therefore never knew when they were being observed.

geography belonging to a group of people. These maps that describe the body, the ecosystem, and the nation are not simply more-or-less accurate delineations of how space is configured but are the result of struggle and contestation, not just about the boundaries or ownership of space but about the very nature of space itself.

Let's consider the map of the diseased body in contemporary Western culture. The Western map of the body is premised on the diagrams of Western medicine. In this mapping, the body is an enclosed space that, as described earlier in our discussion of the body, has internal organs and chemical-electrical flows that determine its health and well being. The health of the body is largely considered to be an internal affair in which even toxins or diseases that enter from the outside are primarily dealt with as a problem of the immune capacity of the individual body. This immune capacity is considered to be the result of a combination of factors within the body, inclusive of genetics and the current chemical composition of the body. The mapping is such that medical intervention is almost always premised on the individual body that requires chemical or surgical intervention. Even the 'holistic' approaches of Western medicine still use the individual map of the body to guide regimes of relaxation, massage, meditation, and diet.

Of course, the field of public health and epidemiology focuses on the body within the larger context of the ecosystem, both social and environmental. However, this work again largely concentrates on the distribution of diseases across individual bodies and on the ways in which social forces such as schools, clinics, and government agencies might discipline such bodies to prevent the spread of disease throughout society. Classic examples of this work include the efforts in the United States to construct various social problems such as youth violence as disease processes that can be deterred through social interventions that educate individual bodies. A less prominent aspect of epidemiology, which begins to challenge this map of the body as a thoroughly separate space, is research that looks at the relationship between bodies and the environment. This is, however, highly contested space. As an example, take the disease of cancer. In the classic mapping of the body, this disease is indicative of a failure of either genetics or immune capacity. In an environmental mapping of the body, the complex interrelationships between high levels of toxins being produced in the environment by global capital and their impact on the body constitute a map that situates the body in a much larger field. Such a mapping, of course, is immensely problematic for the dominant power structures of late-stage capitalism because it implies that the health of the body requires intervention into the ways that products are manufactured and distributed. Lest we think this is simply an academic distinction without political implications, we should note that the funding for cancer research is heavily weighted against the environmental map.[4] This has a significant impact on how cancer is treated and the perceptions the public holds about its causes.

Geographies of Mental Illness

A similar example of the mapping of disease concerns the proliferation and distribution of 'mental illness' among young people. Again, this mapping is predominantly produced on diagrams of the individual body. The rise in depression, anxiety, bipolar disorder, and even oppositional defiant disorder, we are told, is due to chemical imbalances or genetic predispositions in the developing body of the individual. When the question is raised about recent rises in the number of young people affected, the answer is given that the reason we have not seen these diseases to this degree before is because we have not had the tools to properly diagnose them. Intervention is again at the level of the individually mapped body. The question might well be asked, as it has been about cancer, whether such exponential increases in disorder might be related to environmental factors, but research in this area is also minimal, with a great emphasis on the Western medical model. Once again, this has significant implications for practice, as many of the ideas that youth workers hold about the behaviours they see in young people are premised in this biomedical mapping of the body.

To situate the body within the environment and to move away from this individualistic biomedical mapping, however, is to struggle against the status quo. In fact, the distribution of bodies across the spaces of nations and territories has an immensely contested history that extends well into the present moment. The mapping of living bodies such as animals and plants throughout the nineteenth century produced them as available for harvesting and exploitation. As soon as a species was 'discovered' or mapped, consideration was given to its utility for the emerging industrial and mercantile capitalist projects. The mapping of living bodies as commodities or raw materials was accomplished with extremely limited regard to the complex interplay

---

4 See Evans (2006).

of life as ecology with its own parameters of health and well being. Such mapping led and still leads to the extinction of whole species.

It was and is similar thinking about people that led to the Atlantic slave trade and to the current distribution of labouring bodies (child and adult alike) across the globe. The mapping of bodies as useful or not useful produces concepts of life or living bodies as expendable or irrelevant.[5] In the conquest of the Americas, this led to the genocide and forced relocation of native peoples who, as Hardt and Negri (2000) point out, were considered to be a part of nature that was in the way, like a rock or a tree, and needed to be removed. In current practice, this leads to the radical economic and political exclusion of the poor of the barrios and ghettos or the disenfranchised of the refugee camps.[6]

Diagrams of Inclusion and Exclusion

These patterns of exclusion and inclusion are mapped on diagrams of belonging. Such maps permeate our concepts of community and identity. The affiliation to the nation state, as discussed above, is one such example. The nation state, however, is in increasing crisis as alternative modes of affiliation challenge its hegemony. The increase of ethnic and religious affiliations create new maps of belonging that exceed the boundaries of the nation state and produce global interconnected networks of perceived community. Similarly, Maffesoli's (1996) notion of the neo-tribe comprised of people who loosely affiliate along subcultural or political lines comprises another global network that goes beyond the parameters of the nation state.

> I think we are a lot like tribes – different groups in the cities. Skinheads and punks have crews but not gangs – gangs all based on crimes but crews based on hangin' out and having a good time. I think we are a lot like tribal cultures – you have certain things to express you are in this crew, certain things to express you are in a band – your jacket. (Gary)

This is not to say, however, that the nation state has lost its force as an instrument of inclusion or exclusion. Indeed, the most dominant groups in society within late-stage capitalism rely on the existence of the nation state to regulate flows of bodies across borders to their

---

5 See the discussion of 'bare life' above.
6 See Luhman (1995); Hardt and Negri (2004).

advantage. Of course, these groups of super-capitalists continually strive to reconfigure the democratic liberal nation state to their own ends by emptying the state of regulations and limitations for capital, while increasing its ability to exclude and regulate the labour and consumption of bodies. One might argue, as Naomi Klein (2004) and Hardt and Negri (2004) do, that the U.S. military intervention in Iraq is not a battle between nation states but an attempt to gain control of the nation state for experiments in new forms of capitalism, free of restriction and constraint.

Mapping the Subjectum: Rhizomes and Heterotopias

In the quote that opens this chapter, St Pierre asks, 'How can we escape the "politics of space," the inevitable striation of mapping?' The short answer is that we escape the inevitable striation of mapping through the map itself. In this space of contestation and subjection to geographies and mappings determined by dominant power regimes through the deployment of boundaries, limits, and affiliations, there are what Deleuze and Guattari (1987) refer to as burrows or rhizomes comprised of multiple entrances and exits – what Foucault (1986) calls heterotopic spaces. These are the spaces of the subjectum, or the spaces that constantly exceed the definitions of boundaries and limits. They are spaces of production that are fluid and ever changing in composition and duration. That is to say, they are geographies that are produced by the flows of life that traverse them. Every bounded geography is shot through with such spaces. The nation state, for example, would like to portray itself as a well-contained and bounded space. It wants to suggest that its borders are well established and clear. The immigration services, laws, and regulations imply a tight control over the flows of bodies between states, and yet we know that the nation state is in fact porous; that bodies flow across borders in huge waves of immigration and exodus.[7] Even the most totalitarian regimes with the most draconian punishments for border violations have spaces along the border where bodies cross back and forth.

Similarly, youth-adult relations as they are played out in homes, schools, and shopping malls create bounded spaces with regulations that purport to control flows of bodies through the corridors of schools, restrict access to shopping malls, and control the exits and

---

7 See Hardt and Negri (2000).

entrances to home through curfews and sanctions. Yet such boundaries are also quite fluid, with multiple violations and highly permeable boundaries. Even within the bounded spaces of enclosure and discipline there are what Deleuze and Guattari (1987) describe as spaces we can enter 'by any point whatsoever; none matters more than another, and no entrance is more privileged' (p. 3). In this kind of space, each entrance links to another, and each new entrance into the space modifies the map. This is the mapping of the rhizome, a structure that spreads under the ground in all directions at once and connects to everything.

Such a rhizomatic map is very different from the mapping of boundaries and states we have been delineating thus far. Indeed, Deleuze and Guattari (1987, p. 12) suggest that the rhizome is the actual map, while what we have been describing they call a tracing. The map of the rhizome is constantly being disrupted and recreated, or in Deleuzio-Guatarrian terms, deterritorialized and reterritorialized. Space as we know it is disrupted (deterritorialized) and then recreated as a map of the familiar (reterritorialized) only to be disrupted again (deterritorialized). Maps, they suggest, are constantly drawn and redrawn as we come to know geography in new ways or from different vantage points. Tracings, on the other hand, attempt to reproduce space as it actually exists, or try to make a direct copy of the territory under observation. Such tracings attempt to fix space as solid and static. The nation state, with its insistence on the fixity of its geographical coordinates and the right to defend its boundaries to the death, is just such a tracing.

It is important to note, however, that the rhizomatic map is not free of the lines of order and control, because it is, as we pointed out above, connected to everything, including the regimes of dominant power. The burrow functions as an endless interconnected maze that splits off in all directions and can be entered from any point. This open system offers entrance to all parties, including both enemies and friends (Deleuze & Guattari, 1987). The rhizome, however, offers a constantly shifting map that provides endless avenues of flight from encroaching domination. As Delueze and Guattari point out, 'Every rhizome contains lines of segmentarity, according to which it is stratified, territorialized, organized, signified, attributed etc., as well as lines of deterritorialization down which it constantly flees. There is a rupture in the rhizome whenever segmentary lines explode into a line of flight, but the line of flight is part of the rhizome' (p. 9).

Such rhizomatic spaces riddle the striated and controlled space of the home, the school, and the urban landscape with hidden geographies. These geographies are brought into being by accidental encounters with unmonitored space that can be reclaimed for the purposes of an evening, a season, or an indeterminate time of occupation. This is the space of what Deleuze and Guattari call the nomad. The nomad's primary definition lies in the function of occupying and holding smooth space. It is with this definition that we engage our opening chapter quote once again, in which St Pierre refers to the notion of smooth space and claims that there can be no liberation even in such a space, but that there can be new possibilities of deterritorialization.

But what is this smooth space? In the simplest terms, it is space per se, or space that is not yet defined, stratified, or territorialized. To occupy and hold such space is to sustain space as contingent possibility; that is, to claim space as a constantly open construction in which each new body that enters redefines it and extends its possibilities in a new direction. In fact, I would argue that youth subculture has always functioned within such space. The nomadic occupation of smooth space is the reclamation of geography in the school bathroom, the corner of a building, the empty lot behind the shopping mall, the abandoned building in the middle of downtown, or the sidewalk in front of the club. Such occupation at least momentarily disrupts the habitual usage patterns and tracings of repetitive behaviour and deterritorializes the space as unpredictable. This is the moment at which youth enter a public area and induce by their simple presence a certain sense of anxiety. Such anxiety is generated by their status as a cultural space between, a definitional smooth space that holds the capacity for unpredictable appropriation of predictable spaces. Within the shopping mall, for example, much effort is expended in writing regulations and deploying security forces so as to assure that the space is properly segmented and does not revert to smooth, unpredictable space through the introduction of unregulated youth.

It is within the constant reconfiguration of striated and smooth spaces that the world of youth subculture is formed and reformed. Such spaces constitute an outside to the inside of the dominant culture. These are spaces that can be momentarily appropriated and taken out their accustomed context. They are separated from their common usage, as ordained and specified by the dominant society, and recommissioned to the uses of the bodies that cross them. Of course such bodies are not just youth, but can also include the bodies of other marginal groups such as the homeless, the transient, the addict, and the prostitute. In this regard, such space produces an outside to the bounded space of the mapped and striated world. Such an outside 'is not another site, but rather an offsite that erodes and dissolves all other sites ... The outside is never exhausted; every new attempt to capture it generates an excess or supplement, which, in turn, feeds anew the flows of deterritorialization and releases new lines of flight' (Boundas, 1994, as cited in St Pierre, 1997, p. 370).

The notion of space as burrow, rhizome, smooth, or outside becomes central to our interest in geography as subjectum or creative force. As we recall, the subjectum is always comprised of relations of force. In the case of youth, that force is constituted through youth-adult inter-actions wherever they collide across the geographies of home, school, parks, streets, shopping malls, etc. These collisions constitute a dance of negotiated space through which various formations of youth geog-raphy emerge. Such formations include the striated spaces that produce sports teams, cheerleaders, choirs, hall monitors, honour stu-dents, prom royalty, and class clowns. They also include contrary or alternate formations, the various deterritorialized spaces of flight that produce subcultures or neo-tribes. These alternate configurations of youth exist in spaces of unrecuperated potential that constitute fron-tiers outside the boundaries of the known, thought, or practised world existing between youth and adults.

In other words, these alternate configurations occupy space that we have previously called the event horizon. In this sense, the spaces occupied in squats, behind the gym, in the private spaces of cars or bedrooms, in illegal clubs, or abandoned urban landscapes become open to a constantly shifting array of new possibilities. These possibil-ities are produced through the combinations of the specific types of space engaged by youth and the type of youth-bodies engaging it. It is important to remember here our discussion of bodies and identities. Each body and each identity is unique and singular. Therefore, as a body engages a space, say an empty warehouse, it will produce that space differently from any other body. Similarly, subcultural 'scenes' produced by the combinations of multiple bodies across a particular space will create a unique and unrepeatable pattern of possibility for action and creativity.

This is, of course, smooth space and as such defies any set definition. This is why any attempt to define a 'scene' according to its geography of origin will ultimately be unsatisfactory. The definition of such a scene lies in an area of absolute impenetrability belonging entirely to youth subculture. In other words, because it is space in constant production or flight it cannot be fixed or traced with any degree of accuracy.

In this sense, youth subculture is operating 'on the plane of immanence,' where there is no hierarchical structure for delineating and codifying description. This is a space of thresholds, not boundaries. In this type of space, youth produce themselves and the space they occupy through cracks and fractures in the surface tracings of the dominant culture. These cracks open into the burrows and rhizomes constituting lines of flight through irregularities in the compounds of disciplinarity such as schools, families, and workplaces. Such irregularities seem to be most prolific at the moment of transition between dominant regimes of power. This is not to say that there are not always openings into the rhizomatic; after all, Deleuze and Guattari imply an infinitude of entrances and connections. It is simply that in the space between one regime of power and another, irregularities seem to flourish for a period of time as dominant power figures out how to operate new regimes of discipline and control.

This is certainly true of our own postmodern period, where irregularity has become so endemic that the new regimes of control must incorporate its logic into the regimes of discipline they deploy.[8] This may be one explanation for the chaotic condition of rule under postmodern capitalism, with its wars, economic scandals, huge prison populations, genocides, and ever-shifting array of regulations, borders, and laws. Perhaps it is as Negri (2003) suggests, that each manoeuvre to dominate is responding to a revolutionary act that preceded it. In other words, as we noted above, the logic of rule must always frantically follow behind the burrows and rhizomes of the subjectum, attempting to seal the entrances and cover over the irregularities. In the space between systems of control, the proliferating creative irregularities of the subjectum operating in an increased field of smooth space require a chaotic scramble of response by the emerging regime of domination.

In this sense, the smooth space occupied by the youth-as-nomad is composed out of the residue of worlds that are infinitely ending. It is created out of the moments where the maps are 'torn, reversed, adapted to any kind of mounting, reworked by an individual, group

---

8 See Hardt and Negri (2004).

or social formation' (Deleuze & Guattari, 1987, p. 12). This fundamentally mutable map creates space as probable contingency; as any sort of possible map. Such space is a world to be taken from within a site unavailable in its actuality, even to those who live within its parameters.

Heterotopic Geographies

To clarify this last comment, we turn to Foucault and his writing on what he called heterotopias. In his short essay 'Of Other Spaces,' Foucault (1986) makes a distinction between utopias and heterotopias. Utopias are unreal places that do not actually exist. They are ideal forms that hold a relation to society either as a perfection of certain existing forms or as an alternative to the current configuration of the social. Common notions of the nuclear family as a space of constant harmony and nurturance, or schools as spaces of open and uncontested learning are examples of utopias in our current thinking. Utopias are certainly a kind of map. But it is an odd mapping of a world that doesn't exist. This is not to say, however, that utopic maps don't have political or actual force. Indeed, one might even say that they have force well beyond what might be expected, given their mythical nature. The utopic maps of schools and families, for example, have an immense influence on the political landscape of young people's lives. The variation between the utopic map of the ideal school and the reality of actual schools drives policy and funding decisions, which have real-life implications for young people.

The utopic school, like the utopic nuclear family or even the utopic young person, is an interesting case in point because it does not necessarily reference a utopic future space. Instead, it refers to a utopic golden age when schools actually taught, homes functioned smoothly as happy refuges from the hard, cruel world, and young people were compliant and respectful subjects.

Of course, no such space has ever existed. Schools, homes, and youth have always comprised contested space. Indeed, one might argue that it has been precisely these spaces that have fomented insurrection and revolt. The women's movement began in a revolt against domesticity, the recent uprisings in Los Angeles regarding immigration were centred in secondary schools, and of course the ongoing contestation between the dominant regimes of power and young people operate across the spectrum of the social. Despite all of this, the utopias of false memory and constructed history have tremendous political force in attempting to reinstate the well-functioning discipline of a time that never existed.

In contrast to the utopia, Foucault proposes what he calls a hetero-topia. This space, he argues, is made up of actual spaces 'which are something like counter-sites, a kind of effectively enacted utopia in which the real sites, all the other real sites that can be found within the culture, are simultaneously represented, contested and inverted' (1986, p. 26). Foucault locates these counter-sites outside of all of other sites even though he says they exist as real places. This should sound somewhat familiar to us as similar to the description of smooth space as an outside to the dominant mappings of the domi-nant culture. The space produced in the rhizomatic formations of the subjectum, through the appropriation and occupation of smooth space, is also a space that exists outside of all other spaces. It is important to note here that the spaces of youth subculture as exam-ples of such smooth space are not utopic, but are actual and real places that we have identified as schools, homes, warehouses, clubs, sidewalks, and so on. Youth subcultures do not represent anything ideal. Instead, they are self-producing social formations that operate as Foucault's counter-sites.

Foucault goes on to clarify his concept of heterotopias by suggesting that they are like mirrors. Mirrors are also utopias, in that they are machines of representation; what they represent is like the ideal school and family, not a real place but what he calls a 'placeless place ... in which I see myself where I am not in an unreal virtual space' (1986, p. 26). In other words, the mirror produces a sense of reality where there is none. I can see myself behind the surface but I am not actually there, just as we can see ourselves in the mythical nuclear family as if it were real, even though it never existed. Indeed, we can even create our memories so that they reflect this mythical family, covering over the struggles and fights, the disharmony and sacrifice to create a smooth surface onto which we can project our utopic vision. In this we can see ourselves reflected on the surface but we are not really there.

Foucault goes on to suggest, however, that mirrors are also hetero-topias. The mirror, he argues, does exist in a relationship with the viewer. The image projected on the surface of the mirror reflects back to the subject, who views it in a way that functions to 'reconstitute myself there where I am' (1986, p. 26). This is reminiscent of the role of evocation (discussed in chapter 1) and its similar effect. The mirror is impenetrable, we cannot see into it, but it reflects us back to ourselves in ways that bring us to ourselves in new perspectives. This is the interaction of body and space as mutually constitutive. The body interacts with the mirror to produce the mirror as a virtual space in which multiple possibilities of self knowledge are created. Of course, the mirror by itself has no such capacity. It is simply smooth space without feature until it is engaged by a body. To the degree that the body uses the mirror to confirm pre-existing tracings of identity, the space is that of the subjectus. To the degree the body uses the mirror to open up creative potentials of self production, the mirror is one of the tools of the subjectum. In this sense, the space of the mirror is both absolutely real and absolutely unreal.

In a very similar way the worlds of youth and adult within contemporary society function as both utopic and heterotopic spaces. As I have pointed out, the very categories of youth and adult are 'placeless places' that don't actually exist except as utopic ideals. The subjects that inhabit these unreal categories function within them in very similar ways to Foucault's mirror. That is to say, these categories are spaces that have both utopic and heterotopic functions that are absolutely unreal and absolutely real. Over the past few chapters we have been tracing these functions as they operate in terms of identity, body, time, and now finally space. In each of these arenas we have noted the material and actual immanent constructions and productions of the subjectum, and compared it with the representational and transcendent world of the subjectus. I have argued that youth and adults function simultaneously at both levels at all times. Each living being is both subjectus and subjectum. However, I have also argued that if we are interested in a political project that flees and repudiates domination, an investigation of the functions of the subjectum are quite useful.

In the opening chapter to this book, I discussed the problems involved with colonial language and the ways that it produces subaltern subjects as unable to represent themselves. I suggested that like the mirror, colonial language holds a double function in that linguistic representations are always a bit utopic because they can't fully capture the actuality of experience. In this, they are placeless places like the mirror. However, I also argued that language could reflect us back to ourselves through evocatory forms that don't attempt to represent but instead to stimulate response and creativity. At the end of this long exposition of theory regarding the identities, bodies, time, and space involved in youth-adult relations, I want to suggest that youth-adult relations are also heterotopic. That is to say that like the mirror, each encounter between a young person and an adult has the capacity to reflect back to both parties a new set of possible self knowledges that can become the foundation of new relationships, perhaps even of new worlds. It is to this possibility that we will turn in the next chapter.

6 Hybridity and Flight: My Reflections

In this chapter we turn to the interviews. These conversations took place in St. Paul, Minnesota, late in the fall of 2001. In all, I talked with six youth who identified as either punk or skin. Three of them had, at different points, identified as both punk and skin and three identified only as punk. They were evenly split along gender lines. All of them had a history within the punk or skin subculture of at least four years.[1]

The interviews were conducted at my home and lasted approximately thirty to forty minutes. One youth requested that her first interview be deleted and replaced by a second interview, to which she brought handwritten answers that she read aloud. The interviews were structured around a standard set of questions which each of the youth spontaneously noted as being 'interesting' and 'good questions.'

To begin these reflections, I want to engage the kind of the heterotopic space produced by the collisions between youth and adults just discussed in the previous chapter. In particular, I am interested in how such space is constitutive of both a surface that refuses any interpretation of the other, and at the same time creates the other as a mirror that reflects one back on oneself. It is on just such a surface that I engaged the conversations that form the basis of this chapter. I had known these young people for a number of years through my son David, who had been both a skinhead and a punk. They had all spent time at my house, and we had brushed by each other as we came and went to work, school, and conducted the other functions of daily living.

Given the frantic pace of life, however, I had never really had a chance to sit down and talk with them in any depth. This was a bit

---

1 See the preface to this book for more information on these young people.

ironic, since my job at the time was as the clinical director of a large youth service organization that worked with runaway and homeless youth. I spent my days and many evenings doing nothing but talking to young people and the adults in their lives. However, as many youth workers discover, this time away from home created the youth who were closest to me as the furthest away in some sense.

My work with runaway and homeless youth nonetheless gave me some excellent perspectives and tools for engaging the world of skins and punks that I was about to encounter. For example, in my work I had come to understand that the dance between young people and adults was a delicate negotiation of power, just as we have noted in the theoretical discussions so far. Having seen thousands of interactions between young people and adults over twenty years as a youth worker, I was well aware of how easy it was for both young people and adults to speak for one another; to come to believe that they knew exactly what it meant to be this kind of adult or that kind of youth.

In deciding to talk with my son and his friends about being skin and punk, I wanted to be careful about entering into this dance of power. After all, as we have been discussing, each and every fragment of space, identity, time, and embodiment between adults and youth is rife with elements of subjectus and subjectum. Every engagement is a highly contested arena rife with the dangers of colonial subjectification in which the adult writer, whether a researcher writing an ethnography, a clinician writing a case note, or a teacher writing an evaluation, holds the power of the final say in writing about what occurred.

In light of this complicated relation of power and hegemony, I want to be clear that the following remarks are a not a simple accounting of what occurred between me and the punks and skins I came to know, but a complicated mirror reflection of what I heard from the punks and skins who were generous with their time and perceptions, and who opened their world to me and made me welcome. Like all heterotopic spaces, the world I will attempt to describe is both absolutely real and unreal at the same time. Certainly the engagements between myself and the youth at shows, clubs, back alleys, at the house, and finally in the interviews were very real and created a network of highly valued relationships that have continued beyond this writing. However, the reading I will give of the interviews here is a description of what I saw on the surface of the mirror. That projected image is unreal except to the degree that it produces new self-knowledge for me as a youth worker or for you as a reader.

In this sense, this writing constitutes the edge of my own reflection and holds a singular utility for me in my practice as a pedagogue and youth worker. For me, these reflections are a kind of youth work, in that they constitute a text through which the transformations of my own subjectivity involved in adult-youth social relations, over the past two years of this project, are charted, outlined, and extended. Like the world of the subjectum, youth work as a liberatory praxis can only be known through its transformative effect from the inside. In other words, we can only work with others based on what we know of ourselves. As we have discussed with respect to Spinoza, the only way we can know the state of our own being is through our collisions with other bodies. It is through these collisions that we can come to know what we share in common. For Spinoza, that common element was the creative force of life itself as expressed uniquely and idiosyncratically in each body. In terms of youth work, this means that as adult youth workers we can only bring our own particular creative force to our engagement with youth; we have nothing else to share. We can only learn about that force in relation to youth work, however, through our encounters with young people. These encounters, then, are potentially transformative from the inside of each subjectivity.

For me, these collisions evoke my performances of myself as ethnographer, pedagogue, youth worker, parent, communist, and old white guy. However, each collision also evokes past configurations of self in the hidden performance of memory in my internal/unconscious/hallucinatory evocation of my own youth as it lives within and through my identity and my praxis now. Put in another way, youth-adult relations reflect back to each subject a projection of time, like the mirror of Dorian Gray. In each collision, we see reflected to us fragments of who we have been or might become. For each young person, an encounter with an adult evokes a world of potential futures to be embraced or repudiated. For each adult, each collision evokes what we referred to earlier as the becoming youth of every age; that is to say, not a return to an actual world of childhood remembered, but instead a reminder of the potentials of the subjectum or of youth as creative force.

In a sense, these reflections should be read as the kind of poetic evocation we have already described in previous chapters (Tyler, 1986). As Scheper-Hughes points out, 'The ethnographer, like the artist, is engaged in a special kind of vision quest through which a specific interpretation of the human condition, an entire sensibility is forged ... In the act of "writing culture," what emerges is always highly subjective, partial and fragmentary – but also a deeply felt and personal – record of human lives based on eyewitness and testimony' (Scheper-Hughes, 1992, p. xii).

This artistry of writing culture, or in this case subculture, calls for a complicated and delicate relation between the text and subject. Such a relation does not confine the subject within grids of specification but opens spaces through which the constitutive relationship of writer and subject can be seen in mutual production of themselves and the reader. In other words, in describing what I see in the heterotopic space of my relation to skins and punks, I want to open new possibilities for adults, not produce new subjects for objectification.

To accomplish this, I have to be aware that the subjects (in this case the skins and punks of my interviews) as authors of the original text (the interviews) are in a particularly precarious position. Their distance from the actual creation of the final draft makes them completely dependent upon my transparency or lack thereof. Their knowing, as constituted in the text, is only available through the lens I provide. The context and perspective of this lens is critical as a medium of translation for defining who the 'other' is and how they come to be known. To the degree that this relationship is inclusive of my own complex process of incomplete knowing, such translation becomes provisional and evocative. To the degree that this relationship is portrayed as an interpretation given by me as objective observer of the 'other,' such complexities are at best obscured and at worst lost altogether.

Both types of text are 'fantasy,' as Steven Tyler (1986) notes, but fantasy without being fiction, for such fantasies are 'the evocation of a possible world of reality' (p. 139). This evocation is precisely the distinction between Foucault's utopic and heterotopic spaces. The utopic writing of the skin and punk world produces them as a certain kind of ideal subject that never actually exists – a pure fantasy. The heterotopic writing produces a record of the possibilities an encounter such as an interview evokes in terms of alternative real spaces that actually exist but are buried beneath the surface of the dominant culture.

What I wish to engage in the heterotopic text that follows is a reflection that is neither to be found in the original interview transcripts nor in any interpretive final research text. It is instead an evolutionary document that finds its final meaning to be infinite within the multiplicity of interpretations brought by the reader. Like the collisions of bodies, the relationship of a reader to a text is one of creative potential. The reader is not a passive recipient of the knowledge passed from the text in a unified voice of truth and certainty. Instead, each reader creates the text anew through his or her own unique reading, premised in what Deleuze and Guattari (1987) call 'becoming.' That is to say, each reader encounters the text at a particular instant in the age of the body. The body responds to the text out of its singular constitution at that moment. The elements of the text that are selected as meaningful are those elements that promote the continuation and extension of the body's expressive capacity at the moment of the encounter. In this sense, each reading of the text produces an infinitude of texts that, like the rhizome, have endless numbers of entrances and spread in networks of interconnecting meanings in all directions at once. Thus it is with you, the reader, that the polyphonic and multivocal aspect of this process holds the greatest potential.

That said, my writing here cannot avoid a certain reductionism, simply because it is impossible to textualize any experience completely. Conversations and interviews cannot be fully apprehended either in their moment of actuality nor upon reflection. Indeed, once I have written the text, my experience of the heterotopia, my reflections and interpretation, the dynamic process of evolutionary understanding becomes unavailable within the text. In this respect, the 'text is not only not an object, it is not the object; it is instead a means, the meditative vehicle for a transcendence of time and place ... Its meaning is not in it but in an understanding of which it is only a consumed fragment' (Tyler, 1986, p. 130).

Like all meditations, this evocatory reflection requires a textual framework, a rhythm and a sensibility. To satisfy this requirement, I have chosen a framework from Foucault to guide my exploration.[2] Foucault may seem an odd choice for a poetic evocation of subculture. It might be argued that his rhythms are irregular and stuttered, his frameworks are diagrams of structured minutia, and his lyrical style one of the arcane and dusty backrooms of libraries. However, I would argue that Foucault, like Marx, is interested in a reading of the social that privileges a certain political project I propose is useful here.[3]

Such a project concerns the delineation of the mechanics by which domination functions. Certainly this was Marx's project in his writings about industrial capitalism. Deleuze and Guattari hold a similar

---

2 Based on Foucault's recommendations for interrogating texts in *The Archaeology of Knowledge* (1972).

3 The same interest is expressed by Deleuze and Guattari in their writings on capitalism and globalization.

concern in their descriptions of the apparatuses of capture in *A Thousand Plateaus*. Likewise, Foucault made it his life project to diagram the modes of appropriation and domination hidden in the most mundane of social mechanisms. In a debate with Noam Chomsky, Foucault stated it this way: 'It seems to me that the real political task in a society such as ours is to criticize the workings of institutions that appear to be both neutral and independent; to criticize them and attack them in such a manner that the political violence that has always exercised itself through them can be unmasked so that one can fight against them.'[4]

Part of this unmasking includes analysing the ways in which certain social forms come into being at certain historical moments. Foucault (1975) argues that such objects arise through a complex collision of forces: economic, social, historical, and technological. He suggests further that each of these collisions is a random event that creates a rupture in the existing social fabric. Such ruptures challenge the dominant construction of history as a smooth evolutionary process of progress under existing regimes of power. As a result, such ruptures must be covered over and assimilated into the discursive frameworks of sovereign power. Part of Foucault's project is to outline how this process of assimilation, appropriation, and domination functions.

However, that is only part of Foucault's project. The other portion concerns the force such ruptures provide for the political action of what he refers to in the quote above as 'fighting them.' Here, he proposes that each rupture contains within it the capacity of resistance. This in our terms is the relationship between the subjectus and the subjectum. Such a relation, as we know, is one of ongoing struggle, resistance, and flight. In the section that follows I will delineate youth subculture as an object of rupture and flight that has particular significance in our own historical moment.

Towards an Archaeology of Subculture

Foucault Inquiry #1: *Determine how and when the object (in this case youth subcultural performance) emerges as a discourse. Show how it is conceptual-*

---

4 The debate was broadcast on the Dutch television program *Human Nature* in 1971 and is currently available on YouTube under the title 'Justice vs. Power – Chomsky vs. Foucault.'

ized and created as different from other descriptions of the same kind of phenomenon.

The rise of punks and skins as subcultural formation has been taken up extensively as both a historical (Knight, 1997; Marcus, 1989; de la Haye & Dingwall, 1996; Hamm, 1993; Moore, 1993; Marshall, 1994) and a sociological phenomenon (Leblanc, 1999; Hebdige, 1979; Brake, 1985; Hall & Jefferson, 1975; Wood, 1999; Sabin, 1999). I will not belabour the discussion by attempting to replicate or extend these excellent tracings of subcultural trajectory through the late twentieth century. Rather, I would like to explore subculture in the way I mentioned above, as a moment of collision and rupture with unique political possibilities.

In doing this, I will be tracing along an edge of current work in post-subculture theory (Bennett, 2000; Maffessoli, 1996; Muggleton, 2000; Hills, 2002; Stahl, 2003) that engages a sociological understanding of youth social formations within the historical period of postmodernity. While my project here is sympathetic to and even engages some of the same terrain theoretically and methodologically, I would argue that there are some key differences between the post-subculture work and my writing here.

In the first instance, post-subculture theory situates postmodernity as a largely ideological cultural production and argues against a Marxist economic analytic in which subcultures represent class interests.[5] I would agree that a simple reductive Marxist reading of subculture as representative of heroic class struggle is both inadequate and possibly misleading. That said, as a post-Marxist communist scholar I will argue here for a fundamentally economic analysis of subculture as an indication of the ruptural possibilities for resistance, flight, and struggle within the moment of postmodern global capital. In this, I hope to begin to formulate the beginnings of an answer to the perennial question in postmodern scholarship: what happens to politics in postmodernity?

The second instance of difference I have with post-subculture theory is in its predominant analysis of subcultural formations as primarily discursive, as discussed earlier with respect to the ideas of Bourdieu and Butler.[6] Since these arguments were extensively developed in pre-

---

5 See Weinzierl and Muggleton (2003).
6 See Klein (2003).

vious chapters, suffice it to say that I will argue for subcultural formations as auto-poetic or self-producing rhizomatic formations that
mobilize the force of the subjectum against the dominating logic of the
subjectus, rather than as culturally determined inscriptions on the
body of the subject.

Finally, this text will not define youth subculture by a particular
music or fashion.[7] Instead, I will propose that music and fashion are not
only ideological constructions but also modes of affiliation that
produce systematic networks that have both political force and potential. Certainly this aspect of youth subcultures as an expanding
network is well represented in the post-subculture literature,[8] but the
political force of such affiliation is, from my perspective, reduced to the
level of an ideological carnival of representations. Such a reading, while
not entirely unfounded, traces the punk and skinhead movements as
transformations of music and form in ways that I would argue obscure
their social relations within the new modes of production that some
have called late-stage capitalism (Jameson, 1991) and others simply
'empire' (Hardt & Negri, 2000). In this same light, I will not be sketching out punk or skin through examining the major scenes or famous
bands, but premising my remarks on my experience with a small group
of young people who perform punk or skin in their daily lives.

To engage the economic implications of youth subcultures within
late-stage capitalism, let me begin by arguing that it is not simply coin-
cidental that the skinhead and punk subcultures arise precisely in the
late 1960s, in the midst of significant economic and social shifts in both
Britain and the United States. The year 1968 has been noted as the
beginning of the postmodern era of production (Negri, 1996b). The
features of this shift in social forms and relations under an evolving
and rapidly proliferating new mode of production had an immense
influence on young people and the social forms in which they were
embedded. At the minimum, the old economics and social structures
of industrial capital, with its worlds of factories, unions, and fixed
multi-levelled class structure, underwent and continue to undergo significant alteration. In this transition between industrial and postmodern economies, both the bourgeois managerial class and the working
class begin to lose force as social forms.[9]

---

7 See Weinzierl and Muggleton (2003).
8 See Stahl (2003).
9 See Negri (1996b).

This loss of class force is part of a larger change that marks a shift from the disciplinary enclosures of modernism such as race, gender, class, and sexuality to the new modes of production. This new way of organizing the world is built on the advancement of computer technology as it transforms first the factories and then the financial systems, while concomitantly profoundly altering the purpose and meaning of media and shifting the ways in which common sense is constructed in society at large. All of these changes have significant impacts on the worlds of society and politics. In these realms there are two large effects that are quite familiar to us by now. First, this new mode of economy and production creates the most complete system of global domination ever imagined while simultaneously creating new possibilities for the radical assertion of life force. For us, it is here that the forces of subjectus and subjectum come into full profile.

For the subjectum, this shift creates ruptures, schisms, and fractures across the disciplinary mechanisms of industrial capitalism. As Foucault would suggest, these ruptures in the capacities of schools, workplaces, and homes to discipline the subjects within them allows previously subjugated social forms, artificially segregated alternative social formations, and previously disciplined feelings and emotions to erupt and multiply within the spaces created by the breakdown of disciplinary enclosure. As we might imagine, given the theoretical discussion so far, these changes allow for performances of previously contained explosions and collisions of subjectivity in terms of body, time, and space.

This historical moment, which Hardt and Negri (2000, p. 25), following Marx (1993), have referred to as the moment of total subsumption, is the moment of crisis between the modes of production. In this moment, all modes of the social come under the domination of capitalist logic. For those interested in political projects that propose an alternative form of life, this is a dark moment indeed. One might well understand the abandonment by certain social theorists of any hope for Marxist or communist projects.[10] The turn to the purely postmodern mode of analysis in some post-subculture theory is one arena where hope for a revolutionary politics of subculture loses force.[11]

I would argue for a more optomistic reading of these events based on three concepts we have engaged so far: the notion of resistance in

---

10 See Clark (1975).
11 See Stahl (2003) and Weinzierl and Muggleton (2003).

Foucault, the importance of the pass-word in Deleuze and Guattari (1987), and the concept of struggle in Negri (2003). But let's begin with Marx. Marx proposed that capitalism is made from an irresolvable set of contradictions (1978/1992, pp. 146–201). In short, he suggests that capitalism cannot deliver what it promises to deliver. Such contradictions only become fully obvious at the moment of capitalism's full extension across the social realm. At that moment it becomes impossible for capitalism to obscure its contradictions by pointing to less well-developed economic forms that it can claim as inferior. Of course, this hides from view the fact that through war, economic embargo, colonial invasion, and even genocide, the forces of capitalism often produce such systems as inferior specifically in order to assure its dominance. Leaving this aside, however, in the moment of its full domination there is only capitalism and at such a moment its fatal flaws, according to Marx, will lead to its collapse.

Of course, many will point to the fact that the collapse of capitalism has been predicted unsuccessfully for over one hundred years. Capitalism has shown a remarkable ability to mutate and resolve its contradictions as they become obvious. What is missing, however, in this rather neutral accounting of capitalism's 'success' is the brutality of its regime and its long-term effects. If Foucault (1975) is correct and resistance is always produced at the same moment as domination, then the force of resistance to capitalism has its greatest potential at the moment of capitalism's greatest triumph. Similarly, if Deleuze and Guattari (1987) are correct and each escalation of the 'order-word' produces a new set of pass-words that indicate new burrows and rhizomes of flight from discipline, then new forms of politics and life are being produced under the surface of domination at a rate previously not known. Finally, if Hardt and Negri (2000) are right and capitalism has no capacity to produce anything because it is simply an abstract system of appropriation and domination, then capital is dependent on leaving spaces open for undominated life to produce new forms for it to appropriate. This set of conditions leads to a central contradiction for capitalism at the moment of its greatest triumph: how to simultaneously control life under its regime of complete domination and yet leave life free to produce new modes it can appropriate. This struggle between life force in its modes of creativity, resistance, and flight and the full force of capitalist domination, I would argue, constitutes the historical background for the emergence of the subcultural form in the late twentieth century.

The subcultural form holds two aspects that are of interest to us here: the first is that of a certain prophetic quality, and the second is as an event horizon or experimental zone for new political forms. In the prophetic instance, we have to rethink our traditional notions of what prophecy means. Rather than thinking of prophecy as the ability to see the future through revelation of a pre-designated set of events put in motion by an outside power, we can understand prophecy as the ability to know the future through its already-existing aspects in the present. Put in another way, prophecy of this latter type is an example of what we have talked about before as intensive time; that is to say, the kind of time that holds all events along the horizon of potential becoming. In this kind of time, as in Foucault's heterotopic space, there are alternative real moments of the future occurring under the surface of the present. For example, one of the youth I interviewed made the following remark:

> I think a lot of the theory behind, like the bondage and everything was because of the disgust appeal going with how it started. They would rip up their clothes and shred it and paint it and do everything, because that's what you weren't supposed to do at the time ... it made people like, repel away from you in a different way. (Tony)

Certainly the negative, ironic, and intentionally repellant aspect of punk has been more than thoroughly documented in the subcultural, post-subcultural and postmodern literatures. However, I am interested in another aspect of this statement: the subcultural formation of punk as scavenger of the discarded forms of youth subculture. I would argue that on the one hand, this scavenger formation prefigures the extension of capitalism itself as a scavenger into the very margins where punk and other subcultures (hippies, hip hop, metal heads, goths, etc.) have staked their claim, and on the other hand, it holds immense potential for new worlds outside capitalism.

This is a complicated statement, however, because it raises a complex argument that Negri makes (2003) about the moment of resistance. The question that Negri asks vis-à-vis new social forms is whether or not resistance is a reaction to domination or whether it precedes domination. Like many philosophical assertions, this one seems a bit paradoxical: how could resistance come before domination? Obviously, common sense tells us that it is a reaction to domination.

What Negri is getting at here, however, goes back to the idea proposed above that capitalism, or any system of domination for that matter, produces nothing in and of itself. Such systems are always completely dependent upon living subjects to produce the things they use to rule and proliferate. This is why Marx (1978/1992, p. 94) describes capitalists as parasites or 'pimps.' Because it cannot produce anything, whatever capitalism deploys in both its economic and political aspects must be produced first by the subjects living within its regime of power. Under these conditions, Negri (2003) proposes the following sequence: first, living beings produce something that has the possibility of operating as an alternative to capitalism; this form is then noticed by capital, which takes steps to dominate it so that it does not obtain sufficient force to create a viable alternative to the existing system. At the moment that capitalism begins to discipline the new form, that form becomes resistance. This is also why Foucault (1975) says that resistance and domination occur simultaneously. They occur at the same time because until there is a moment of domination, life force is simple assertion. It is only with the intervention of domination that life force becomes resistance. That is to say that life always holds the potential of resistance prior to any specific mode of domination. Of course, the specific form resistance takes is produced out of the social and material environment of a particular historical moment.

So the punks scavenge the rather bleak environment of Britain in the throes of deindustrialization and a failing national empire and produce an alternative form of emotional and political economy. They abandon the attempted solutions of conventional forms and politics, beginning by disassembling clothing, music, and style, then reassembling these in new forms. Of course this has been articulated in the subcultural and post-subcultural literature as the postmodern art of bricolage or pastiche.[12] Indeed bricolage, the art of taking whatever is at hand and creating something, is particularly apt here.

What hasn't been as well articulated is the notion that punk prefigures the postmodern habits of capitalism itself; not just as resistance but also as source. In other words, punk (along with many, many other emerging social forms of the time) produces a new mode of culture that is both responsive to new articulations of the economy and that produces new forms which that very economy will use in its own proliferation. Once capital appropriated the art of scavenging the social on

---

12 See Clark (1975).

a global scale for bits and pieces of emerging culture that it could sell back to its subjectus citizenry, it quickly put punk and other new forms into creative flight.

In this sense, the rise of the discourse of punk as a resounding 'fuck you' constituted and constitutes an ongoing moment of resistance from which punk itself must constantly flee. On the level of social form, punks express the absolute negation of all previous modernist formations. In the absence of coherent modernist social form in the transition between modes of production, punk performs and prefigures the crisis of capital as a system that has extended its imperialist limit to its end and must now cannibalize its own production to survive. As one of the youth I interviewed put it,

> Punk was about poor kids being fed up with shit. And just saying fuck everything. We're going to do it our way and we're going to have fun about it too. You know, it was, really punk was a bunch of kids who lost hope and decided to do their own thing. (Frank)

Here, punk is evocative of the lines of flight delineated by Deleuze within the society of control. Each moment of resistance constitutes an appropriable subject that can be discovered, domesticated, and sold back to subculture itself. However, neither the appropriation nor the sale is ever final, because the site and moment of resistance is quickly abandoned to capital as new forms are created through flight. This is the politics of postmodernity; a guerrilla war fought underground through the assertion of creative life force that produces new sets of affiliations that network the globe. Punk then both prefigures such a politics in its earliest productions and continues to extend this politics through its proliferating new cultural and political manifestations.[13]

In contrast, I would argue that the skinheads, as a series of ruptures, evoke a range of modern and pre-modern social formations. Their movement across the social is one of explosion, collision, formation, and dissolution from singularity into multiplicity and back again. This sort of pattern should be familiar to us as the activity of de-and re-territorialization. The skinhead community is not a simple reactionary formation, as has been proposed by those authors who have focused on the racist, Nazi edge of the culture (Hamm, 1993; Moore, 1993). Rather, as I discovered in my talks with young skinheads, it is a

---

13 See Thompson (2004).

complex hybrid formation of dissolving and resolving boundaries along a pre-modern tribal-warrior social formation. The skins, at one level, are profoundly engaged in an attempted recuperation of the disciplinary enclosures of family, class, gender, sexuality, and race. In this regard, it is not surprising that they are profoundly nationalistic, as their struggle mirrors in a significant way the tensions of the nation state embedded in a proliferation of global capitalist formations.

> Skinheads are very much Americans. But, I mean, skinheads like most of the working class don't fit into culture but are the backbone of America. I mean, we all speak English. You know, we all have our jobs, we all do our little thing, you know? And I mean I believe that this is a great country. I may not like a lot of the people but I still believe this is a great country. You know? And I think it would be even a greater country if everybody could just fucking get over their goddam little squabbles and get along and that's what I say by everybody just needs to be the same culture. 'Cause if everybody could just deal with their bullshit then everything'd be fine. At the same time I take pride in my heritage but it doesn't have anything to do with my culture right now, here. That's heritage, there's heritage and there's culture. You know? It's like whatever you want to do in your own house is your own house, but it's like when I say part of the culture I mean you need to do the things that in America are, well the laws for one that are set are for certain reasons. Like female circumcision. That's not okay in America. That needs to stop. English. That's what we speak in America. If you want to be able to talk to people you need to learn how to speak English. You know, people constantly say it's so hard, well I say everybody should just speak goddam English. But you know, I was over in Europe a couple of months ago, you know, and people would get so angry at me for not even trying to speak their language. And nobody was getting upset with them, they'd just be like, well, you know, he's trying. Well fuck that! It's the same way in every god damn country, you learn the language. And Americans got this whole PC bullshit going on where everybody has to be so forgiving of everyone else and nobody has the right to say settle down and do something. (Gary)

Like the nation state, skinheads are caught in a historical moment of profound contradiction. Their roots are in the postcolonial formation between working-class British youth and Jamaican British dockworkers. Their musical forms derive from the subjugated colonial communities of the Irish and Jamaican working class.[14] Their warrior-tribal formations and tendency to violence are antithetical to any nation state social agenda outside of open warfare. Skinhead political forms stretch across the spectrum from anarchist-communist to the national front–Nazi skins. This political tension is only partially resolved by the traditional skinhead practice of separating politics from skinhead identity.

> Politics is a bigger burden to the cult. It's like a maggot that has eaten its way to the core, leaving the cult in the tatters it now finds itself in. Today's cult has been ripped apart by tin pot politicians from both the left and right. I haven't a clue who the winners are, but it's bloody obvious who the losers are. Us. Fortunately, the skinhead cult doesn't stand or fall on one rotten pillar, and more and more skinheads are beginning to see no politics as good politics. (Marshall, 1994, p.5)

These contradictions, both in skinhead subculture and in the modern nation state, have always existed. It is, however, in this moment of total subsumption that they erupt as productive social forces on the surface of the social realm instead of existing as a muted social tension that must be denied within the forms of the disciplinary.

What then distinguishes the discourse of skinhead and punk subculture from the discourses of adult culture? I would argue that in this moment of postmodern production, there is increasingly little difference between the margins of punk and skin subculture and the centre of adult bourgeois culture. This is not to say that there are no significant differences, but the differences are of degree and not substance. As the youth I spoke with noted, even body piercing has gone mainstream and tattoos (discretely placed) are not at all unusual among younger adults who would never dream of calling themselves punks or skins. As one of the skinheads put it,

> In reality you can be a skinhead without actually being one. The old idea of what a skinhead used to be about is being ignored or forgotten about. Nowadays you can be a skinhead with a full head of hair. Times have really changed. (Betty)

---

14 See Hebdige (1979).

The primary difference in the way subcultures are distinguished from adult or dominant cultures is in the performance of adult-youth relations within the domain of the developmental. It is in the discourse of adult superiority, driven by the Hegelian arrow of time we call maturity, that the differentiations of discursive formation take shape. It is not that the elements of youth subculture, such as fashion, hard core rock, tattoos, and piercings cannot be found as an integral part of adult culture. It is rather that the discourse of developmental maturity mutes the emotional intensity of these discourses, sending them fleeing into capitalist formations of unfulfilled desire, or to use a more specific term, 'need.'

Foucault (1975) has pointed out that the disciplinary society has, as an integral part of its ability to internalize and shape subjectivity, the persistent availability of the marginalized classes (the delinquent, mad, sexually deviant, racially inferior, poor, etc.). He argues that this is a structural necessity for the disciplinary society, as it sustains within view what those living at the centre of society must not become. In this moment of total subsumption, I would argue that the functions of such margins shift. Youth and its array of proliferating subcultures are no longer constituted as a primarily disciplinary form (although they still serve this function internal to youth itself); rather, the margins are sustained as sites of alternative production. In other words, it is in the very fabric of marginalization and oppression that subcultural forms proliferate. This creative proliferation cannot occur within the dominant cultural discourse without risking massive social upheaval and disruption to the regimentation of dominant modes of production. However, as we noted above, since capital is increasingly dependent upon cannibalizing its own social realm, it must sustain margins of pure creative productivity, which it can appropriate and distribute across the surface of its global circulation.

In this respect, subcultures that exist in the margins among disenfranchised and marginalized groups no longer serve as a negative impetus for internal self-discipline. Instead, subcultures have become productions of desire that are advertised and sold by association with goods and services as yearnings and needs for a certain kind of emotional freedom and liberation from the constraints of at the centre of capital.[15] Youth

---

15 For an excellent examination of this process, see the February 2001 Frontline documentary *The Merchants of Cool* (available at www.pbs.org/logbin/pages/frontline/shows/cool).

subculture, in short, becomes an offshore factory of raw affect that produces the objects of emotional cathexis for those living at the centre of the culture. I would argue that this is the central organizing feature of subcultural discourse at this historical moment.

Foucault Inquiry #2: *Describe how this body of knowledge and practice determines who can speak and with what authority. Who gets to describe youth subculture and how is this recognized as a voice of authority within the society?*

The question of who can speak on behalf of youth subculture is a highly contentious one. The positioning of punk and skin knowledge as the knowledge of the delinquent, the adolescent, the barbaric, situates it in a contentious and conflicted relationship with the knowable world of the dominant culture. The traditional academic disciplines such as psychology, sociology, and anthropology that produce texts about marginalized and disenfranchised others have tended to portray youth subculture within dominant frameworks of ideology and politics. In fact academic researchers, ethnographers, and sociologists have only had a moderate degree of success in trying to write from a position very close to the lived text of subcultural life. George Marshall points this out in *Spirit of 69: A Skinhead Bible*, in one of the rare moments when he suggests an academic text as a reasonable resource for understanding what he calls the skinhead cult:

> The book (*The Painthouse*) looks at different aspects of the gang's life ... In doing so it dispels many a myth about skinheads, not the least that they've been racist from day one. Paki-bashing went on just like it did in other areas, but there were also blacks in the gang. Sadly though it also creates a number of myths, particularly in the eyes of those who see it as some sort of definitive study on skinheads ... It never pretends to be that, and the opinions of the gang are no different to those shared by generations of street corner kids. (Marshall, 1994, p. 16)

Journalists have had even less credibility, as they have tended to focus on the sensational aspects of subcultural experience. Skinheads in particular, because of the violence of the crews and the Nazi political edge of the subculture, have elicited profound moral panic from both the popular media and the academic community. Such attention is an ongoing feature of skinhead life. As one of the young people I spoke with put it,

> I can't always go around and be like, 'I'm a skinhead, I'm a skinhead.'
> Because you know, a lot of people when they hear the word skinhead
> they're like 'Whoa, racism. That means that they hate colours.' You know
> or whatever. It's like, that worries me sometimes because for instance
> when I'm on the city bus or something I can't be talkin' about, 'Oh, hey
> you know that skinhead so and so ...' because right away you'll have
> people lookin' right at you. (Alice)

At the same time, the overwhelmingly negative treatment by the
media has served to both bond disparate elements within both punk
and skinhead communities and shape their perception of themselves
as under perpetual attack.

> All the bullshit used to get right up my nose, but now it's just water off a
> duck's back. Another cutting for the scrapbook and that's about it. You
> can't help but laugh really, because if you start to take any of it seriously,
> you are giving ignorant journalists far more credibility than their drivel
> deserves ... To misquote my old mate Oscar Wilde, there are lies, damned
> lies and skinhead stories. (Marshall, 1994, p. 4)

Nonetheless, it is not unusual for skinheads and punks to have read
extensively in the literature of their subculture, both popular press and
scholarly writing. In fact, both subcultures have their own indigenous
literature in books such as *Spirit of '69* (Marshall, 1994), *Pretty in Punk*
(Leblanc, 1999) *Skinhead* (Knight, 1997) *Rotten: No Irish, No Blacks, No
Dogs* (Lydon, 1995); zines such as *Flipout, Cooties, Rude International,
Hardcore Ink, Worst, Kontrol*; along with websites and pamphlets.
However, because of the extensive array of positioning among skins
and punk crews, textual authority here is highly contested as well. As
one young skinhead put it,

> I mean, ask yourself, in the rap subculture and hip hop subculture and
> the hippy subculture there is no Oi [laugh]. No, it's totally unique 'cause
> in those cultures there is no Oi, there is no Hammerskin which is Nazi,
> there is no RASH which is Red Anarchist Skinhead, there's no GASH
> which is the funniest of all, GASH if you can make sense of this, then I
> don't know, it's Gay Aryan Skinheads, they're Gay Skinheads. How does
> that work? (Frank)

Indigenous, scholarly, and popular texts that simply attempt to trace
the historical trajectory of music, fashion, and style are on the whole

less contentious than texts that critique the subculture, even from the inside.[16] More textual authority is given within the subcultures to texts such as George Marshall's *Spirit of 69: A Skinhead Bible* that attempt to clarify what are perceived as popular misconceptions:

> Hopefully this book will go some way towards putting the record straight about the skinhead cult. Not because we want to go down in history as wronged innocents, and certainly not to impress some twat of a Sociology professor. This book has been written for no other reason than to give skinheads themselves a written history of the cult, but I'm no expert on anything. Just a skinhead trying to provide other skins with as truthful account of our history as I can ... this book is a celebration of the skinhead way of life. (1994, p. 5)

It is important to emphasize the textual heterogeneity of the lived experience of the subcultures in question here. In a recent performance of the play *Lipstick Traces*,[17] the history of punk was traced through its philosophical and musical lineages. Such a presentation gives the mistaken impression of a coherent and progressive movement through time of certain ideological lineages and formations. However, in the last moments of the play, the various elements of philosophy and musical lineage were explosively combined with the personal narrative of all of the players, including the narrator herself, who until that moment had attempted to give an accurate and factual history of punk as a movement and musical form. The performance of this heterogeneous assemblage of personal, factual, and historic narrative combined with the music itself in an accelerated intercise of explosions and collisions that for me was a more accurate portrayal of subcultural text than any linear account.

The question of who can speak is constantly in tension with the complex heterogeneity of the margin as production. Any effort to gain textual authority within the subculture promotes immediate flight from the moment attempting to be spoken. Subcultures as poetic formations of flight hold a textual authority that has no centre except the absolute moment of production. As such, textual authority holds its

16 Leblanc's *Pretty in Punk* was read in whole or in part by most of the interviewees over the period that I knew them. None of them felt that the intensity of the critique of male gender bias within punk was warranted. While few informants stated that the bias did not exist, they simply felt the focus on it was overstated.

17 Performance by the Rude Mechanics in Minneapolis, January 2002, based on the book *Lipstick Traces* (1989) by G. Marcus.

only validity in the performance of subjectivity in each moment, by each collective assemblage of identities, times, bodies, and space. That is why this text, which I am writing and you are reading, can never be about skins and punks, but can only be an evocation or an echo, which like sonar helps us locate ourselves in this cultural moment as we sense the movement of punk and skin rupture in its flight.

Foucault Inquiry #3: *Describe how 'grids of specification' are derived. How are performances of body, space, time, and identity divided from dominant descriptions?*

As I have suggested above, the grids of specification for punks and skins are largely premised in the discourse of biological development that constructs them as adolescent. As adolescents, they are produced as an array of hyper-emotional subjects that have very little control over their impulses, sexuality, rebellion, and other actions. However, punks and skins are also to some degree voluntary exiles from the mainstream culture. Factors like race, ethnicity, gender, or any other form of observable difference inherent to their unadorned subjectivity do not determine their exile. An argument could be made, of course, that skins and punks are a class phenomenon and to some degree that may be true.[18] However, this assertion is confused by the fact that skins and punks also come from middle-class and even upper-class backgrounds.

> I mean you can be as much as a skinhead as you can possibly be but it's going to be different because the times are different and you have to kind of adapt that to modern-day living ... modern-day life. I think it's much more common not to come from a really working-class background, espe- cially in Minnesota 'cause I didn't and I mean, in all reality back in the day most skinheads were very working class and came from that – but nowadays I think that's much less common so that's more of a modern way of skinhead. I think that's just something you fit with. (Betty)

Indeed, the grids of specification that form the skin and punk sub- cultures, I would argue, lie outside the traditional disciplinary frame- works of the biological-social-political. The modes of analysis that attempt to overlay the tracings of class, gender, and socio-economic

---

18 See Muggleton and Weinzierl (2003); Bennett (2000).

status seldom give a satisfactory reading of the skin-punk experience. Yet the attempt to read such 'scenes' as purely postmodern is not thoroughly satisfying either. After all, the moment of the postmodern is simply a space between things – it is neither modern nor whatever is to follow the modern. It is simply a term used as a place marker in the absence of a clearly defined and coherent social world. In such an indeterminate space we find that social forms such as skin and punk hold traces of modern, pre-modern, and postmodern elements.[19] In this kind of social terrain, the old grids of specificity become highly contingent but no less forceful. Certainly, as we have discussed in previous chapters and this one, the new grids of domination with their flexible nets of capture and appropriation, infinitely malleable language structures, mutable forms of identity, and new hierarchies of privilege hold extreme force. However, this is the description of the grids of the subjectus. We might now ask, what is the grid of the subjectum?

As we know, the grid of the subjectum lies within the ability of youth as creative force. That is to say, it is an auto-poetic or self-produced grid of specificity. In terms of skins and punks, this youth-determined grid of specification might well be called the terminally social disease of being different. As one of the interviewees stated,

> I think a lot of kids, you know, even before they're punks or anything like that, a lot of kids kinda start out being weird, you know what I mean. They're just like, 'Well, I'd better dye my hair and wear all these bracelets and stuff like that because I want to be different.' (Sue)

This difference, rather than being a source of shame or intruding as a command to conform, spurs a radical departure from the norms, not only those of the dominant culture but from the norms of youth subculture as well. This difference is manifested as ongoing performance and as such once again prefigures postmodern subjectivity within late-stage capitalist culture, as we have outlined above. These performances take place primarily on the body.

> Punks are sort of crazy about their bodies. I mean, the crazy coloured hair, the Mohawks, the I don't give a fuck attitude. I mean, it's just like

---

19 By pre-modern I am referring to nomadic and agricultural social systems that pre-date European modernity.

saying fuck you, fuck your conventions, and fuck whatever you want to think if you want to look at me and not like me for it, well, I don't care. You know, because we don't need you. You know? (Tony)

This performance of radical alienation, expressed fully upon the body of the subject, can be read as a reversal and reclamation of a body alienated from its labour within the Taylorist modes of production in the disciplinary society. The bodies shaped by the factory, the family, the school, and other spaces of confinement are rejected by punk and re-formed as hybrid assemblages that repudiate any need for disciplinary acceptance. Punk not only accepts the panoptical gaze of society (Foucault, 1975), but revels in the public displays of deviance it affords. Punk doesn't care that others are watching, because the gaze from the outside is not worth their time. If you don't like what you are gazing upon, then fuck off!

Most people aren't worth your time anyway and it's like, me personally I thought it was one of the greatest ways to root people out anyway on who I really gave a fuck about anyway. Because I mean, if somebody's not going to give you the time of day because of the way you look? Then fuck them. (Tony)

Within this realm of radical alienation and voluntary exile, performance begins to form the body as art; that is to say, it is expression that is creative but not communicative (Deleuze, 1995).

I think with tattoos it's a kind of expression it's an extension of our leather jackets, you know a piece of art – a kind of extension. I think that the idea behind it would be that I have always felt that I wanted to be able to tell other people I didn't want to be part of what they were doing without having to say it – but the clothes definitely and by behaviour say I don't want to be part. You get a lot more negative attention – there's quite a lot of people would rather not talk to you. (Tony)

This performance of art on the body that does not have an interest in communicating but only expressing mirrors a similar movement in modern art to turn your back on the audience, like Miles Davis, and play only to the band. There is an indifference to response outside of the limited circle of other artists who understand that your art doesn't mean anything that can be spoken or defined. It is to be experienced, not understood; shared, not analysed; and celebrated, not showcased. In punk, one of the grids of specification internal to the subculture is an unwillingness to care about ascription of value to what you do.

> I think after a certain point punks really stop caring in the same sort of sense. Like you stop caring if people look at you and you stop caring if people like, don't want to talk to you, people make snap judgments about you. And I think it actually gives you more of an aggressive stance on other people. Like you're more likely to be on defence when you're talking to other people and you're more likely to, like, you walk more aggressively and you just ... 'cause you have to 'cause people otherwise confront you on a lot of things. I think definitely like in how you carry yourself and everything and a lotta punk girls will like not care like what like whatever Abercrombie, [a preppie fashion outlet] like football guys. If she wants to wear short skirts she doesn't care because people who are looking at her they don't mean anything to her so it doesn't matter. And, plus if you're wearing a short skirt and you're punk you're less likely to get hit on because you're a punk and therefore unattractive to other people so you don't have to worry about other people looking at you as much. (Sue)

If the punk performance is one of turning away, the skinhead movement is one of head-on confrontation. The art on the body and clothing in skinhead subculture is centred on affiliation and exclusion. It is a tribal marking of territory, both subjective and cultural. It is a tracing of a certain history of both the immediate subjectivity of the body as well as its lineage – geographically, culturally, and politically. This expression of multiple and hybrid forms of belonging that might include a combination of tattoos, buttons, patches, boots, and braces are not designed to communicate to the outside (although they may hold significance within the skinhead subculture itself). However, this is not to say that it does not express a certain positioning vis-à-vis the non-skinhead world. This positioning is not a turning away, but an active physical engagement with the world around them.

> I think skinheads use their bodies more in a physical sense ... Skinheads tend to use their bodies as sort of a way to say what they think and you know, it's like if you're going to have your pride, you can't really say you're proud of something unless you're willing to put it on you. (Gary)

This active assertion of skinhead culture as a force of subjective production holds in tension an array of modernist subjective and social formations as well as valorized disciplinary enclosures. The performance of skinhead includes an attempt to recuperate and sustain performances of race, family, ethnicity, gender roles, working and class identity. Along with this is a voluntary re-entry into the disciplinary enclosures of the factory, the labour union, and the nuclear family.

I think it would be a mistake to assume, however, that these returns are inherently retrogressive movements. Without question, the right-wing skinhead performances of Nazi ideology, the violent attacks on immigrants, sexual minorities, and people of colour are regressive and intolerable on every level. At the same time, the majority of skinheads I have met and interviewed do not subscribe to or participate in these performances and are instead attempting to recuperate the structures and enclosures of modernism as hybridized assemblages of alterity to what they perceive as the nihilistic movement of postmodern capital (Wood, 1999). Movements such as Skinheads Against Racial Prejudice attempt to revitalize working-class values outside the historical collusion with whiteness (Roediger, 1991).

> I identify racially, not so much racially because I'm white, not so much about race but the countries where my ancestors came ... I'm not so much proud of what my race is, but where I come from. I think it's really cool, like, I don't identify myself racially. (Frank)

Perhaps the most intriguing aspect of the grids of specification within the punk and skin subcultures is their auto-poeisis or constantly evolving self-production. These groups highlight the rise of subcultures since the mid 1960s as voluntary associations whose grids of specification are located and generated from the inside. The dominant culture has no particular need to extrude these particular young people any more than it generally marginalizes youth as a whole. However, as we have noted above, once these margins are created from the inside by the youth themselves, capital quickly follows behind each developing grid to exploit whatever is created within.

Foucault Inquiry #4: *What relationships are established between institutions, economic and social processes, behavioural patterns, and systems of norms that allow for the appearance of the object? What are the conditions of post-ality that allow for these particular hybridized performances?*

Punks and skins are produced exactly between the institutions and the economic and social processes of the postmodern world. That is to say that they are produced as what Casarino (2002) has called immanent or potential interference: 'Immanent interference ... is the questioning movement of a practice towards itself; it is the manner in which a practice repeatedly folds back upon itself in an attempt to come to know itself; it is the fold of being by which a practice thinks itself as a practice' (p. 28).

Punks and skins are precisely this reflexive praxis within the postmodern moment of total subsumption within capital. In this, they are 'characterized by an intertextual and intercultural deconstructionist thinking ... by a recodifying and decentering of history; by heterogeneous or hybrid thought ... not exclusionary, rather ... includes multidimensionality ... capable of unmasking ... the irrefutable truth, as contradictory and irregular' (de Toro & de Toro, 1995, pp. 17–18).

The deterritorializing movement of punk deconstructs the world of the modern and experiments with new forms along the edge of nihilism. Skinhead moves along a trajectory of reterritorialization in which it attempts to recuperate in hybrid form the structures, enclosures, and fragments of modernism that postmodern capitalism has released into rhizomatic flight. Both subcultures represent interrogatory practices in which the late-stage capitalist social realm asks itself the central questions of limit and threshold.

In a sense, the central question of punk is how far can this go, while the central question of the skinhead is how much can be salvaged from the wreckage. Both performances are constructed out of a spiralling return of infinite recycling. In this sense, these subcultural performances are both produced by and fully productive of the conditions of possibility for institutions, economic and social processes, behavioural patterns, and systems of norms.

Both subcultures, in their separate but related forms, interrogate the postmodern social world. In this, they don't simply challenge but actually engage the social world through assembling a mix of cultural icons from across the globe. Both skins and punks scavenge society for the material out of which they will fashion their performances. In this moment of the dying modern and the birth pains of the as-yet-undefined world of post-ality there is, of course, loss. This loss is deeply imbued into the subcultural worlds of the youth I spoke with. It inheres itself in each moment of negation and recuperation, but perhaps has its most powerful effect in the affective realm. In the performance of punk and skin on and through the body, there is a disdain for the gentle, the beautiful, the sweet, the kind, the innocent, and the hopeful. In its place there is pride, strength, celebration, loyalty, love, and affiliation, but perhaps most of all rage. As the skins and punks in the interviews put it,

> Skinheads is one of the few subcultures where pride in who you are is the most important part ... It takes valour to fight back, it takes valour to stay in this subculture. Even though everybody's kicking you down, spitting on you and beating you up ... I mean, a skinhead is probably one of the toughest subcultures there will ever be. It's a boots and fists subculture ... In general it's like everybody's so scared of us and so scared, you know them skinheads, they're violent ... Skinheads are really about respect for yourself and respect for your friends and it's a very close-knit community. Respect means you don't fuck with your friends ... you got your friends back ... and it doesn't really matter whether you win or lose, it's the fact that you had the balls to stand up to it. (Frank)

> I see that punk is like a whole group of people working together to try to, you know, just have a place for themselves. I mean the punk community is probably one of the closest-knit ones you'll ever deal with ... Punk culture, I think is living life to the fullest ... Basically punks have a negative outlook, a negative outlook on everything ... I mean it's just like saying fuck you, fuck your conventions and fuck whatever you want to think if you want to look at me and not like me for it, well, I don't care. You know because we don't need you ... Most people aren't worth your time anyway. (Tony)

The rage of skin and punk subcultures is a rage of betrayal; a rage of trust misplaced; a rage of a world promised but not delivered; a rage of being left on one's own to create the world. This rage, I would argue, is not necessarily a negative thing. It serves as a savage negation of the transcendent and is very probably the necessary affective precondition for whatever revolutionary possibility lies within this moment of historical transition As Johnny Rotten said at the end of the Sex Pistols' last performance at Winterland, 'Do you ever feel that you've been cheated?'[20]

---

20 Documentary *The Filth and the Fury* (2000, New Line Home Video).

Beyond rage, loss, and betrayal, however, there is transformation. In the interviews with the six youth about the subcultures to which they belong, I did not discover anything I could describe as static formations of culture or identity. Instead, I found fluid, mobile, heterogeneous assemblages of everything these youth engage. These interviews, for me, are a portrait of becoming. They are becoming youth, becoming adult, becoming community, becoming nation, becoming multitude, becoming relation, becoming man, becoming woman, becoming culture, and finally, but not only, becoming pure and material possibility. It is within this space of becoming possibility within youth subculture, I would argue, that a new politics of youth-adult relations might be found.

In the last meeting with these six youth, we sat around my dining room table and discussed this chapter. We laughed, joked, ate chips and pizza, and I asked them for their feedback. This is what they said when asked to give advice to adults who want to work with youth:

> I think you should get to know the kids you're workin' with really well and try to see where they're comin' from and why they are doing what they're doin'. Put yourself in their shoes and see if you would do the same thing and if you understand ... kinda role-play it almost ... like really try to see where they're comin' from. (Tony)

***

> I would say that just because you're old doesn't mean you have a buncha knowledge. I know a lotta people who are like fuckin' 60 and are fucking idiots. Just because we're young doesn't mean we are fucking stupid and don't know what we are talking about. You know a lot of us are fucking mature and know a buncha shit. (Frank)

***

> I think it's really important, like if I was talking to an adult who was going to be working with kids, especially about this topic – it's not a phase! Every time an adult like sees a punk they're like goin', oh they're goin' through their angry phase. They always think it's like really childish and they don't realize there are adults who are like punk and still are skinheads. They're always assuming the kid thing and I think that's wrong. What they could do is like talk to kids about what they do on a

daily basis instead of, you know, like what do you think about the grand perspective on things instead of what we do on a daily basis, like drink beer and play video games and eat pizza and little stupid things that would probably get overlooked but it's us and it's a big part of who we are is really all the boring things and shit like that. (Sue)

***

Talk to kids, not at them – don't be condescending. Don't just say well you'll get over it cause you're young. Talk to them one on one. Never say when you're older you'll understand. Talk to them like you would a friend. Don't be overprotective – let them do their own thing but at the same time offer guidance – tell 'em what you think is right but don't force it on them cause they're gonna do what they want anyway. Keep your distance. Cause we're gonna make our mistakes and learn from them. (Frank)

***

Don't always prejudge – just 'cause you are skinhead doesn't mean you are Nazi. Saying that as a punk is pretty important. And not all punks are flag-burning little idiots, fighting against the system any way they can, just rebelling to be rebelling. So basically throw out all your notions you had before, throw away all that you got from TV. Look at it from the perspective of like completely new. Look at the person – not even what subculture they belong to as an individual. Stereotypes are usually really bad things. Everybody who has seen *American History X* [21] thinks they know what skinheads are. It's not even accurate, but you take everything you get from the media and it does have an influence on what you think about something. So just throw all your misconceptions out. (Tony)

---

21 1998 film, New Line Cinema.

PART TWO

Creating Spaces for Radical Youth Work

7 Nomads and Refugees: Youth and Youth Work

It could be said that working with people is best done in the space between things. This space comprises a zone of indeterminacy that is pure potential. It is a moment in which that which has happened is over, and that which is to come is not yet. In such an opening, between the solid edifices of history and knowledge, lies a highly mobile and transitory encampment of nomads, gypsies, and refugees from all that is known to be the truth. Somewhere in this shifting terrain of hazy vision and uncertain movement lie the incomplete and unfinished revolutions of the past. Deep within this space of liberatory potential reside the unrecuperated alternatives to all that comprises the empire of now.

These alternatives can only be held in the space between things and by those who inhabit such places. This is the power of the minority; all those created as 'other' who live between the lines that order and structure the dominant culture. Subcultural youth are created within this 'otherness' and as such (along with other minorities) hold in tension the abandoned alternatives left behind by the victors of cultural, economic, and political struggle. This residue of past struggles for equity, dignity, and liberation are encoded within the creative expressions of subcultural youth identity, as we have discussed in our previous investigations of time, space, and embodiment. This encoding functions in much the same way that Western society makes sense or non-sense out of madness. That is to say, following Bateson (1972), that the language of the schizophrenic and the expressions of subcultural youth are immediately appropriated, interpreted, and overcoded by the dominant culture, based on the cultural positioning of both the speaker and the message, without full investigation of the message's local meaning.

What is clear, however, in the case of both psychosis and youth sub-culture, is that the message delivered is both unsettling and often disturbing. Messages of this type, whether from prophets, visionaries, madmen, or youth, are often ignored, interpreted, or appropriated. As Bateson (1972) points out, 'Disturbing information can be framed like a pearl so that it doesn't make a nuisance of itself' (p. 435). Of course, it is just such nuisance that youth workers are hired to manage. In fact, we might say that those who work with youth live between the potential for liberation implicit in the creative force of youth and the dominant society's mandate to 'frame [it] like a pearl.'

This struggle between the forces of creative desire and the mandates of the subjectus has shaped the world of youth-adult relations in both practice and theory. In a slightly different context, Negri has stated that 'every innovation [of capital] is a revolution which failed – but also one which was attempted' (1996b, p. 158). I would propose that this applies to the regimes of youth work as well: every innovation in youth work is a revolution that failed, but also one that was attempted. All advancement within the technologies of assistance to young people is appropriated out of the revolutionary struggles of the youth. The following quote can be read in the same sense: 'The more radical the innovation is, the more profound and powerful were the antagonistic proletarian [youth] forces which determined it and therefore the more extreme was the force which [the youth work profession] had to put in motion to dominate them' (Negri, 1996b, p. 158).

In *A Thousand Plateaus*, Deleuze and Guattari (1987) outline the difference between a limit and a threshold. They state that 'the limit designates the penultimate marking a necessary re-beginning, and the threshold the ultimate marking an inevitable change' (p. 438). It is in the nature of capital and its agents of capture, such as the 'helping professions,' to extend its own limits without crossing the threshold that would change it radically and irrevocably.[1] The appropriation of the revolutionary impetus of youth – the subjectum – by the knowledge regimes of the 'helping professions' that produce the subjectus has traditionally functioned along this axis. The question is, can youth work become something else?

---

1 This idea owes much to its elaboration by Dr Casarino of the University of Minnesota, in a lecture given 30 November 2000. It should also be noted that Foucault's notions of 'biopower' and the role of social sciences in constructing regimes of knowledge are critical here as well.

Youth and Youth Work: A Brief and Particular History

Youth work began with the creation of 'adolescence.' This cultural distinction of an age group between children and adults began in the nineteenth century (Perrot, 1997, p. 68) and was established as a distinct developmental stage of life in 1904 (Hall, 1904). Until that time, there was no clear distinction between youth and adults. It was only with the advent of the Industrial Age that youth, or young adults, became adolescents. In pre-industrial societies the transition from child to adult was without an intermediary period (Mitterauer, 1986). While there were certainly concerns over how young people comported themselves, they were subject to the same disciplinary and supportive societal forces as older adults.

This began to change as young people joined the factory workforce in Europe in the late eighteenth and early nineteenth centuries. According to Mitterauer (1986), young people were one of the largest workforces within the early factories and mills. As they experienced the appallingly poor working conditions, they began to organize as a political force. The first organizations formed specifically to 'work with youth' were given the task of de-politicizing their activities and 're-patriotizing them.' Luzzatto (1997), in outlining the revolutionary activities of young people in Europe during the French Revolution and the struggle for labour rights in Germany, England, and France, describes the situation as follows:

> The fact remains, however, that young people inspired fear throughout the nineteenth century. Everything seemed to conspire to make young people untrustworthy ... Hence the urgency of instituting a kind of delaying tactic, of postponing the moment when young men could assume political and social responsibility ... a heterogeneous, but clear image emerges of a restless or rebellious youth ... [It was] at the very moment when youth lost the role it had played in traditional societies – a culturally recognizable role and a factor in social cohesion – that [youth] began making political demands and thus became the object of political denunciation. (pp. 174–5)

While political denunciation certainly constituted one of the ongoing societal discourses relating to adolescence, another discourse was forming that has had even greater relevance to the development of youth work. This was the shift away from youth as a societal issue to youth as a particular biological and psychological stage in life. This new concept is what Foucault (1978/1990) has referred to as nineteenth-century biopower. Ann Laura Stoler (1995) describes biopower as the 'disciplining of individual bodies' and 'the global regulation of the biological processes of human beings. It is this "technology of power centered on life" that produces a normalizing society' (p. 33).

The development of biopower allows a group of people such as youth to become objects of discovery, categorization, and observation. It is this shift that allowed for the creation of the 'modern or psychological' adolescent (Hall, 1904). I have discussed the impact of these developments on young people at length in the examination of youth and subculture in Part One. Now I want to outline the effects of this process even more directly as it pertains to youth-adult relations within the field of youth work. Indeed, I will argue that it is with the advent of the observable, definable, and discoverable adolescent that modern youth work was born. The field of youth work was and is deeply shaped by the development and construction of ideas and 'truths' about youth or adolescents throughout the modern industrial period. These ideas have not only shaped the world of adolescence, but also the world of the youth worker.

Youth Work: Definition, Struggle, and a Proposal

The field of youth work is multifaceted in practice, theory, and location. In its simplest sense it 'brings the world of ... adolescents together with the world of adults' (Arieli, 1997, p. 1). This can take place working in residential treatment centres (Arieli), street outreach (Oliviera, 1995), day treatment, emergency shelters (Gershowitz & McFarland, 1990), as well as in schools, churches, and community centres. Across these diverse locales, however, the mission of the field becomes more diffuse.

Some believe that the role of the youth worker is liberatory and should focus on the amplification of 'youth voice' or on the legitimization and explication of 'youth subcultures.' Others state that youth work 'brings together ... those who are ... "not properly socialized" – whom the prevalent educational and care approaches seek to change – together with those who know the "proper" social codes and are expected to generate the desired change in the ones who don't by intervening in the course of their maturation' (Arieli, 1997, p. 1). These radically differing views should be very familiar to us as the subjectum and subjectus. This struggle between subjectum and subjectus produces an ongoing tension in the field that has direct bearing on the lived experiences of youth workers and their subsequent co-constructions of youth. These divergent codes and meanings about youth also have an impact on how youth workers conceive of themselves and what work they believe themselves to be doing. It is through these 'knowings' that the youth worker comes to understand his or her world, and it is these beliefs that shape their lived experience. Perhaps even more importantly, these understandings deeply influence the lens through which youth workers view youth and how they make sense of what 'youth' means.

The production of the subjectus within the field of youth work stems from what Foucault (1972) has called a 'fellowship of discourse.' This kind of discourse is involved in the production of 'truths' that yield certain kinds of power (p. 227). The role of the youth worker is constituted at the intersection of a number of cultural discourses. Many of these have to do with the marginalization, categorization, normalizing, pathologizing and de-politicizing of youth. Others have to do with the construction of 'truth regimes' and 'disciplines' displayed in discourses about professionalization, maturation, progress, rationality, science, medicine, expertise, and social control. The identity of the youth worker is comprised of these intersecting discourses that affect their descriptions of themselves, their roles, and how they come to understand their relationship to the youth they serve.

This induction into certain kinds of knowing about youth constructs youth work and youth studies within the frameworks of European modernity, the colonial imperialist project, and Euro-American capitalism. These frameworks formulate youth and youth work as a process of accommodation, exploitation, or resistance (Brake, 1985; Hall & Jefferson, 1975; Hebdige, 1979; White & Epston, 1990; Willis, 1977). Within this way of knowing, youth becomes an observable object in a dialectical process of development that is hinged on the relationship of resistance or assimilation to the dominant structures of modernist knowledge or capitalist development.

In this sense youth, youth work, and youth studies are sustained and developed within a system that is designed to penetrate and overcome; or what we have described as the subjectus. The power of modernity in this instance lies in its ability to produce ultimate truths about youth that include young people's resistance and the colonial ability to 'capture' such resistance and turn it to its own ends.

However, despite the apparent pervasiveness of modernity and its effects on youth, youth studies, and youth work, its theoretical foundation is being radically altered. The world is entering an age in which the old structures of imperialism, modernism, the nation state, capitalism, and their respective regimes of truth are mutating. We are moving from the colonial and modern to the postcolonial and postmodern. As we have noted previously, 'Post, in fact, marks an end, and the beginning, of a new field of inquiry which unsettles and undermines previous theoretical discourses and forms of inquiry, while drastically providing an open-ended field of possibilities (de Toro & de Toro, 1995, p. i). We have surveyed some of the limitations of the postmodern approach in discussing post-subculture studies. Now we can take a look at some of the possibilities postmodernity opens up for youth work, in which this shift into 'post-ality' allows for a re-conceptualization of youth, youth studies and youth work. Within this entirely different framework, the conception of youth is no longer based on regimes of truth through which youth can be known in some essential way, nor is youth a singular identity that can be discovered.

Youth Work under the Society of Control

Current youth work dilemmas are often framed as concerns about how to best to discipline young people. Work in residential programs, schools, family studies, and education for work and community development tend to focus on either how to discipline youth effectively or how to create frameworks that allow them to escape the mechanisms and gaze of discipline. Such frameworks were certainly applicable and important within modernist industrial capitalism, in which the discipline of the individual subject was of central importance (Durrant, 1983). Deleuze (1995), however, argues that the age of the disciplinary society is past. He suggests that we are moving instead towards what he calls a 'society of control.' The parameters of this society include 'forms of control,' which are defined as 'inseparable variations forming a system ... whose language is digital' (p. 178). In other words, within the regimes of global capital, discipline is no longer dependent on consistent rules or practices. Instead, discipline is brought about through the deployment of anxiety. The subjectus is produced as a subject of a highly uncertain marketplace in which the rules are constantly changing. The subject of such a regime is induced into believing that they must constantly accommodate such change or fall behind and lose their place in the evolving world of work. Success in such a world is not judged by how well one follows the rules or given morality of the system. Instead, the 'controls are digital,' which is to say that one is judged by one's numbers; in other words, one's credit rating or financial worth. Deleuze goes on to state that within the emerging society of control, 'controls are a modulation ... continually changing from one moment to the next' (p. 179). In other words, control is implemented by constantly changing the codes that signify success or stability. It is a bit like living in a giant casino: the minute you think you have figured out how the game is run, the house changes the rules. Definitions of success such as high school graduation shift and lose meaning in the marketplace, so that now a university degree is required, but then that in turn loses its force and is replaced by the requirement of the 'right' degree. Lists of degrees that will guarantee a job this year are posted in the media, but such lists are constantly changing: a degree in computer science was the ticket to success until that bubble burst, and now people with those degrees are back at school retraining for a new career.

In this sense, Deleuze tells us, control societies are made up of 'endless postponements' (1995, p. 179), 'codes and passwords,' and 'dividuals' rather than individuals. These 'dividuals' are not in a binary relationship with the 'masses' but are components of 'samples, data, markets or banks' (p. 180). In such a society, 'marketing is now the instrument of social control,' and 'control is short term and rapidly shifting, but at the same time continuous and unbounded' (p. 181). In such a society, we never fully arrive at a career, a relationship, an identity, or even a home. In our careers we are told to train and retrain as the demands of 'the marketplace' change the need for different skill sets and whole fields of endeavor shrink drastically or disappear entirely. Our identities are increasingly made up of a shifting set of codes that include our student ID numbers, computer pass codes, passport numbers, social insurance codes, security codes for work and home, and, finally, our credit ratings. In this way, Deleuze suggests, we are no longer individuals but simply bits and pieces of marketing data. Our worth to the fully capitalist society has nothing to do with our character or moral behaviour, but only with how much we contribute to the ubiquitous economy. We can never find a space into which such controls don't penetrate: every part of our life is available to the marketplace, including our schools, homes, computers, relationships, national identities, and certainly our workplace. In each of these arenas we experience the constantly changing codes of expected economic behaviour. Within such a society, I would argue, the concern with resistance and discipline that is a feature of contemporary youth work is no longer relevant.

Disciplinary Youth Work

Skott-Myhre and Gretzinger (2006) have argued previously that youth work, as traditionally practised, is laden with preconceived notions and fear of the same young people it sets out to serve. Adolescents have come to occupy a space of otherness within our society through the production and reinforcement of dominant discourses of fear, idleness, and political and democratic marginalization. Consequently, youth workers often believe that it is their responsibility to control the very people they set out to serve. Such a system of 'care' becomes a project designed to digest those on the outskirts, to convince both the youth and themselves of the benefits of buying into the dominant social system.

This relationship between capitalism as an economic system and youth work as system of social control produces practices of youth work based on set standards of normalcy. Through the distribution of normative dominant standards and the regulation of dress, speech, ideology, and the body, youth work becomes a system designed to reproduce and facilitate goals that sustain the status quo. Youth who successfully and seamlessly enter the system are rewarded with privilege as a method of furthering and dividing a category of people that, when united, could make substantial social change.

For example, within the field of youth work there is a general consensus that young people ought to be taught to be good citizens. We generally mean by this that they should join the dominant culture with a minimum of disruption. To that end we attempt, in many programs, to teach them discipline and respect for the authorities (adults) who are working with them.

However, this is more complicated than it may appear. If we are simultaneously attempting to prepare our young people for democratic citizenship, in which they exercise their rights as human beings, and at the same time show them that submission to authority, over which they have no democratic input, is the way to be successful, we are operating in direct contradiction to our own intentions. More importantly, we are building an addiction to certain forms of dominance by confusing submission to authority with respect. It is important to note in this regard that respect is as a relational quality found between equals, whereas submission always occurs between unequal levels of power. The promise of a respectful relationship between youth and adults cannot be built on a platform of submission. To use the term respect when one really means submission is to discount the actual lived experience of submission through a simulation of respect. It is precisely this sort of confusion that produces the antagonisms often experienced between youth and adults in youth work programs. Respect cannot be achieved through submission, and yet we push discipline and subjugation to others as the path to mutual respect between youth and adults within our programming.

Youth Work and Resistance

What if we were to resist the conflation of capitalism and youth work? I would argue that unfortunately, the modes of analysis utilized by both traditional youth studies and by most youth work practice orientations do not account for the speed of mutation inherent in the new regime of control. A review of the literature (Skott-Myhre & Gretzinger, 2006) revealed that even the most radical youth work approaches were still driven by notions of representative democracy derived from ideas of developmental capacity. The notion that capitalist youth work can be resisted through an increased but adult-regulated youth voice cannot provide any real resistance to domination. In addition, as I have argued above, in the moment of total subsumption each and every social formation produced by resistance is immediately appropriated by the regimes of capital and turned to its own ends.[2] In fact, even if a viable youth-adult challenge were mounted within an agency, by the time resistance or challenge could be mobilized, all the definitions will have shifted to accommodate, enclose, and incorporate the new knowledges made available from the new youth subjectivity or youth work practice.

One possible answer to this dilemma is offered in Deleuze and Guattari's notions of lines of flight. The rhizomatic burrows of the lines of flight suggests a sense of multiplicity and infinite possibility of escape that may be flexible enough to break free from the mutating elements of control. Massumi (1996) offers the line of flight as absolute subjec-

---

2 I will have more to say about this later.

tum in stating that 'effective escape is nothing less than the perception of one's vitality, one's sense of aliveness or changeability (often signified as freedom)' (p. 229). This again allows for a flexibility, energy, and stamina that are required to engage in flight from an ever-shifting landscape of control. While a full explication of a youth work or youth studies based on 'lines of flight' is beyond the scope of this book, I would like to outline three principles upon which such a practice might be developed.

Multiplicity of Self

In discussing the lines of escape from a 'dominant atmospheric semiotic,' or a world in which all meaning is absorbed and regurgitated through capitalist logic, Deleuze suggests we need to flee signification entirely. He uses the example of Don Juan in Carlos Castaneda's *Tales of Power* (1991). Deleuze paraphrases Don Juan's injunction to the young anthropologist Castaneda regarding his constant need to create coherent meaning out of his experiences: 'Stop! You're making me tired! Experiment, don't signify and interpret. Find your own places, territorialities, deterritorializations,[3] regime, and lines of flight! Semiotize yourself instead of rooting around in your prefab childhood and Western semiology' (Deleuze & Guattari, 1987, p. 139).

In other words, Deleuze is suggesting that we need to create our own meanings for events without using predictable frames of reference based in the existing dominant language structures. This is a tremendous problem for developing a field of youth work that can actualize a new world outside capitalist logic. The demand often heard by community-based youth workers that academics use 'common language' and not jargon certainly holds some merit. However, there are traps in the 'common language' of capitalism that reproduce the very system political youth work is attempting to challenge. New worlds require new linguistic structures and definitions that are seldom found in 'common or plain language.'

It is important to remember that in the society of control, the 'dividual' is an infinitely mutable element of marketing. As such, any fixed identity becomes captured by capital and used to its own ends. In a

---

3 As we discussed in Part One, 'territorialization' and 'deterritorialization' are Deleuzian terms referring to the ways in which all formations are organized and taken apart by the creative force of desire.

youth work of flight, identity must also become infinitely mutable but along lines of flight outside of capital. Youth work must focus on the development of a multiplicity of identities, each responsive to the control levelled through the multiple projection of the marketplace. Lines of flight should be located idiosyncratically and creatively. They cannot be found in the existing metaphors of capital, the confines of disciplinarity (family, work, school, etc.), but rather in the deterritorialization of such identities constructed and abandoned through a conversation that explores infinite possibilities of shifting identity. These lines of flight must provide multiple exits as the society of control appropriates and assimilates each new identity. Points of convergence between various lines as well as the convergence of each line with power must produce a bifurcation or rhizomatic of identity with infinite creative potential.

Hijacking Speech

In his essay 'Control and Becoming,' Deleuze states, 'We've got to hijack speech. Creating has always been something different from communication' (Deleuze, 1995, p. 175). Youth work must move away from communication as a central metaphor. Conversation must become creative, not communicative. In this, we must form a poetic praxis of youth-adult relations. Our conversations should break apart and explore the myriad possibilities inherent in each word, each turn of phrase. Conversations between youth and adults should explode and open lines of escape out of both the spaces and the content of each utterance. Deleuze said, 'The key thing may be to create vacuoles of noncommunication, circuit breakers so we can elude control' (p. 175).[4]

Conversations about and frameworks for youth work and youth studies should not remain content with making sense, but aim at breaking sense into new configurations that have sufficient velocity to escape the market's encroaching assimilation of new language. Definitions must be mobile and transitory, evocative not definitive. New codes or passwords must be constantly generated within the idiosyncratic life world. Such codes must mutate and provide a counterpoint to the codes and passwords of the marketplace. They must close off access to the lines of flight that have been taken and frustrate the

---

4 The Williams Burroughs short film *cut-ups* (1964) is an excellent example of how vacuoles of noncommunication function.

agents of control. Such a use of codes may be found in the creative expressions of youth subcultures that must constantly mutate to avoid the capture of capital.

Creating Believable Worlds

In 'Control and Becoming' (1995), Deleuze states that we have lost the world and our sense as a people: 'If you believe in the world you precipitate events, however inconspicuous, that elude control, you engender new space times, however small their surface or volume ... We need both creativity and a people' (p. 176). A youth work of flight would concern itself with the recovery of both a people and a world. Conversations would explore the parameters of culture, struggles, history, art, and poetry. This would not be a 'romantic return to culture,' but rather an exploration of the assemblages,[5] the component pieces, the evocative histories that might be assembled in a creation of a mobile culture in which lines of flight can be located. Such an evocation of culture is not an archaeological project, but a project that involves art as a 'war machine'[6] that has to do 'with a particular way of occupying, taking up, space time, or inventing new space times: revolutionary movements' (Deleuze, 1995, p. 172). Youth work and youth studies would comprise conversations in which a collaborative construction of culture as an art form would be explicated. The creative force of such a pastiche can be found in the performance of the hybridized uses of time, space, and body within youth subculture today.

It is out of these performances that an exploration of the groundwork on which a 'youth work of flight' might be premised. A focus on youth subcultures as performances of postcolonial hybridity has the capacity to demonstrate how these performances can provide new avenues for teaching adults (particularly youth workers) how to collaborate with youth in challenging the dominant ways of knowing. Through this, possible discursive frameworks in youth subculture can be produced that will provide avenues for challenging the 'capture' or

---

5 'Assemblages' is a Deleuzian term referring to the constellation of components which come together to form people, events, emotions, ideas, music, painting, identity, or anything that falls within perception.
6 'War machine' is a Deleuzian term for the revolutionary impetus within all peoples and histories.

appropriation of work, community, and family by capital. Such opportunities for challenge are important for reformulating a youth work and youth studies discipline based in the world of the subjectum, which has the capacity to respond to the radically shifting global environment that impacts youth, their families, and communities. An exploration of the subjugated knowledges within youth subculture provides one example of how the world of youth might collaborate with the world of adults in transforming or reclaiming our lives at the material and political level.

8 Creating a Youth Work of Flight: Barbarians, Boundaries, and Frontiers

To think about youth and youth work is to return to the ambiguities of the Battle of the Teutoburg Forest. It was here that the Germanic tribes defeated the Roman Empire in 9 CE and halted the further expansion of that empire into their territory and into northern Europe. The military defeat, while successful in halting the Roman occupation of more territory, did not prevent the expansion of Roman influence on culture, law, politics, and economics. Indeed, the Battle of the Teutoburg Forest marks the end of tribal structures in what was to become Europe. It also set in place an ongoing ambivalence in the European psyche between the barbaric and the civilized.

To work within the relations of force that constitute youth-adult interaction is to constantly revisit this historical abyss that obliterated the tribal history of Europe. It is to re-enter the colonial problematic in its purest binary manifestation: the Roman and the barbarian. Though other colonial projects have created 'others,' even barbaric 'others,' none have had the same far-reaching impact as the Roman construction of barbarism and civilization (Wells, 1999). This construct has many different registers, all of which operate within what might be called the European colonial project. For our purposes, it is important to note that this project produces many of the central constructions of otherness with which we must concern ourselves if we are to rethink youth work.

Indeed, at the centre of various permutations of otherness (including race, ethnicity, gender, sexuality, and youth) is the primary move of the tribal peoples of Europe from being barbarian to being Roman. This move by a conquered people to adopt the mantle of empire and tools of colonization has been central in the production of European colonial modernity. It has had important effects on shaping the structures of disciplinarity – internal and external – to Western subjectivity. In its most basic manifestation it has created an absolute repudiation of the tribal, as found in the writings of Western philosophers as diverse as Marx, Freud, Nietzsche, Hegel, and Locke.[1] It has also produced a model of civilization based on the Roman model of law, which gives preference to the functional over the aesthetic and maintains an ongoing oscillation of the 'tension between Romulus and Numa: Romulus, the symbolic figure of Roman expansion and Numa, the symbol of law and order of limits' (Whittaker, 1994, p. 10). This binary tension between what Deleuze and Guattari (1987) have referred to as oppositions between the 'nomadic war machine' and 'the state'; 'the arborescent' and 'the rhizomatic';[2] the process of 'territorialization' and 'deterritorialization' or 'striation and flow'[3] runs 'deep in Indo-European culture' (Whittaker, 1994, p. 11). Whittaker, in writing on the relationship between the Roman and the barbarian, refers to this tension and struggle as 'paradox.' I would argue that the tension is far more dynamic and productive than this suggests and that it has been instrumental in reshaping the anxiety of European indigenous post-colonial subjectivity (derived from Roman occupation) into formations of sovereignty and empire.

These formations continuously and dynamically reshape the relationship between the barbarian other and the colonial centre along specific trajectories of capture and appropriation. Within the history of post-tribal Europe these projective extensions of boundary and frontier or centre and periphery have been produced within the movements and developments of capitalism. The infinite array of production, originating out of the colonial, neo-colonial, and postcolonial productions of capital, is the result of the struggles of those who would resist its appropriations. As Wells (1999) points out in *The Barbarians Speak*, 'The native peoples of Europe played a much greater role in the formation of the societies of Roman Empire Europe than we would think' (p. ix).

---

1 Each of these writers dealt with the issue of the primitive or barbaric with outright suspicion, derision, or disdain without ever identifying the tribal roots of Europeans as the defining moment of the barbarian.

2 'Arborescent' refers to tree-like hierarchical structures, in contrast to the rhizome which, as we have discussed, runs under the ground and splits into multiple off-shoots each time it is cut.

3 'Striation and flow' is the force of structure and release.

In short, the barbarian, through failed struggles against empire, provides the very material through which empire is able to expand. Indeed, as we have noted before, it is through the appropriation and assimilation of revolutionary impetus that capital continually expands (Negri, 1996b). In this context, we can begin to look at how this expansion functions in youth work as a complex mapping of boundaries and frontiers, limits and thresholds.

Youth as Frontier

Youth, as a subject within the historical and contemporary terrain of the colonial, constitutes a particular territory, boundary, and frontier. Youth work and its closely aligned disciplines of psychology, psychiatry, sociology, and social work map this territory, both because they intend to sketch its outlines and because they cannot help it. They can't help it because each conversation that an adult has with a youth subjects the youth to a cartography of understanding. In this sense maps open territories, even though, as Korzybsky (1941) has pointed out, the map is not the territory itself. Nonetheless, mapping opens frontiers and frontiers are not easily bounded once engaged. As Whittaker (1994) points out in *Frontiers of the Roman Empire*, 'a frontier [is] not a line to stop at, but an area inviting entrance, by definition never still – a process, not an area or boundary' (p. 5).

It is here on the frontier, an area comprised of both lines and zones, that youth and youth workers oscillate in the ancient pattern of control and liberation, flow and striation, webs of discipline or capture and lines of flight (Deleuze & Guattari, 1987). This movement between youth and adults is comprised of both limits and zones. That is to say that on the frontier where youth and adults meet, limits are defined by lines that separate and differentiate levels of bureaucratic order and administration; zones, by contrast, unite and integrate those who are culturally diverse (Whittaker, 1994, p. 72). The space constituted by youth, as we discussed in Part One of this book, creates subaltern territories which then become subject to the administrative lines of dominant culture or the homogenizing influence of zoning, which creates groups of youth as being fundamentally the same. This is reflected in the creation of groups such as jocks, punks, Goths, gang bangers, and the like.

This ordering of territory is never finally completed because the territory is in constant contestation, struggle, and flight. As such, it produces a frontier space of indeterminate control that invites entrance because it has no capacity to hold a firm boundary. Those youth who are indigenous to the territory and are constantly slipping into frontier must negotiate both the lines and zones inherent in their 'discovery' by the academic, cultural, and professional communities who are putting them on the map.

It is here, in this dance of negotiated space, that youth subcultures emerge. It is important to remember that these formations of youth into subcultural components are not modes of resistance (Hall & Jefferson, 1975), exemplaries of class oppression (Willis, 1977), modes of aesthetic expression (Hebdige, 1979), nor even postmodern performances (Butler, 1990) but are, I would argue, complex machinic assemblages which function as reservoirs of unrecuperated residues of failed possibility (Negri, 1996a). These residues are those practices, performances, beliefs, and ideas that 'have been subordinated, excluded, or held in abeyance by forces and according to necessities' (Derrida, 1988, p. 21).

This space of unrecuperated potential is the frontier that lies just outside the boundaries of traditional youth work. It is the unknown, unthought, unpractised realm of possible youth-adult relations. It is also, as we noted in our discussion of Spivak and subaltern speech, simultaneously an area of absolute impenetrability belonging entirely to youth subculture as well as an area that is already assumed to be within the infinite expanse of capital's unrealized empire (Negri, 1996b).

According to the central construct we have defined so far, this space of unrecuperated potential interacts with zones and limits in complex ways. For example, it criss-crosses the zone of homogenization with lines of flight that escape into the impenetrability of absolute refraction. In other words, each generalized category of young person, whether punk, skin, jock, or cheerleader is riddled with exceptions to the assertion of sameness. These exceptions are radically unique to each person and cannot be interpreted or fully understood from the outside. However, as we have noted before, each idiosyncratic expression of creative force has the capacity to reflect back new possible formations to the observer, provided they relinquish any generalized knowledge of the subject in view.

That said, each social formation of identity carries within it the history of struggle out of which it was formed. Youth subculture carries the deepest motifs of colonial and postcolonial ideology. The figure of the unknown and savage interior that must be brought to the light of civilization intersects and cross-pollinates with the anthropological impetus to preserve and valorize the noble savage and his or her potential contributions to world culture. In other words, we hold ambivalent feelings towards the productions of youth subculture: we want to valorize and preserve it while at the same time wanting to civilize it and make it more palatable. This ambivalence saturates our models of developmental and assets-based youth work, where we try to rework the productions of youth into formulations that are productive to the dominant society as assets or future potentials. There is, however, another kind of youth work that moves underground at the margins of disciplinary and colonial youth work.

Towards a Minoritarian Youth Work

This subterranean subject is the youth worker who enters the territory of youth with the understanding that to do so is an inherently subversive activity. It is subversive, not because the goal is to politically re-enfranchise or empower youth, but because the worker is there to be radically altered as an 'adult' through interaction with youth. This work might be called a 'minoritarian' youth work. I use 'minority' here as it is defined by Deleuze and Guattari (1987) in *A Thousand Plateaus*: 'Minorities are not necessarily defined by the smallness of their numbers but rather by becoming or a line of fluctuation, in other words, by the gap that separates them from this or that axiom constituting a redundant majority' (p. 469). Stated another way, the minority comprises those subjects that elude a definitional category set by the dominant culture. This is the gap that separates and creates as entirely impenetrable the becomings of the minority (in this case, youth subculture). As such, it operates fully outside of colonial logic and holds potential for a different set of relations between youth and youth worker.

This gap containing youth subculture and youth work as minority functions within a terrain filled with the structures of language. In youth work it is language that 'shapes events,' since the world of youth-adult relations is built almost entirely through conversation, interaction, and conversation about interactions. As we have discussed, language constructs young people as three-dimensional bio-structures that grow and die on the surface of the biological plane. For a youth work rooted in the colonial scientism of development, assets, and evolution, language reflects biology and is constrained by concepts of processes such as brain development, hormonal balances, and biological capacities.

This relation of force produces the linguistic bio-structures that are outlined by hierarchical rules; lines of frontier that outline and shape (order and administer) the trees whose branches structure and hold the levels of logical typing about youth, adolescence, delinquency, assets, development, and so on. These levels in turn form eco-zones that 'unite and integrate' their seemingly heterogeneous elements by establishing the pattern that connects them through a complex array of repeating patterns and predictable trajectories. In other words, these zones reduce the infinite complexity of difference that composes each subject down to descriptions of sameness and repetition. Through this reduction, the singularity of each young person can be composed into a group definition of composite behaviours through which each subject can be connected to a group of subjects that ostensibly predetermines their possible or at least probable sets of behaviours.

In his book *Three Ecologies* (2000), Guattari points out that these eco-zones, which produce the singular subject as simply an instance of the group, integrate the individual's unique and idiosyncratic psyche into a set of homogenizing descriptions. Such descriptions produce the sameness of description in what comes to be called adolescence or youth. Any time we think we can know what is true about a young person based on their group identity as an adolescent, we are entering into such an eco-zone. It is important to remember that it is in the nature of the frontier to abrogate and dissemble boundaries. In this respect, these lines and zones create large webs of capture that operate on the same plane of frontier as the photograph. That is, they contain and subject all that is within the frame to the context and moment of aperture.

It is to this moment of capture that Guattari speaks. Arguing against the cybernetic and systemic theorizing of Bateson, which has informed so much of 'systemic' youth work,[4] Guattari argues against a zone that homogenizes action and enunciation through frameworks determined from the outside that contain and structure behaviour. He argues that such zones are created following ruptures, in the predictable patterns

---

4 I am thinking here of the influence Bateson had on therapies derived out of the Mental Research Institute, such as Systemic Therapeutics, Brief Therapies, Solution Focused Therapy, Strategic Therapies, etc. See Wilder-Mott and Weakland (1981).

of development that pre-exist before understanding. In other words, there is no smoothly functioning system that produces certain kinds of social subjects. Subjects are produced through ruptures, breaks, and accidents that are then smoothed over in the description that follows. Such descriptions might well be referred to as a zone of context, in which the rupture is explained away by a description of the surrounding circumstance. For example, we can explain the rupture of creative behaviour that exceeds the boundaries of the classroom through using the biological context of bad chemistry or attention deficit disorder.

In this respect, one might say that the zone of context is a construction driven by anxiety. It is a cartographic covering over of the abyss that is no-thing. In other words, describing a given phenomenon is a way of obscuring the fact that the phenomenon in question is not really anything that can be described fully. By the time we have described what we see (which is always partial at best), the object has already become something else. In addition, without description an object is not yet anything and as such might well be anything or everything. Stated in yet another way, that no-thing which precedes description is pure immanence.

On such a plane of immanence there is no 'overall hierarchy for locating and localizing the components of enunciation at a given level.' In other words, in such a space there is no ability to claim structure, no patterns to connect, no zones and lines that erode and contest boundaries; instead there are thresholds. The plane of immanence is pure frontier without order. It is, as Whittaker pointed out: 'not a line to stop at, but an area inviting entrance, by definition never still – a process, not an area or boundary.'

The plane of immanence is where things 'become' through ruptures in the logical levels of the world that is constantly no more. It is composed not out of trees of logic and empirical sense, rising majestically towards a realm of transcendent perfection, but rather out of rhizomes of non-sense, spreading in infinite extension along the plane itself. This, then, is a world of pure 'minority' taken on its own terms, 'detached from the surrounding world and closed on itself like a hedgehog' (Guattari, 2000, p. 54). This is the world of youth subculture; the world of the nomad and the refugee. It is the space within which youth and adults collide and produce one another. It is a world constituted of relations of force – a world of power. Such a world of power sets the conditions for the field of youth work: its possibilities and its sets of dominating forces.

9 Power and Its Effects

In *The History of Sexuality* (1978/1990), Foucault describes power as the product of force relations. He argues that power is not the province of one person or another but manifests itself in all aspects of human endeavor. For Foucault, power is somewhat like electricity. It is not something you can locate as an object, and yet it is present in every aspect of the world. Power, like electricity, is only visible at points of resistance. But its points of visibility are not its only points of productivity.

Obviously, this is not the traditional sense of power commonly found in Western thought. Foucault argues that our modern sense of power continues to be linked to monarchical concepts of centralized power. We continue to define power by what he refers to as its 'points of terminus,' conceptualizing it not in any complete way but only by the points at which it becomes visible. Foucault challenges the idea that power works according to laws or institutional conventions. Referring to a critique of the 'legal' applications of power, he questions the basic premise that power is lawful: 'Real power escaped the rules of the rules of jurisprudence ... the legal system itself was merely a way of exerting violence, of appropriating that violence for the benefit of the few and of exploiting the dissymmetries and injustices of domination under cover of general law. But this critique of law is still carried out on the assumption that, ideally and by nature, power must be exerted in accordance with fundamental lawfulness' (1978/1990, p. 88).

This traditional concept of power is central to the rule-based structures that formulate youth work as a process of discipline and consequence. Rule-based structures conceptualize youth as being in need of adult supervision and regulation. Foucault, however, does not subscribe to this idea of power as bound by law or order. He states that power is not 'a mode of subjugation,' 'a group of institutions or mechanisms that ensures the subservice of the citizens,' or 'a general system of domination exerted by one group over another' (p. 92). Instead, he proposes that power must be understood as 'the multiplicity of force relations immanent in the sphere in which they operate and which constitute their own organization; as the process which, through ceaseless struggle and confrontations, transforms, strengthens, or reverses them; as the support which these force relations find in one another, thus forming a chain or a system, or on the contrary, the disjunctions and contradictions which isolate them from one another; and lastly, as the strategies in which they take effect' (1978/1990, p. 92).

This description of power as both diffuse and profoundly local has tremendous implications for youth-adult relations. Foucault is talking about power as made up of relationally constructed aspects of force that constitute a process that is transformative within a local sphere of influence. This relational process has no fixed outcome. It might 'form a chain' or 'isolate them from one another,' but its productions have no finality, no end point. Power, therefore, is not a commodity but rather a process with somewhat random results. As a process it has no fixed point at which it can be located with any certainty. 'Power is not something that is acquired, seized, or shared ... power is exercised from innumerable points' (p. 94).

This notion of power as diffuse both in location and identity wreaks havoc with our traditional notions of power relations. We tend to think of power as residing within someone or some institution. We talk about it as though it was a quantity that some people have and others do not. Its exercise tends to be linear. We use it or bring it to bear on others or to enhance or transform ourselves. If there are multiple sites of power, they are generally thought to be in conflict with one another for primacy; hence the term 'power struggle,' which has such currency among youth workers and the institutions that attempt to 'serve youth.'

Power from Below

Power in traditional 'colonial' youth work is tied up with 'will' and individual assertion.[1] Power is intimately associated with notions of

---

1 I am coining the term 'colonial youth work' to mean youth work premised on colonial constructions as delineated here.

evolution and progress; to be power-full is to be on the 'top of the heap.' Here again, Foucault looks at the matter differently:

> Power comes from below ... the manifold relationships of force that take shape and come into play in the machinery of production, in families, limited groups and institutions, are the basis for wide ranging effects of cleavage that run through the social body as whole. These then form a general line of force that traverses the local oppositions and links them together; to be sure, they also bring about redistributions, realignments, homogenizations, serial arrangements and convergences of the force relations. Major dominations are the hegemonic effects that are sustained by these confrontations. (1978/1990, p. 94)

This vision of power being formulated among youth as they go about their daily lives, establish the structures and practices of their family life, and carry out involvements in the community has direct implications for the theorizing of youth subculture. Foucault is suggesting that the world out of which youth-adult relations are generated – the world of school, work, family, and community – is not subject to power that is imposed by any kind of elite. No one defines for the other how his or her world should be constructed. Rather, it is in arranging and making meaning from daily living that power is engendered. It is here that the dualities that have reverberations throughout the culture are constituted – male/female, black/white, gay/straight, self/other, and so on. How each of us attempts to enforce our vision of the world constructs the confrontations that comprise the centre and periphery of what is true. Through a multiplicity of such confrontations, hegemonic truths are formed and given power. As a result, the force-relations of youth work must be rethought at the profoundly local level of each youth-adult interaction. It is in these confrontations, not through the world of agency administration or government policy, that the hegemonic constructions of empire are formed.

This complexity of formation does not lend itself to simple causal models of power. There is no single application of intentionality that can be pinpointed and challenged. While each exercise of power has its objectives, they are hard to tie to any singularity of origin or authorship. 'Power relations are both intentional and non-subjective ... there is no power that is exercised without a series of aims and objectives ... yet it is often the case that no one is there to have invented them, and few who can be said to have formulated them' (Foucault, 1978/1990, p. 95).

Power and Resistance

Power is therefore neither singular in origin nor a trajectory. Power is constantly being generated at an infinitude of localities throughout a society or culture. The generation of power cannot be tied to any particular person or group of people. No one stands outside of power. Everyone is involved in its production and distribution. It is important to remember, however, that power is also multiply productive. While on the one hand it generates through confrontation across society certain hegemonic constructions of truth and practice, on the other hand it ties together and brings into being resistance against such ideas and practices. Such resistance, however, is not separate from power. It is, instead, an integral part of power relations and the ongoing construction of power itself. As Foucault states,

> Where there is power there is resistance, and yet, or rather consequently, this resistance is never in a position of exteriority in relation to power ... one is always 'inside' power, there is no 'escaping' it ... [The existence of] power relationships ... depends on a multiplicity of points of resistance: these play the role of adversary, target, support or handle in power relations. These points of resistance are present everywhere in the power network ... There is no single locus of great refusal, no soul of revolt, source of all rebellions, or pure law of the revolutionary. Instead there is a plurality of resistances, each of them a special case. (1978/1990, p. 96)

The idea of a 'plurality of resistances' calls into question some of our most dearly held notions of political and revolutionary practices and belief. In my reading of Foucault, the notions of large hegemonic constructions of resistance and dominance such as 'class struggle,' 'national identity,' 'gender- and race-based struggle and resistance' begin to break down. These constructions are the terminal points of long and complex processes of local confrontation. The focus of revolutionary action at such points may have little impact on their power. These hegemonic constructions only apply power; they do not generate it. Power is generated idiosyncratically in every interaction between human beings. Effective resistance to such power must occur at the local level.

In this regard, any effort to confront youth-adult relations of force that is based on consensus about the 'truths' which comprise our world only amplifies the terminus points of power. To shift this dynamic, local knowledge of alternatives and individual modes of both youth and youth-worker resistance must be employed. Resistance cannot be consolidated into ideology without resulting in a loss of these idiosyncratic knowings. Effective resistance can have no centre and can hold no truth without generating yet another type of power that will in turn generate further resistance.

In this regard, Foucault sees resistance as unstable and continuous. Rather than envisioning an effective resistance in the sense that power will be overcome, Foucault sees power and resistance as involved in an ongoing restructuring of society with no ultimate end or particularly desirable outcome. Resistances 'are distributed in irregular fashion: the points, knots or focuses of resistance are spread over time and space at varying densities, at times mobilizing groups or individuals in a definitive way ... more often one is dealing with mobile and transitory points of resistance, producing cleavages in society that shift about, fracturing unities and effecting regroupings, furrowing across individuals themselves, cutting them up and remolding them, marking off irreducible regions in them, in their bodies and minds' (p. 96).

This is the landscape that Foucault portrays in the *The History of Sexuality*. It is this shifting topography of individual, familial, political, physical, moral, and conceptual practices and beliefs about sexuality that Foucault uses to illustrate the fractured unities and regroupings of people's most intimate contacts. Here he outlines the ways in which each of us are cut up and remoulded in our thinking and our body practices. Through his explication of this history he outlines the productions of power, the 'mobile and transitory points of resistance,' and the consolidation of such resistance into cultural and societal hegemonies that have echoes into our own current practices and beliefs.

This analysis of power and resistance creates youth, youth subculture, and youth work as conduits, points, or knots in the grid comprising the constructions of both power and resistance. As such, the process of youth-adult relations is intimately tied to issues of power and resistance. This is not a process of exploring the meaning of certain behaviours or histories. Nor is it an explication of human motivation. Instead, it is an exploration of what Foucault has called 'subjugated knowledge': the relationship of hegemonic 'truth' to 'local knowledge.'

Desire and Power

In his essay 'Desire and Pleasure' (1997a), Deleuze examines Foucault's analysis of power and resistance as outlined in *The History of Sexuality* and *Discipline and Punish*. A complete outline of his analysis goes beyond the scope of this project, but I would like to take up several key points as they relate to the notion of power and resistance and what Deleuze refers to as 'lines of flight.'

This is a complicated endeavor, however, in that even in the differences between Foucault's and Deleuze's thinking there is a certain give and take, an interpenetration of concept, which makes their differences difficult to cleanly distinguish. Yet I would argue that an exploration of their differences could be productive in producing variable readings that lead in new directions for explorations of our conception of power.

One of the primary points of divergence between Foucault and Deleuze as identified in 'Desire and Pleasure' is that Deleuze sees desire as preceding power. Desire is made or unmade out of the plane of immanence, or what he calls the body without organs (1997a, p. 189). What Deleuze means by this is that desire springs out of the force of life to produce and create prior to any structuring of that creation. He goes on to claim that the manner in which desire is produced includes the apparatuses of power, but that such apparatuses will be organized according to the ways in which desire distributes its components. For Deleuze, power follows desire in that desire is what drives the world into being through creative force. In other words, the mechanisms of power must be situated within the different components of the ways desire lays out the world. The articulations of power operate through the reterritorialization of the components of desire that also includes 'points of deterritorialization.' The mechanisms of power do not assemble or constitute, 'it is rather the layout of desire that would spread throughout the formations of power.' Deleuze argues that power is 'an affect of desire' rather than desire being a production of power (p. 186). In sum, power is the way in which desire is structured, while desire determines the distribution of power.

This centring of desire has several key implications for Deleuze in relation to Foucault's analytic. For example, whereas resistance is mutually constitutive with power in Foucault's analytic, Deleuze maintains that the phenomenon of resistance is not an issue (1997a, p. 188). He sees lines of flight and movements of deterritorialization as primary determinations, 'since desire assembles the social field' and 'it is rather the mechanisms of power that are both produced by these arrangements and crushed or sealed off by them.' (pp. 188, 189). Here we move out of the arena of youth-adult relations as simple resistance to domination and into the arena of youth subcultures as pure flight.

Where Foucault sees simply resistance, Deleuze talks about lines of flight and resistance as one and the same (1997a, p. 191). However, it is hard for me to see flight and resistance as being one and the same. For example, Foucault's notions of power are premised on a system in which power is a relation of force from which there is no exit. There is only resistance that creates other forms of power. For Deleuze, desire and the lines of flight are becomings that are an endless process of opening and closing folds in the plane of immanence, in which lines of flight provide the release of the fold. These lines of flight are to be found in the cracks and crevices of the folds, in the multiplicity of spaces between things. Foucault's resistance, however, is located not in between, nor outside, but as an integral part of the fabric of power.

Whereas Foucault sees power as a relation of force, Deleuze sees desire as 'an assemblage or arrangement of heterogeneous elements that function as process not structure or genesis.' Desire is an event, not a thing or a person (p. 189).

> Above all it [desire] implies the constitution of a plane of immanence or a 'body without organs' which is solely defined by zones of intensity, thresholds, gradients, flows. This body is as much biological as it is collective and political; the arrangements of desire are made and unmade on it, and it supports the cutting edges of deterritorialization or the lines of flight of the arrangements ... If I call it the body without organs it is because it is opposed to all the strata of organization – those of the organism, but also the organization of power. (1997a, p. 189)

This is a crucial point of difference. Deleuze's description of the assemblages of desire as productive of a constant flow of deterritorializations is quite different from Foucault's descriptions of power as constitutive of what Deleuze would call reterritorializations. This difference is critical to an understanding of the complex interaction that takes place at the frontier of youth subculture. The frontier, as a cartographic extension of the colonial youth work boundaries of biopower, constantly inscribes its logic on the domain of the frontier and on the subjectivities residing there. The minoritarian collective assemblages of youth subculture engage desire through radical and idio-syncratic creative expression that deterritorializes or explodes these inscriptions.

Power and Desire in Youth Subculture and Youth Work

These distinctions between resistance and lines of flight have a particular resonance for thinking about youth subcultures. Does one see youth subculture as a point of resistance, in which new productions of power lead to alternative knowledges that can be used to challenge the crystallized knowledge of the 'state' or institutional knowledge? Or does one see subculture as a line of escape from certain territorializations or structures? Is there in fact a difference? Perhaps the difference lies in the type of society in which one is embedded.

As we have already noted, in the interview titled 'Control and Becoming' (1995), Deleuze states that we are 'definitely moving toward "control" societies that are no longer exactly disciplinary' (p. 174). He discusses Foucault's work as it related to the disciplinary society and its use of the technologies of confinement, noting that Foucault foresaw the end of disciplinarity and the beginning of control. Control societies 'no longer operate by confining people but through continuous control and instant communication' (p. 174). Such a society works through 'open sites' and 'continuous training' (p. 175). People are constantly monitored and speech and communication are 'corrupted' or captured by capital (p. 175). Identity is established through consumption and debt. In such a society, your identity is your credit rating and is accessible wherever you are, twenty-four hours a day.

How does this shift to a control society affect the issues of power, resistance, desire, and lines of flight for youth, youth subcultures, and youth work? How does such a constellation affect the development of youth work and youth subculture in today's society? I would like to propose that the two questions are interrelated.

Youth work is constructed as a technology of conversation. As such it has been deeply involved in the production of knowledge, power, and resistance. It has also long been created through the productions of desire and has aspired to create lines of flight. In the disciplinary society, the concerns of youth work were related to the confines of the school, the jail, the treatment centre, and the family. Its mission, depending on the orientation of the youth worker, was either to accommodate or normalize youth to the regimes of discipline or to assist them in avenues of resistance. The focus was on the development of singular identities that could either accommodate or resist. Histories consisted of singular individuals who struggled or had 'problems' to 'solve.' Conversations were designed to open and clarify communication in hopes of developing new meanings or understandings that could challenge hegemonic constructions of identity or purpose.

Within the society of control, these dimensions shift and bring different valences to the endeavor of youth work. Without the focusing element of confinement in the school, the workplace, or the family, individual identities begin to fragment. This fragmentation brings youth of multiple identities to youth work. The role of desire is joined with that of consumption, bringing youth whose desiring discourse is deeply laden with metaphors of capital. The nature of relationships is no longer bounded by identification with a certain role and brings youth whose relational field is transitory. The smooth history of the individual youth becomes fragmented and discontinuous, bringing young people of hybridized lineage. Problems and solutions become linked to an unstable field of shifting identity and desire, resulting in youth with a changing multiplicity of 'problems.' The nature of delinquency and madness proliferates and expands to include a dazzling array of categories unbounded by disciplinary needs but premised instead on youth work as an arena for the production of the consuming subject.

This portrait of a 'society of control' fully subsumed within capital (Negri, 1996a), creates a world of pure frontier with boundaries that are provisional and interpenetrated. As I have outlined above, this is concurrently the world of youth subcultures and youth work. It is a moment of immanent but perpetually delayed revolution. Each revolutionary impetus to significantly alter the colonial pattern of youth-adult relations is created and subsumed within the growing sphere of corporate or capital-driven youth work. If we are interested in challenging this pattern and undoing the impact of empire on youth-adult relations, it is important to consider both the modes of appropriation that are being used to defuse revolutionary potential and the possibility of escape from such appropriation.

10 Appropriation and Escape*

In order to think about escape and capture as revolutionary becomings in the context of youth and youth work, it is important to examine several questions. How do we conceptualize the revolutionary impetus? What constitutes a revolutionary idea? How is such an idea created in a form that can be appropriated and exploited? What are some possible tactics of response to such appropriation? And finally, how does this affect the problematic of revolution itself?

Revolutionary Impetus

The impulse towards revolution within youth work and youth sub-culture is a complex dynamic comprised of an immense array of inter-actions, historical conjunctures and ruptures, contradictions and antagonisms, some of which we have outlined above. Such an impulse precedes and is integral to revolutionary praxis. As an impulse, revolutionary youth work would be carried through on the basis of mate-rial realities combined with beliefs about those realities. To the degree that the dominant culture, the state, or the current mode of production appears impervious or impregnable, the impetus to revolution will be thwarted by a sense of powerlessness or cynicism. As Jameson states, 'To understand why the concept of revolution has fallen on hard times today ... there can have been few moments of modern social history in which people in general have felt more powerless: few moments in

* Material from this chapter was previously published in 2005 as 'Captured by capital: Youth work and the loss of revolutionary potential,' *Child and Youth Care Forum* 34(2), 141–57.

which the complexity of the social order can have seemed so forbidding and so inaccessible, and in which existent society, at the same time that it is seized in ever swifter change, has seemed endowed with such massive permanence' (Jameson, 1996, p. 38).

I would argue that youth work is permeated with this sense of powerlessness. The disciplinary edge of youth work with its rules, diagnostic categories, therapies, spaces of containment/confinement, and over-coded descriptions of youth has constructed edifices of capture which constantly seem to overtake and render impotent any effort to crack their surface. At the same time, the impetus towards revolutionary youth work can also be seen as a constant dynamic force that may ebb and flow but never disappears or is entirely defeated. Such impetus generates a range of anti-hegemonic ideological constructions, which are generated by the historical epoch, particular material conditions, and the mode of production. This impetus resides outside of reactive considerations of dominant cultural formations and within subjectivities formed alternatively to such constructions as youth subculture or radical youth work. Alternative subjectivities of this type include conscience and belief, which 'under particular historical conditions can move mountains or break down the wall of a particular form of domination. Only in this way are revolutionary ideologies ... conceivable' (Haug, 1987, p. 74).

It is, however, the particularities of historical conditions and forms of domination that reduce the revolutionary utility of such alternative or subcultural subjectivities. In addition, although such subjectivities may include anti-hegemonic beliefs and impetus, these may be included without being fully revolutionary in the sense of the full destruction of the existing order of things. However, in spite of any given historical conditions that make revolution unlikely, there has always been the possibility of revolutionary collaboration between youth and adults. In the tradition of Western democracy it can be seen as far back as the French revolution, in which many of the key figures were youth working in collaboration with adults, or in the early organizations of factory workers, many of whom were children and youth. The 1903 children's march on Washington during Teddy Roosevelt's administration, led by the indomitable Mother Jones, is another example. More recently, the American civil rights movement of the early 1960s and the global revolutionary upheaval of 1968 were collaborations of youth and adults. The early punk movement collaborated with elders of the Beat movement such as William Burroughs, and the recent uprisings against global capitalism and the U.S. incursion into Iraq have also included youth and adults working together. In fact, the early youth work movement, as exemplified in organizations such as the National Network for Runaway Youth, held revolutionary and political goals of societal change built from youth-adult collaboration.

The political force of these historical movements, however, appears to have bypassed much of the current field of youth work. It is difficult to find a collaborative youth work with overt revolutionary political intention. In fact, it is difficult to find a youth work organization whose primary goal is the liberation of the youth and adults involved. There are of course notable exceptions, such as the youth workers in Brazil who have been willing to give their lives for the street youth that they serve. On the whole, however, the field has lost much of its revolutionary potential. In fact, many of its most revolutionary ideas such as peer culture, street-based services, free shelter, community-based programming, and poverty programs have been appropriated as mechanisms of control and capture in which youth are seduced into contact with 'helping professionals' and then defined, diagnosed, and rehabilitated as bourgeois citizens of late-stage global capitalism.

For example, in transitional living and job programs, youth work serves many disadvantaged and marginalized young people. These young people have been exploited at many levels on the street and in their families and communities. We offer programs ostensibly designed to offer them an escape from exploitation. I would argue, however, that what we actually do is to make them available to another form of exploitation: exploitation by global capital. Each time that we offer a course in job skills without including a section that explains the exploitative nature of youth employment within multinational corporations, we are complicit in the continued exploitation of these youth. When we train youth to work for corporations that do not pay benefits or offer a living wage, without having provided classes on labour organizing, we are complicit with the status quo.

Of course, it goes without saying that it is difficult for youth workers to approach such issues within agency contexts, because the very working conditions that they would be training youth to challenge exist within youth work itself. This is most certainly one of the reasons that our training within such agencies focuses so consistently on differences and boundaries between youth workers and youth. What would happen if youth and youth workers realized their common status as exploited workers within global capitalism? Put in another way, how have youth and youth workers been constructed within global capitalism in a way that keeps their political interests separate and opaque? What has happened to the revolutionary potential of youth work and what can be done about it?

To answer these questions I would like to pursue further the issue of global capitalism and its increasingly comprehensive influence over youth service programming. In order to address the issue of capital and its ability to appropriate alternative forms and practices, we must consider youth-adult collaboration as a possibility for revolutionary becoming, or the liberation from exploitation for both the youth and adults involved. In seeking a framework for this discussion, it seems obvious that the models of neo-liberal capitalist democracy and its extension, global capitalism, need to be examined. These economic forms have shaped the social and institutional environment of youth work in dramatic ways over the past twenty years. What lens affords us the analytic tools necessary to examine the impact of capitalism and its effects on the revolutionary liberative potential of youth-adult collaboration? I would argue that the best analysis of capitalism and its modes of appropriation, capture, control, and exploitation remains that of Karl Marx and the Marxist and communist writers who have followed capitalism's development over the past 500 years.

There are those who would say that communism and other forms of radical economic and political change are finished and bankrupt. They would assert that the 'failure' of the Soviet Union signals the triumph of capitalism as the ultimate hegemonic force within the contemporary world. They would argue that it is the role of youth work to accommodate youth successfully to the world of capital; that it is the function of the youth worker to assist young people in obtaining those skills, tools, affective states, and social identity that will allow them to thrive in the 'new world economy,' and that there is no reasonable alternative to this investiture in capital.

Global Capitalism and the New Communism

It is certainly true that capitalism has considerable force at this moment. Its appropriative and exploitative capacity seems relatively boundless. However, I also see this moment as one of opportunity for revolutionary youth work. The demise of state forms (such as the Soviet Union) that have been identified as the defining constructions of communism open as many spaces as they close. While capital has certainly shown its ability to flow into these spaces with some speed, the demise of these systems also 'allows us to uncover and indeed to constitute, as though for the first time ... a whole range of alternative communist trajectories, projects and histories' (Makdisi, Casarino, & Karl, 1996, p. 4).

This opportunity for a new communism is in profound contradiction to the current historical moment of production known as global capitalism. This moment, in which the capacity for appropriation and exploitation has reached epoch proportions, signals either the point in history at which capital has proven itself as a thoroughly successful endeavor, or the point at which its inherent contradictions and antagonisms are approaching full revolutionary possibility. In either case, the level of capitalist development is extremely high and this has significant implications. 'When the capitalist process of production has attained such a high level of development so as to comprehend every, even small fraction of the social production, one can speak, in Marxian terms, of a "real subsumption" of society in capital. The contemporary mode of production is this subsumption' (Negri, 1996a, p. 152).

In this moment, it is important to investigate the manner in which capitalism, in its effort to 'comprehend every, even small fraction of the social production,' appropriates and exploits the revolutionary potential of projects such as youth work and how this appropriation by capitalism shapes and defines the parameters of revolutionary, liberatory response. To do this requires a step-by-step analysis of the methods by which capital appropriation actually functions. If we can understand the way in which capitalism's machinery of appropriation functions, then perhaps we can discover new modes of escape and ways in which to accelerate the development of new forms of exploitation-free existence for both adults and youth.

Exploitation and Appropriation

The first step, in Marxist terms, to appropriating and exploiting any object by capital is to create what is called surplus value. Surplus value can be defined as whatever is beyond the material conditions necessary for one to live. In other words, it is that which one is required to do that goes beyond what is needed to satisfy one's unique conditions of lived experience. When we ask young people to mute their creativity within schools, agencies, and group living arrangements by disciplining their musical expression or the ways they use their bodies through clothing, tattoos, and piercings, we produce them in ways that are valuable to the program, staff, or adult culture but are not valuable to them. In this way we produce a value beyond that which they would produce for themselves and which is only useful to someone else. Similarly, when we ask youth workers to modify their creativity and actual human contact with young people in order to meet the rules and regulations of the agency, we are producing their work as valuable to the agency in ways that may not be valuable to them or the youth. This is what is called surplus value. In the case of youth or youth work, it is accomplished through the mechanism of ideology.

The Question of Ideology

Ideology is the world of ideas and concepts that have been separated from their actual lived material practice. For example, in neo-liberal democratic societies such as the United States, citizens are inducted into an ideological set of beliefs about living as democratic citizens. And yet when I ask youth workers to define the places in their life (family, work, school, church, etc.) where they experience democracy in relation to the material conditions of their lives (wages, housing, benefits, etc.), in a way that actually allows their active participation, I find the lived experience of direct democracy absent. The ideological construction of democracy is radically separated from the actual day-to-day experience of the youth worker. This, of course, is then replicated within the relations between youth and adults in agency contexts. All democratic practice is carefully restricted so that neither youth nor adults have any actual democratic input into the material aspects of their work. At the most basic level, for example, youth and youth workers are not democratically included in the process of money distribution within their agencies.

The ideology of youth work is also separated from the revolutionary practice or potentials of youth work by divorcing it from the actual lived material conditions of youth-adult relations and hiding from view its involvement and collusion with the dominant mode of production; specifically, global capitalism. For example, agencies and organizations that work with young people often exclude both young people and youth workers from decisions about how money is raised and from whom. This knowledge can hide from view significant influences on agency practice and policy based on the interests of funding sources, such as corporations or government agencies, with overtly capitalist interests. The most blatant example of this is the increasing insertion of brand-name logos and curriculum into the public schools.

It is important to note, however, that if youth workers and youth can stay connected to the material conditions that drew them together in the first place and sustain the capacity to modify their relationships as conditions change, together they hold profound revolutionary potential. As Marx points out with respect to an early mode of production (feudal society): 'The production of ideas, of conceptions, of consciousness, is at first directly interwoven with the material activity and the material intercourse of men, the language of real life. Conceiving, thinking, the mental intercourse of men appears at this stage as the direct efflux of their material behaviour' (Marx, 1978/1992, p. 154).

In other words, it is what youth and youth workers do together that produces a social effect and creates a certain force. This force, if it stays connected to the actual material conditions of its origin, has direct use in shaping the life and lived conditions of the people who produced it. This creative function of labour is defined in Marxist terms as non-alienated labour, or labour that retains what Marx called its 'use value.' This creativity of practice and thought remains significantly related to actual material and social relations. To use our earlier examples, to the degree that youth and youth workers insist on the implementation of actual democratic practices within the agencies and organizations that have a direct impact on their lives and are actually involved in decisions about funding sources and their influence, youth work holds 'use value.' In this sense, then, 'use value' is that creative force which is only useful to the youth and youth workers themselves and cannot be exploited by someone else.

For creative 'use value' to be useful to capitalist interests it must be transformed to an 'exchange value.' To do this, the creative products of youth work must be separated and alienated from their source in the work itself. Capitalism must create conditions in which need, desire, and production are confused with one another. This means that both youth and youth worker must lose track of what it is they actually produce and their central role in that production. Both groups must come to believe that they cannot create the world outside of the belief systems, values, and systems of control that make up the current capitalist system. They must confuse their own material desires, through which they create their life, with the produced needs of capitalist-driven consumption. They must come to believe that their efforts and creativity are inadequate to the demands of their life. Furthermore, they must come to believe that it is only through the benefits of the current system that they stand any chance of succeeding in life.

To ensure this belief in the face of consistent economic losses for both youth and youth workers within countries at the centre of neo-capital democracy, such as the United States, youth work is produced as a response to fears about youth. This places youth workers in the position of believing that their primary role is to protect and serve (which, ironically, is the motto of the police in the United States). Therefore, instead of youth work becoming a project of building shared relationships and community through creative collaboration, youth work becomes based on the need of adults to control youth out of fear and anxiety.

This process removes youth-adult collaboration from its status as a creative force in relation to its 'use value' and instead harnesses it as a mode of translation between object, desire, and production. Put another way, the desires that we all have for genuine engagement with other people, freedom from poverty, direct rewards from our work, and the liberation of our time to do the things we truly love are all placed by capital in a perpetual future that can only be accessed by the very few who win the lottery of capital merit.

Youth work, instead of working to demand that this future become immediately available to the majority of youth and youth workers, instead acts as a mechanism of deferral. In other words, youth workers are used to perpetuate the beliefs and ideologies that defer relation-ships, economic equity, social justice, and rewarding work through programming that emphasizes boundaries, no physical contact, rules, deferred gratification, employment in minimum-wage environments, and an unwillingness to analyse the economic conditions of the youth and families we serve.

This kind of production of the field of youth work as an ideological machine that reproduces the values of alienated life, or life separated from its own creative potential, thus produces not only the object (youth as social terrorist) but also the manner of consumption (youth work as control, protection, assimilation, and safety), both objectively and subjectively. Production thus creates the consumer. Or as Marx puts it, 'Production not only supplies a material for the need but also supplies a need for the material' (Marx, 1993, p. 92). This is the func-tion of ideology. It is the transformation of the use value of youth-adult relations as creative force for social change into their role as a translation agent between exchange values that benefit the existing dominant system of exploitation on behalf of global capital. 'It is value rather that converts every product into a social hieroglyphic. Later on, we try to decipher the hieroglyphic, to try to get behind the secret of our own social products; for to stamp an object of utility as a value, is just as much a social product as language' (Marx 1978/1992, p. 322).

This transition, however, is fraught with contradiction. Social hieroglyphics such as youth and youth work have both revolutionary and reactionary impetuses. The ideological constructions of capital carry within them the seeds of revolution. Every idea carries within it its opposition. If an idea can be reconnected with its material origin and overcome its alienation, its use value has revolutionary potential. 'To the extent that ideologies are necessary they have a validity which is "psychological," they organize human masses and create the terrain on which men move, acquire consciousness of their position, struggle, etc. To the extent they are arbitrary they create only individual "movements," polemics and so on' (Gramsci, 1971, p. 377).

Ideologies, because they are derived out of the shifting terrain of the social, are unstable. This instability makes them available for both appropriation by capital as well as utilization for creative revolutionary purposes. They are often 'transitory,' and 'different, even contrary functions are overdetermined in them' (Haug, 1987, p. 87). Ideology – or within the current mode of production, the capture of creative performance and the force of lived experience by capital – is crucial to the revolutionary impetus. As Hall points out, 'The problem of ideology ... concerns the ways in which ideas of different kinds grip the minds of masses, and thereby become a material force' (Hall, 1986, p. 119). The question is always, what kind of force and to what end?

The Revolutionary Force of Lived Experience

I have mentioned the idea of 'use value' in a number of different places in our discussion so far, but here it may be useful to discuss its implications more thoroughly as it relates to ideology and the revolutionary potential of youth work. The force of lived experience, of creative performance, or the actual engagement of youth and adults in relationship (as an exchange value) is constrained within the parameters of its utility to capital. The force of youth-adult collaboration as a use value 'has value only because human labor in the abstract has been embodied or materialized in it' (Marx, 1978/1992, p. 305). This means that for youth work to have 'use value' it must directly correspond to the satisfaction of actual individual material desires, such as liberation and belonging, and not the desires of capital.

It is the positioning of individual desire outside of capital that creates and sustains the radical creative individuality and opaque insularity of both youth subcultures and youth work along the edges, such as street outreach. The performances and concepts driving both movements are built out of the actual material conditions of the individual youth and worker. They are driven by liberatory desire; an immanent becoming on the edge outside of desiring capital.

The use value of an idea only becomes 'true in practice when it reconquers its independence of presupposition through alienation through the incessant changing phases – but which are not less real – of appropriation through alienation' (Negri, 1991, p. 52). In other words, the practice and concepts of youth work must reassert their independence from the constraints of capital appropriation and the resultant alienation. This reassertion of independence frees these practices and concepts from the exploitative definitions of capitalism and takes them back in their original relation to the shared lived experience of youth and adults as an infinitely creative community struggling together to produce the world. This is why 'capital only sees use value as an "abstract chaos" which is opposed to it, and the only form in which use value permits capital to conclude it within itself, is the form of irrationality' (Negri, 1991, p. 68). Capitalism cannot afford uncontained or undisciplined creativity. The creative force of youth and adults in a collaboration directed towards their own interests operates, by definition, against the desires of capital.

This tension can be seen clearly in the relations between 'youth work on the edge' and the agency structures in which such work is embedded. Within the administrative structures of such agencies, there is a constant fear that unmonitored and unregulated youth work such as street outreach or the drop-in centre will 'devolve' into chaos. It is feared that unmediated relations between youth workers and youth will result in youth workers 'going native.' Such a prospect is particularly feared because the youth worker may 'mistake' their loyalties and place their relationship to the youth before their obligation to the agency. Under such conditions, the liberatory potential of the free exchange of ideas on the edge of the outside between youth workers and youth must be captured, mediated, and structured.

Youth work, when captured by capital as an exchange value, is forcibly removed from its infinite potentiality and 'becomes value only in its congealed state, when embodied in some object' (Marx, 1978/1992, p. 316). The idea of 'liberation' therefore becomes embodied in the objectified form of an agency model, a 'safe' space, or a marketable creative form based on youth subculture, such as spoken word poetry, a treatment manual, therapeutic innovation, or marketable 'intervention.' Along these lines, liberation may be presented even more insidiously in the paid-for services of a therapist, human service agency, or program that promises a certain kind of liberation for a price. This complicated exchange value situated in the intersection of psychotherapy, youth work, and corporate capitalism is amply illustrated within the context of 'total quality' management: 'In any case, what other meaning can we give to the capitalist slogan of "total quality" if not the attempt to set to work all those aspects that traditionally it has shut out of work – in other words, the ability to communicate and the taste for action ... There is none so poor as one who sees her or his own ability to relate to the "presence of others" or her or his own possession of language, reduced to wage labor' (Virno, 1996, pp. 192–3).

The value of a concept such as liberation 'is, in itself, of no interest to the capitalist. What alone interests him is the surplus value that dwells in it and is realizable by sale' (Marx 1978/1992, p. 383). The extraction of the surplus value of concepts such as freedom, liberation, equity, justice, and so on, is one of the capitalist's most effective adaptations with which to combat the rising contradictions and antagonisms of a mode of production in which the material reality of these ideas as use value to young people and their families and communities is thin indeed. How then does this extraction occur?

Modes of Appropriation and Exploitation

It is important to expand the above statements about capitalism to state even more clearly that the goal of capitalism has nothing to do with liberation, equity, democracy, or justice. For the capitalist, 'growing wealthy is an end in itself. The goal determining activity of capital can only be that of growing wealthier, i.e., of magnification, of increasing itself' (Marx, 1978/1992, p. 270). To the degree that the aforementioned qualities of life occur as a result of this mode of production, the capitalist welcomes them. To the degree they begin to interfere, they must be either harnessed or extinguished. Capital is not inherently opposed to liberation or democracy; it is rather opposed to their interference in the sacred activity of producing wealth. Therefore, the freedom inherent in a subjectivity defined through use value is an anathema to capital. Concepts and relationships must have an exchange value, because within capital, concepts and people's relations become commodities in the translation of use value to commodity. As Marx points out, 'The commodity only realizes itself as exchange value, in so far as its owner does not relate to it as use value. He appropriates use values through their sale, their exchange for other commodities. Appropriation through sale is the fundamental form of the social system of production' (Marx, 1993, pp. 881–2).

How then are the use values of the revolutionary potential within youth work transformed into exchange values? In my analysis there are four central steps to this process. First, the revolutionary concept of youth work must be matched at the level of desire/alienation; it must then be conflated with an existing form of capitalist ideology; the mutated concept must then be appropriated; and finally, whatever original potential there was in radical youth work can then be emptied and bankrupted.

Matching the Level of Desire/Alienation

In order for revolutionary or radical youth work to be transformed from its 'use value' into an 'exchange value,' it must be reconfigured within the parameters of young people's relation to capital. Therefore, it must work as a palliative to alienation or provide relief from the anxiety of desire. Radical youth work cannot provide an actual alternative to alienation or fulfill an actual desire, because this would mean constructing an alternative to the mode of production, one in which youth are no longer alienated from their lives, families, and communities, and are able to independently fulfill their desires without the mediation of capital.

As a result, any idea that proposes the actual independence of young people or the creation of space in which young people are free must be reconfigured into a dependence upon capital. The capitalist or agent of capital must take a mediating role between youth and their freedom. Whatever ideas of freedom, liberation, or democracy are harboured within the revolutionary consciousness of youth must be intercepted and put into the framework of the capitalist mode of production. Marx outlines this when he states that the capitalist 'puts himself at the service of the others' most depraved fantasies, plays the pimp between him and his need, excites in him morbid appetites, lies in wait for each of his weaknesses – all so he can demand cash for this service of love. Every product is a bait with which to seduce away the other's very being' (Marx, 1978/1992, p. 94).

This perpetuation of alienation and the construction of mediated desire extends particularly to those instances in which innovation threatens the existing mode of production. In these instances it is critical that capital separates youth or youth workers from the innovative idea and eliminates any revolutionary possibility. 'The more radical the innovation is, the more profound and powerful were the antagonistic proletarian forces which had determined it, and therefore the more extreme was the force which capital had to put in motion to dominate them. Every innovation is a revolution which failed – but also one which was attempted' (Negri, 1996b, p. 159).

Conflation with an Existing Form of Capitalist Ideology

The critical move in producing alienation is the separation of the revolutionary idea from its material base in lived experience. Youth-adult collaboration cannot be connected to the actual life of youth or youth work in such a way as to promote a decrease in the sense of radical separation from society at large. Mechanisms such as laws that only apply to youth, double sets of rules and standards within facilities, theoretical frameworks that radically separate youth and adults as biologically different, and programs that ignore the material conditions of economic privilege, racism, and cultural genocide promote and continue this kind of alienation. In this, youth work and the youth within its boundaries become alienated and disconnected from the material base of its intended field of practice. Once the field of practice is removed from its point of origin, it can be joined with more generally accepted dominant cultural ideologies, such as those from Western bioscience. Such ideologies present themselves as 'truths,' and their aim is 'to present production ... as encased in eternal natural laws independent of history, at which opportunity bourgeois relations are then quietly smuggled in as the inviolable natural laws on which society in the abstract is founded' (Marx, 1978/1992, p. 225).

Revolutionary youth work, now alienated from it revolutionary intention or impetus, is conflated with these 'natural laws' on which society is purported to be founded. For example, the revolutionary idea of youth rights becomes separated from the actual practices of living and is conflated with the abstract world of 'the law' and with the scientific truths of 'development.' Youth rights become an abstraction based within legal codes and determined by biologically defined identities such as child, adult, or adolescent. These biologically defined identities and legal codes are presented as absolute and eternal facts of biology and human nature, when in fact they are culturally specific and relatively recent productions of Western capitalist society.

In this process the rights to certain modes of behaviour, locality, movement, or identity are distributed across a scientifically derived spectrum of constantly shifting developmental stages of 'maturity.' The revolutionary idea of the right to live free from alienation from one's own experience and have the ability to define oneself is subsumed in an ever-fragmenting set of social contradictions and youth-adult antagonisms.

Appropriation

Youth work, now having been uprooted from its connection to a particular historical materiality and conflated with the 'natural laws' of capitalist scientism, is now prepared for appropriation.[1] The appropriation of revolutionary concepts for capitalist purposes consists of a radical alienation of youth work from its original content and context. The practices of youth-adult collaboration become estranged from themselves in such ways that form and content become separated and hold no internal coherence. 'Appropriation appears as estrangement, as alienation; and alienation appears as appropriation, estrangement as true enfranchisement' (Marx, 1978/1992, p. 81).

One example of this phenomenon is the recent effort to 'protect' youth in the United States from the insidious effects of drugs and alcohol by utilizing an assets- or community-based approach. This approach is premised on a survey-driven, expert-determined set of assets derived from the norms of middle-class communities. These bourgeois assets are then marketed to communities across the social spectrum as necessary for healthy community life. The approach takes

---

1 By 'capitalist scientism,' I am referring to the set of ideas based in the logic of Western science that capitalism has used to justify its imperialism and subjugation of those outside its immediate circle of privilege.

little account of idiosyncratic or unique aspects of non-dominant community life that may operate outside the logic of the middle class and its values. The use of 'assets' and 'community' is an appropriation of both terms in a manner that makes neither recognizable in their original historical content. The actual meaning of 'asset' is derived entirely outside of any context meaningful to young people and the definition of 'community' is similarly constructed without youth input.

It is pertinent to note here that just as capital does not generate labour, but rather labour capital, so capital does not generate ideas, but appropriates the revolutionary impetus of new ideas to its own ends. Capital has no language of its own, but 'vampire-like, only lives by sucking living labour and lives the more labour it sucks' (Marx, 1978/1992, p. 363).

For capital to achieve this appropriation, it must be ever diligent in its monitoring of new ideas and new concepts that have revolutionary potential. It must give these ideas enough time to build a certain force or energy before directing that energy to its own ends. In the most cynical instances it is the 'hope' that is the driving force of revolutionary change that is appropriated. One example of this is the ever-increasing multiplicity of advertisements that portray a youth-adult world of racial and gender harmony; a utopian world of peace and happiness in which we wake gracefully to a new dawn and go and buy things. Capitalism monitors our hopes and dreams and then turns them back on us to advance its own agenda. 'This is the boss's curse; those who learn most from the class struggle get ahead. This paradox is the shame of the boss – the perennial spy, who borrows and represses' (Negri, 1996b, p. 167).

Bankruptcy

In the final stage of the transformation of use values into exchange values, the concepts and practices of radical youth-adult collaboration have been thoroughly emptied and dispersed. The centre of radical youth work has been hollowed out and its framework so thoroughly permeated as to render it meaningless. Concepts and practices of lived experience and collaboration such as democracy, labour, liberation, freedom, community, culture, pride, and even revolution itself have been appropriated. The question then becomes, can the concepts and practices of radical youth work captured by this process be recouped, or must they be abandoned?

Tactics of Response

I would argue that the ideals of radical youth work can neither be recouped nor must they be abandoned. Instead, they must be rethought, reconfigured, and then reclaimed. They cannot be recouped because their trajectory through capital has eviscerated their historical moment. Revolutionary concepts and practices that have been appropriated by capital must be retrieved outside the range of capital. This is a significant challenge in this stage of total subsumption, in which 'we are confronted ... by a capitalism composed of diverse and very mobile forms, an agglomeration which is in effect a metasystem or hypercapitalism' (Surin, 1996, p. 184). To undertake a full explication of possible responses is well beyond the purview of this short section. However, I would like to make a small beginning at the level of alienation or radical separation from the lived experience of youth-adult collaboration.

In this moment of total subsumption and ongoing exploitation of youth and youth workers, there is indeed reason for collaboration over shared risks of unemployment, family dissolution, cultural destruction, racism, economic exploitation, issues of addiction, and radical isolation from one's life and community. Yet these shared risks are sometimes difficult to acknowledge, perceive, or share between youth and adults. Part of the reason for this is the ideological constructions of youth and adults as radically separate, as I have described earlier. Perhaps, however, a more profound reason has to do with our limited capacity to continue responding affectively within an environment and society filled with loss, despair, fear, loneliness, and grief.

Youth workers actively engage the worlds of youth and families in struggle with the world of capitalist society, a society that sometimes seems at best indifferent and at worst intent on destroying those people whom youth work serves. This engagement requires the ability to avoid alienation from the actual conditions of lived experience that are encountered. When youth workers themselves encounter similar conditions within their own families and communities, the level of pain encountered within any given day becomes at times unbearable.

I would argue that if a radical youth work is to be constructed that has the capacity to operate in a non-alienated actual engagement with the lived experience of the youth and adults involved, we must find ways to manage the pain of the work. This is a complex and difficult task, but unless we address it seriously, it will be almost impossible to avoid becoming alienated from the actual encounter between two people in community.

Pain is complicated. It is an imminent force, which means it cannot be changed from the outside. It has to be met on its own terms and fully engaged in the actuality of its lived condition. That means that one has to fully accept pain on its own terms without anaesthetic (drinking, drugs, despair, rage, anger, cynicism, shame, guilt, or separation and denial). However, that doesn't mean indulging or wallowing in pain by holding onto it. Pain, like all feelings, is not a stationary or one-dimensional force. It is a force used to take things apart, to disassemble them, and it only sustains itself within things that will not come apart or reorganize themselves at its insistence – bodies and systems, for instance. Pain cannot be outrun without hugely damaging consequences.

Pain requires that you allow it to transform you. You have to open your heart. The temptation in youth work, of course, is to close off the heart in order to protect it from any further assault. This interferes in the development of any kind of actual collaboration between youth and adults, because if you have you closed off your heart or even restricted it, then you cannot feel; and if you cannot feel, you cannot know the world in its actual formation and destruction. You become senseless and your reality is thoroughly ideological and unrelated to the material conditions of the world in which you live. If we are to develop a radical youth work that is a viable liberative force in the streets, the jails, the schools, in our communities, our homes, our families, and our relationships, this will be the work. We must become fearless in the face of pain and suffering; we must become dangerous in our love.

11 Decolonizing 'White' Youth Work

Several authors (Males, 1996; Giroux, 1996) have recently argued that 'youth,' whatever their skin pigmentation, are no longer 'white.' Conversely, my colleague Reggie Harris and I have begun to assert in our consultations with youth workers that social service professionals, whatever their skin pigmentation, are 'white.' Such assertions may appear, on the surface, to be simply polemic provocations within the highly contested area of race in America. I would argue, however, that the attribution of 'whiteness' is critical to concepts of indigeneity, subculture, Western constructions of youth and adolescence, 'otherness,' and the entire arena of subjugated knowledges; that such attribution is deeply rooted in the histories and analysis of colonialism; and finally, that to understand the specific positioning of youth and youth work within the frameworks of capture, power, resistance, and escape outlined in previous chapters, it is useful to examine the history of whiteness as a colonial construction and in terms of postcolonial theory, theories of neo-colonialism, as well as critical race studies.

For most of life I have thought of myself as 'white.' It wasn't something I questioned very much – it was an integral part of my identity. Whiteness was part of my culture, my heritage as an American. The identity of my European lineage was present in my consciousness, but only as an artefact with no actual current status. This alternate identity was an interesting anthropological curiosity; something to be taken to school for display occasionally or referenced as factual but not relevant.

This is not to say that my European roots were obscured from me or denigrated in any way. My father was a first-generation immigrant to the United States and my mother's European lineage was often mentioned. My mother proudly displayed my father's national symbols, cooking, arts and music, and traditional holiday practices. Her own heritage was that of a Mormon American. Whatever had happened in Europe before her people joined the church and came to America was never referred to. She was a product of the great American melting pot, a 'Heinz 57' blend of multiple European cultures into a hybrid called American. What she didn't say and what didn't become clear for me until I was in my early teens was that the melting pot to which we belonged was 'white.' There were no 'others' in her lineage.

I should acknowledge here that the lineage which I am describing as mine is actually my adopted lineage. It is, however, the history within which I was raised and until recently, the only one I could reference with any degree of certainty. It is perhaps serendipitous that as I was researching the history of whiteness, I received a letter detailing my own biological roots as three-quarters Irish and one-quarter Dutch. Which makes me 'white' – or does it?

What and Who Is 'White'?

This turns out to be a complicated question. What and who is 'white' is a relatively new concept. According to Roediger (1991), 'the term *white* arose as a designation for European explorers and settlers who came in contact with Africans and the indigenous people of the Americas ... Its early usage in America served as much to distinguish European settlers from Native Americans as to distinguish Africans from Europeans' (p. 21).

This seems fairly straightforward: 'white' developed as an indication of difference based on skin colour. It was simply an obvious difference noted by peoples coming into contact with one another for the first time. This explanation would make things simple, but it would not be accurate, nor would it explain the profound power and exclusionary privilege of the term 'white.'

To begin to understand whiteness within the cultural context of the United States and Western Europe and its implications for youth subculture and youth work, it is useful to return to the frontier of the colonial project, with its registers of barbarism versus civilization, centre versus periphery, and self versus other. To do this I will examine the work of three authors: David Roediger, Ann Laura Stoler, and Edward Said. Each of these authors conceptualizes the human world as constructed through human perception, belief, and description. Each in their own way is deeply concerned with how knowledge and being are interpretively created. They differ significantly, however, in their approach to analysing these constructions, representing three very different but convergent descriptions of how we construct the world of whiteness. It is in the convergence of their descriptions that the full complexity of an idea such as whiteness begins to become clear.

The Creation of Whiteness

David Roediger's approach to the construction of whiteness in his book *The Wages of Whiteness* (1991) is closely related to critical science, examining the ways that inequitable social structures are created through specific historical processes and how meaning that justifies the economic and social advantage of those in power is created (Comstock, 1982).

Roediger's analysis focuses on the construction of whiteness as a result of the convergent historical processes that created the 'white working class' in the United States. Whiteness for Roediger is a social construction, not simply a fact of difference. He cites the Marxist historian Barbara Fields, who states that 'race cannot be seen as a biological or physical fact (a thing) but must be seen as "a notion that is profoundly and in its very essence ideological"' (Roediger, 1991, p. 7).

The history of this ideology of whiteness is in Roediger's view a reflection of the tensions created by the use of slavery in the United States. Roediger outlines two kinds of slavery: chattel slavery and indentured servitude. Indentured servitude was largely experienced by those non-Africans who were not considered 'white,' such as the British working class and the Irish. 'Low browed and savage, groveling and bestial, lazy and wild, simian and sensual ... were the adjectives to describe the Catholic Irish "race" before the Civil War ... an Irishman was a "nigger" inside out ... the Irish were part of ... a "dark" race, possibly originally African' (1991, p. 133). These 'non-white' peoples were 'transported in abysmal conditions ... sold at auction, sometimes after having been stripped naked ... wholesaled to "soul drivers" who marched [them] through the countryside ... selling them' (p. 30).

In Roediger's view, this early history of indentured servitude and the experiences of Africans in chattel slavery combined with the advent of the American Revolution to create great concern and debate over what kinds of slavery liberty was meant to alleviate. Of all of the 'fathers' of the American Revolution, only Tom Paine and Benjamin Franklin called for the abolition of all forms of slavery. The others argued only for the abolition of 'wage slavery' and as time went on, for the abolition of 'white slavery' (p. 31).

While Roediger's argument is complex, this central historical tension underlies much of what was to follow. If the Irish and the working class were to become 'free,' they must do so by being different than 'real slaves.' If they were to have the privilege and the promise of the new republican country, they must separate themselves from the 'other' who continued to be enslaved. They must justify their freedom by 'becoming white.' And they could only become 'white' in contrast to the 'other' who was not 'white.'

This problematic of what might be called 'the purchase of whiteness' at the expense of those only slightly more marginalized than oneself is a critical element in the youth-adult relations of youth work and in the marginalization of certain youth as dangerous or 'other.' The complex interplay between the youth worker (most of them between the ages of eighteen and twenty-five) and the youth they serve (ages twelve through seventeen) is riddled through with this dynamic. The purchase of adult privilege within the colonial structures of disciplinary youth work involves the acquisition of languages of description such as diagnoses and developmental psychological frameworks that clearly define the youth worker as safely different from the youth served.

The Discipline of Whiteness

Ann Laura Stoler (1995) is also concerned with the creation of the 'other' as a central aspect of whiteness. However, her lens is somewhat different although profoundly related. Stoler's analysis in her book *Race and the Education of Desire* is based on the work of Michel Foucault. While both she and Roediger are concerned with the historical conditions that created the idea of whiteness, Stoler is not interested in how whiteness benefits the privileged class. Instead she is interested in how whiteness is used disciplinarily throughout society, and her focus is the creation of whiteness in the Dutch colonization of Indonesia.

Stoler outlines her project as being concerned with the ways that 'discourses of sexuality articulated with the politics of race.' She is interested in how race and sexuality were involved in the 'cultivation of a European self' and how this self was 'affirmed in the proliferating discourses around pedagogy, parenting, child sexuality, servants, trop-ical hygiene: micro sites where designations of racial membership were subject to gendered appraisals and where "character," "good breeding" and proper rearing were implicitly raced' (p. 11).

Stoler argues that these 'discourses did more than prescribe suitable behaviour; they locate how ... identity has been tied to notions of being "European" and being "White."' She outlines how these disciplinary discourses about what could and could not be done created the 'authentic, first-class citizens of the nation state' (p. 11).

Whereas the tension in Roediger's work is around issues of liberty and slavery, Stoler's concerns are with the creation of the 'other' as a sexualized danger to social stability. She notes the Foucauldian analy-sis of a European society that had 'linked individual sexualities and the security of the social body as nineteenth century inventions ... the very fate of the race and the nation seemed to turn in large part on its sexual practices' (p. 41).

Like Engels (1972), Stoler links the disciplining of sexuality to fear of losing possession of the apparatus of power and resources to non-Europeans through interracial sexuality and the resultant children. In fact, Stoler examines in some detail the ways in which the Dutch attempted to decide which interracial children were European and which were not. She delineates the creation of the kindergarten as a means of removing interracial children from their 'over-sexualized native mothers' so that they could become European (1995, p. 122).

The creation of whiteness as a discourse, however, is broader than these concerns. Stoler argues that the creation of whiteness falls within the creation of the disciplinary society referred to by Foucault (1975) in *Discipline and Punish*. It is the creation of the 'other' that allows for the discipline of the self. The centralized mechanisms of power are dis-tributed throughout the society and constituted within the individual self through the creation of the marginalized and disfranchised 'other.' The disciplining of sexuality is part of the Enlightenment project to exalt rationality, reason, and productivity; to separate mind and body; to place the body under administrative control so that it can be used in the service of the industrial state. It is part of a colonial discourse that de-centres the rest of the world so as to use it as a comparison for what we are not, and correspondingly, for what we must be.

This same formulation is at the centre of the constructions of youth as 'dangerous,' 'hypersexualized,' and 'irrational.' The structures and rules of most modern youth work are based on bio-power and its ability to classify and categorize whole groups of people into developmental disciplinary frameworks. Until recently, the full impact of this was reserved for people of colour, tribal or indigenous peoples, women, and the gay, lesbian, bisexual and transgender population, but lately this effect has begun to spread towards the 'white' youth at the centre: 'The lazy, profligate, hypersexed "teenage mother" is a direct descendent of the black "welfare queen." "Youth violence" has its ancestry in the savagery of "Negro violence." "Teen suicide" and reckless teenage driving derive from the same impulsiveness once attributed to the hot-blooded minority' (Males, 1996, pp. 13–14).

Colonial Whiteness

This decentring and recreation of the world outside of the colonial centre is the subject of Edward Said's book *Orientalism* (1979). Said's central thesis is that the 'Orient' has been created entirely out of the West's imagination. His approach is postcolonial in that it addresses issues of identity, history, and culture that are the direct result of the colonial experience. While his work is a complicated and detailed exposition, within it he addresses the creation of whiteness in relation to the colonial project and its impact on the 'Orient.' 'Along with all other peoples variously designated as backward, degenerate, uncivilized, and retarded, the Orientals were viewed in a framework constructed out of biological determinism and moral-political admonishment. The Oriental was linked thus to elements in Western society (delinquents, the insane, women, the poor) having in common an identity best described as lamentably alien. Orientals are rarely seen or looked at; they were seen ... as problems to be solved or confined or ... taken over' (1979, p. 207).

This process of Orientalization is one that continues to permeate the relations of youth and adults within the world of youth work. The view that youth are not as advanced as adults, not as morally developed, and less able to make reasonable and determined decisions is constructed out the same framework of 'biological determinism and moral political admonishment.' Indeed it might be said of youth, as Said says of the Oriental, that they are created entirely out the imagination of adults. In this relationship the adults are constructed as 'white' and the youth as 'other.'

The relation of the 'white' self to the 'other' is critical in Said's work. It is his contention that the 'Orient' was specifically constructed to serve the interests of the colonial project. This construction obscured and continues to obscure indigenous histories, knowledges, and possibilities. This Foucauldian line of analysis has significant implications for youth-adult relations. Is the construction of youth specifically designed to serve adult interests? Does this construction obscure particular histories of youth, particularly youth-centred knowledge and arenas of youth-derived possibility?

This obfuscation and appropriation, when seen within the Foucauldian frameworks of power and Deleuzian (1987) concepts such as territorialization and deterritorialization, holds mutually constitutive properties for both youth and adults. The properties of colonization, through which indigenous frameworks of knowledge are deterritorialized and reterritorrialized within whiteness, simultaneously deterritorialize the centre and reterritorialize it within the colonial relation. To use Foucauldian terminology, power and resistance are mutually and simultaneously constitutive. In other words, within a postcolonial context, the colonized subject is not the only one affected by colonization. The colonizer, too, is altered by the construction of the 'other.' In Said's view, the colonial 'white man' is outlined as 'behaving according to a code of regulations, and ... feeling certain things and not others ... [it] was a very concrete manner of being in the world, a way of taking hold of reality, language and thought' (1979, pp. 226–7).

This means that the subjectivity of the youth worker as an extension of the colonial or cultural machine is always constituted in relation to the 'other.' The youth worker is constantly created by the naming of that which it is not. The peculiar blind spot within such a subject position is a lack of self-reflexivity. To stand in the centre of the world as an adult and look out upon the world of youth provides a singular view in which youth can be seen but adults become invisible. In Said's terms, it is to become 'white,' which is to become invisible to one's self as a complexity of culture and contradiction. It is to be hegemonically constructed only in relation to the 'other.' The only time adults know for sure they are adults is when they are in contact with another who is different.

This constitution of the self as 'white' obscures important and maybe even crucial historical and indigenous information. The gloss of whiteness obscures the joint historical struggles of peoples comprised of both youth and adults. Such obfuscation would have us believe that our history as adults and parents is the same history as all adults and parents. Any sense of alienation that I feel from Euro-

American late-stage capitalist cultural paradigms of adulthood and parenting is idiosyncratic and psychological.

The logic of whiteness further suggests that adult youth workers have little in common with young people and less in common with subcultural youth. Youth workers as adults are by definition predestined for privilege and power that is unavailable to the youth they serve. Like many social service workers they are placed at the border to parcel out housing, food, medical care, relationships, and franchise according to the rules of engagement determined by colonial relations of force. As such, the role of youth work within this system is to subject the 'other' to the gaze of privilege, or to benevolently allow them access through the same route of disciplinary practices that shaped the youth worker as adult.

However, what if youth workers were to become something more than 'white'? What if each youth worker were to recover a history of colonization and exploitation as well as struggle and the experience of oppression, through an alternative lineage of youth adult relations? This complex legacy would allow the opportunity to both take accountability for the privilege of whiteness and to join legitimately with others in resisting the hegemony of such a description. If youth workers can begin to see the ways in which whiteness hides them from themselves, then perhaps youth work can begin to create an alternate identity. But if the historical struggles of lineage are not available, then there is no personal ground out of which to base a line of flight. From my perspective, if the construction of whiteness was critical to the development of the colonial enterprise, then the deconstruction of whiteness is critical to the decolonization of colonial youth work.

12 Towards a Pedagogy of Radical Youth Work

In the past few chapters, I have been exploring the parameters of what might be called a conceptual framework for a pedagogy of radical youth work. In this final chapter, I will outline and construct a possible framework for educating youth workers. The construction of a pedagogy of radical youth work is a project that has been ongoing since the inception of the field. In this respect, there is nothing new in the project itself. I have attempted to point out, however, that the world in which youth work is situated has made a significant shift in its composition and relations of force. This shift requires that a pedagogy of youth work formulated in this moment needs to take into account youth-adult relations as they are engaged within the world of what we have referred to as the moment of total subsumption. I have argued that skinheads and punks, as subcultural formations, are positioned in particular ways between the worlds of modern and postmodern society. As such, their prefigurative properties in relation to capital development hold significant implications for youth-adult relations and modes of pedagogy. I have also argued that punks and skins are produced between the institutions, economics, and social processes of the world of post-ality. Their uses of body, space, time, and identity are shot through with performances and re-performances of elements of the modern as it traverses the postmodern moment. As such, skins and punks, along with other subcultures and Deleuzian minorities, represent a certain movement in societal relations in which the radical creative expressions of minoritarian groups fold the world of the dominant culture back on itself in a way that opens the possibility of that society coming know itself as pure potential once again. This is the moment of the subjectum.

The reflexive praxis within the postcolonial moment – that is, the moment of total subsumption within capital – holds immense potential for a pedagogy of radical youth work. If, as I have argued, these subcultures are prefigurative performances of the postcolonial, which will recodify and decentre history through heterogeneous and hybrid creative expression, then a pedagogy of radical youth work must engage youth-adult relations as mutually transformative. That is to say, such a pedagogy must reconfigure the traditional role of teacher and student into a transversal relationship that does not exchange information but rather enters into a mutual transformation of subjectivity. A pedagogy that seriously engages such a project would need to abandon any training of youth workers that focuses on youth work as disciplinary or hierarchical. Instead, youth worker training and pedagogy would focus on investigating youth as a pure creative force, available at any age, that holds possibilities for producing new sets of relations that go beyond the categories of youth-adult within the postcolonial moment of capital subsumption.

Such a pedagogy would ask youth workers to examine their own relationships to the deterritorializing movements of postmodernity as they deconstruct the world of the modern and experiment with new forms along the edge of nihilism (as seen in punk). Similarly, this new pedagogy might explore the ways that society attempts to recuperate in hybrid form the structures, enclosures, and fragments of modernism that postmodern capitalism has released into rhizomatic flight (as the skins do). Such pedagogy, as a liberatory praxis, would be concerned with youth-adult relations as central questions of limit and threshold; that is to say, as ways of moving beyond the limits of the existing system through the threshold of new possible social and economic configurations.

Youth work training under these conditions needs to engage the world of youth within the social realm of the postmodern mode of production. We cannot continue to train youth workers to work with young people as though the world has not changed. It is critical that we engage a pedagogy of radical youth work on a new terrain. To do this we need to rethink how we train youth workers to view themselves and the youth they engage. Rethinking radical youth work requires that we need to rethink subjectivity itself. I say this because youth work is a collision between subjectivities: those of the youth worker and of the youth. At the most fundamental level, if change is to occur in youth work praxis it must occur here.

Rethinking the Subject

Here we come full circle to our original concern with the subject and subjectivity. To rethink subjectivity, a radical pedagogy of youth work must seriously engage the worlds of the subjectus and the subjectum. I have argued that the self is structured between the tensions produced by the desire of life to express itself radically and uniquely in every movement of each body, and the mechanics of domination that would turn those productions to other purposes. Any radical pedagogy that hopes to operate on the terrain of the society of control or the moment of total subsumption must address the subjective constitution of the youth workers living within this tension. It must take into account concepts and experiences of resistance, flight, and submission. In this regard, I am following the lead of critical pedagogy in 'conceptualizing schooling as the construction and transmission of subjectivities ... [which] serves an introduction to a particular way of life' (Giroux & McLaren, 1986, p. 317).

I am also suggesting that the intellectual frameworks taught in a pedagogy of youth work cannot stand outside the lived experience of the youth workers themselves, any more than youth can be placed outside these frameworks as objects of observation or transformation. The intellectual concepts and the subjectivities of youth workers must both be seriously engaged if an alternative radical youth work is to be taught. The political formation of subjectivity, developed through the disciplinary apparatus surrounding adolescence, has significant implications for the decolonization of adult subjectivity within the space of youth-adult relations. As a result, the engagement between youth and adults must be engaged as a mutual political project that deconstructs the disciplinary apparatus that produces both adult and youth forms of subjectivity.

In this respect, a subjectivity within radical youth work built upon the framework of the subjectum might well be premised on what I have sketched out, following Deleuze, as the concept of the 'minority.' This kind of minority is defined not by its numeric value but by its positioning in relation to any dominant group that can denumerate the 'other.' The power of the majority, then, lies in its ability to identify and isolate the singular youth or youth subculture as separate from itself, while constructing itself as a diffuse plurality of power that is non-denumerable. Foucault, as we noted earlier, states that the main political task at this historical moment is to unmask the apparently benign institutions that function as just such a majority. As such, teaching radical youth work would entail a detailed examination of apparently helpful and neutral systems such as developmental psychology, behavioural science, mental health, education, and psychiatry, in order to expose the ways in which domination is distributed by these social sciences.

Concomitantly critical to the restructuring of subjectivity within a pedagogy of youth work is the exploration of the minoritarian. As such, radical youth work pedagogy would not explore the traditional definitional worlds of binary relations between the majority and minority sets, but instead would seek to teach methods that explore how one comes to know one's status as a minority, or in another term we have used, as the subjectum. Important here is the realization that such exploration cannot move forward through the usual channels of clear delineation and taxonomic definition. We cannot come to know the minoritarian through general rules or laws, but instead must seek it in the idiosyncratic and peculiar aspects of our singular experience. As Deleuze and Guattari (1987) put it, we must seek out the '"fuzzy" non-denumerable, nonaxiomizable sets, in short, "masses," "multiplicities of escape and flux"' (p. 470). In other words, we must find a radical new mode of empiricism that seeks to explore the very concrete and material manifestations of that which eludes definition; in short, life in motion as creative production. This would become a central focus of teaching and experience.

These fuzzy, nondenumerable, nonaxiomizable sets are those moments in youth work where adults are able to forget for a moment that they 'know' young people. It is the moment when the filters of development, diagnosis, and adolescence fall apart and the dangerous seduction of conflating the visible and the actual is escaped. A pedagogy of youth work would show how youth as pure creative force produces itself as revolutionary effect prior to our ability to perceive its existence. In other words, we must train youth workers to see the effect of life force before they can describe it. In this we must train youth workers to understand their intuitive and emotive capacity to see ahead of language into the possibility of radical new worlds being produced in their relationships in the most mundane of interchanges.

This type of pedagogy challenges not only youth subculture's points of visible capture in identifiable forms and modes, but also the capture of the youth worker within the forms of adult privilege. It seeks to develop, between the creative expressions of young people and the desiring subjectivity of the adult, an improvisatory singularity of call and response – a constant anticipatory emptiness of listening in order to respond. In this listening to respond is a certain kind of slippage in the known moment of the performed event between youth and adults. If youth-adult relations can be formed within the mobile subjectivity of the creative expression, always slightly ahead of perception and hence capture, there is the moment-to-moment possibility of a mutual youth-adult subjective nomadic becoming.

Hazardous Youth Work

Such teaching of youth work always stands in danger and along the edge of the outside. It resides within what Nealon (1998) has referred to as 'hazardous performance.' Such youth work, like the youth subcultures of skin and punk, does not consist of reactions or acts of resistance, but is purely and mutually creative. It is not creative in a way that exploits youth for their creative impetus, like so many youth service programs that engage youth in the arts and then pimp them out to perform messages of adult discipline; rather, it aims to join youth and adults in creative hazardous performances that escape full definition by dominant cultural standards. Not to become punk or skin (although there are adult punks and skins), but to join with punk and skin subculture in one's own creative struggles to become.

To do this, youth work pedagogy would need to examine the central cultural claim of contemporary Western culture that the youth worker is a separable individual. Instead, a radical youth work pedagogy would explore alternate forms of identity such as those discussed in Part One of this book. The individual is a bounded and defined space far too limited for the projects of the subjectum. In its place, we would propose what Hardt and Negri have called the singularity (2004). The singularity is a radically unique expression of life force with its own desire to persist and express. At the same time, it is a singular aspect of the larger expressive capacities of life. This is related to Spinoza's description of the body, in that the singularity gains more force or power to act only through its collisions with other bodies. The singularity is always part of a multiplicity, and the two cannot be separated or opposed to one another but are mutually productive of each other. This model of the subject would require a rethinking of the ways in which we conceive of all configurations of youth work, from the one-on-one exchange between youth and youth worker to the group living arrangements of homes and institutions.

The possibility that the axiomatic role of the youth worker could deconstruct into a transversal relational force without a central identity would form an important aspect of liberatory youth-adult relations. Current relations of privilege and force sustained within the confines of modernist disciplinary youth work that are premised in knowledge of what is and has been would be challenged through the kind of radical negation offered by punk, as a relation of force interested in what has not happened yet. A youth work pedagogy premised in punk might well explore the residue of failed revolutions of being. Classroom discussions on a youth work premised in the radical negation of punk would not focus on the trajectory of founded identity and its historical antecedents. They would instead explore that which has not yet been; in short, 'masses' and 'multiplicities of escape and flux' (Deleuze & Guattari, 1987, p. 470).

Immanent Youth Work

In an immanent youth work, that which has not yet been cannot be found in the psychological constructions of self, but must be sought instead in the 'minority as universal figure, or becoming-everybody/everything. Woman: we all have to become that, whether we are male or female. Non-white: we all have to become that, whether we are white, yellow or black' (Deleuze & Guattari, 1987, p. 470).

This is a pedagogy that teaches youth work premised on no-thing, which must eschew the singularity of self – its 'thingness.' In such a pedagogy, youth workers must become 'race traitors' (Ignatiev & Garvey, 1996), gender traitors, sexuality traitors, and so on. The self and its identities must be immersed in the no-thing of the mass/the people/the cloud. This is the line of flight from the biopolitics of self, race, gender, and sexuality. The teaching of such youth work would focus on the exploration of potential multiple and shifting identities, on decentralizing and dispersing definitions of the self and other. It is here that we can see the full force of youth subculture as prefigurative performances of the postcolonial. In the joint creative performance of youth and youth worker, there is the always the latent possibility of a youth work that recodifies and decentres history through mutual heterogeneous and hybrid performances.

The practice of these creative performances lies in the exploration of an immanent becoming of multiple potentialities for both youth and youth worker. This abandonment of the fixed identities of youth and youth worker that are caught in any given moment is crucial to developing the issue of potential. Potential, as a central thesis for youth work and subjectivity, would be explored by examining the linkage between the single locality of the psychological, marketable self and its psychological and marketable problems and solutions, and how such linkage creates an ongoing recycled form of the subjectus. This exploration of the eternal looping of the self as a desiring problematic shows how just such problematics weave lines of flight into ropes of bondage, fibre by fibre. A radical youth work pedagogy would explore how a youth work that seriously engages what we have called 'flight' would abandon the subjectus to capital and explore the subjectum as immanence, not as the now, but as the 'yet.' Not a transcendent 'yet,' an idealized, perfected self not yet realized, but the 'yet' of nothing: the unthought, undone, unspoken, unpractised 'yet' of infinite possibility. It is the mass of 'yet,' the horde of 'yet,' the twinkle in the eye of nothing.

Youth Work Pedagogy and the Development of the Multitude

As I have suggested above, a radical youth work pedagogy would assert a power of the non-denumerable and the pure becoming of minorities. This is the moment of the subcultures we have been engaging. It is precisely in their identity as community and in their assertion that we must throw all our misconceptions and preconceptions of them out the window that we enter into becoming minority. Pedagogy that functions out of asserting the power of the becoming minority is radically and overtly revolutionary in nature. A pedagogy of exploratory youth work that brings to bear the force of the non-sets against the majority system is a pedagogy that is not concerned with accommodation, assimilation, integration, or compromise. It is instead an active praxis or proposal that suggests, if not demands, that youth work explore a radical alterity to the state and all other axiomatic processes. It is human service no longer concerned with 'healing' within capital, but rather the 'healing' entailed in the alternative ontology of the minority.

The remaining question for a pedagogy of radical youth work that wishes to become minority, then, lies within the encounter of the youth worker and the youth. It is here in the collision of bodies that youth work is practised. If one wishes to enter into the becoming minority, how does one learn and teach how to engage without contestation, capture, or the artificial construction of communality; in short, how does the encounter yield itself to becoming multitude out of dyad?

> It is no longer a matter of utilizations or captures, but of sociabilities and communities. How do individuals enter into composition with one another in order to form a higher individual, ad infinitum? How can being take another being into its world, but while preserving or respecting the others own relations and world ...? Now we are concerned, not with the relationship of point to counter-point, nor with the selection of a world, but with a symphony of nature, the composition of a world that is increasingly wide and intense. In what order and in what manner will the powers, speeds, and slownesses be composed? (Deleuze, 1988, p. 126)

This central problematic engages youth work as purely creative, as sheer affirmation. In this, there is no possibility for dialectical negation, for with that kind negation there can be no full community.[1] To negate the other or oneself is to misunderstand the status of the relationship. There are never two people in the youth work encounter, whether it is a pedagogical encounter or within the field of youth-adult relations; one is always engaging the multitude. To understand this is to return to the plane of immanence-full force as an ontological production. 'The philosophy of immanence appears from all viewpoints as the theory of unitary Being, common and univocal Being. It seeks the conditions of a genuine affirmation, condemning all approaches that take away from Being its full positivity, that is, its formal community' (Deleuze, 1995, p. 167).

To use this pedagogical praxis, it is important to acknowledge that all lines of flight are rhizomatically interconnected and that no knowledge is wrong or worthy of dismissal. All knowledge is useful and productive; much of it is simply incomplete. In other words, the line of such knowledge has simply been truncated or cut off from its full explication. It is the function of a pedagogy of radical youth work to extend such lines.

This productive infinite interconnectivity is the engine of the multitude. It is, fundamentally, the multitude as becoming minority that is engaged in a pedagogy of radical youth work. The praxis of such

---

1 I am making a distinction here between radical and dialectic negation, based on the radical negation of Spinoza.

teaching is to connect backwards, forwards, and to the side without closure or repetition. The encounter engages communities of gender, class, kinship, sexuality, performance, identity, and the unconscious, throwing them like shamanic bones into heterogeneous productive combinations that shift and change with every conversational inquiry. These combinations must be recast out of their repetitive formations of capture within the niche markets of late capitalism or the disciplinary confines of factory capital. Such differences in formations need to 'be made between imaginary crowd aggregates and collective assemblages of enunciation, which conjoin pre-personal traits with social systems or their machinic components (opposing living autopoetic machines to mechanisms of empty repetition)' (Guattari, 2000, p. 61).

A pedagogy that asserts youth work as the action of the multitude means to assert a power without number. This is the realm of desire, which is directly contrary to the logic of capitalism as a system of need. The realm of desire is the terrain of immanence. It is extension and surface without end. It is open and infinite and contains worlds without number, sheer virtuality – the power to act through the refractory nature of the multitude. It stands in opposition to the world of capital that is driven by the logic of numerable scarcity. This world is a realm of addiction to the numeric 'more' to which there is no end.

The realm of desire as the basis of pedagogy and the practice of youth-adult relations produces by extension; that is, by giving itself away, recycling itself through itself in an amplification of difference refracted like light through a prism. Desire is incapable of taking anything back – it is sheer expenditure. There is no possibility of compromise for the multitude as a full extension of desire, because it cannot retreat. It is driven forward by an overflowing force that is absolute surplus. It is just such a surplus that capitalism and other systems of domination wish to contain, control, or direct to their own ends. They would have us believe that all surplus belongs to them and that it is limited and must be allocated and distributed by leaders and state forms; that the world is a lottery in which some win and some lose, but the house controls the distribution of a limited set of resources.

A Pedagogy of Love

In the realm of surplus there are no such limits because the set of resources is life itself and its infinite array of production. It is this surplus that a pedagogy of radical youth work employs as praxis to enjoin those involved to recognize without compromise their essence as community and as multitude. This radical alterity is neither stable, developmental, reactive, nor responsive to any particular historical moment. Its logic is not the logic of measurable time nor diachronic history. It is, to paraphrase Che Guevara, a logic of love.[2] It may seem odd in this moment of scientific pedagogy to speak of a pedagogy of love, but this is a love which functions as pure utility. As Balibar (1998) notes, two of the fundamental aspects of Spinoza's politics are 'thinking of God as necessary ... and loving men and seeking out their friendship because of the reciprocal relation of utility that exists between them and ourselves' (p. 92). This mutual utility is not the utility of appropriation based out of need, but rather a utility of conatus, or becoming. It is a reciprocal utility that allows the becoming multitude to act and in acting, to produce and have access to flight.

Negri and Guattari (1990) have stated, 'Our problem is to reconquer the communitarian spaces of liberty, dialogue and desire' (p. 141). To promote the alternative ontology of the minority it is necessary to open 'communitarian spaces of liberty, dialogue and desire.' The construction of a radical pedagogy of youth work is an impulse in that direction. In its development, it is positioned at a certain space in between, an uncertain space in which the ancient impetus to commune is subsumed within the triumphant moment of capital appropriation. The realm of desire is the absolute affirmation of life itself. It is life without compromise, without mediation.

In a moment when most pedagogy of youth work is designed to accommodate people to their slow and incremental death through the logic of need and addiction, such pedagogy can be called nothing kinder than a hospice movement for the victims of capital. For those teachers of youth work who hold hope for the dying but await a life, a politics, a community yet to come, the kindest thing we can say is that they wait in purgatory. For those who seek the communion of the multitude, they seek, live, and love in the life that is produced and produces in the space between.

Both youth work and pedagogy are, in the end, an encounter; an encounter that involves youth and adults. What kind of an encounter is engaged in this praxis of teaching and youth work? Perhaps we could say it is an encounter of potential; that is to say, a tentative,

---

2 'Dejeme decirle a riesgo de parecer ridiculo, que el revolucionario verdadero esta guiado por grandes sentimientos de amor' (Guevara, 2003, p. 216).

provisional encounter. It might be characterized as an exchange between guerillas whispering in the dark, a subversive encounter that points the ways out, reveals nothing, and in fleeing closes off the entrances behind itself. The dialogues of such a pedagogy are conversations in a cloud, voices muffled, conclusions vague, with an imminent sense of danger. There is no safety in such an encounter. It is unstable and decentred. Finally there is no one there. Finally we all become everyone.

References

Aegerter, L.P. (1997). Michelle Cliff and the paradox of privilege. *College English, 59*(8), 898–915.

Agamben, G. (1995). *Homo sacer: Sovereign power and bare life* (D. Heller-Roazen, Trans.). Stanford: Stanford University Press.

Althusser, L. (2001). *Lenin and philosophy and other essays* (B. Brewster, Trans.). New York: Monthly Review Press.

Arieli, M. (1997). The occupational experience of residential child and youth care workers. *Child and Youth Services, 18*(2), 1–10.

Bakhtin, M. (1984). *Problems of Dostoevsky's poetics* (C. Emerson, Ed. & Trans.). Minneapolis: University of Minnesota Press.

Balibar, É. (1994). Subjection and subjectivation. In J. Copjec (Ed.), *Supposing the subject* (pp. 1–15). London: Verso.

Balibar, É. (1998). *Spinoza and politics* (P. Snowden, Trans.). New York: Verso.

Basaglia, F. (1987). *Psychiatry inside out: Selected writings of Franco Basaglia* (N. Scheper-Hughes & A.M. Lovell, Eds., A.M. Lovell & T. Shtob, Trans.). New York: Columbia University Press.

Bateson, G. (1972). *Steps to an ecology of mind: Collected essays in anthropology, psychiatry, evolution, and epistemology*. San Francisco: Chandler Publishing Company.

Bennett, A. (2000). *Popular music and youth culture: Music, identity and place*. Basingstoke: Macmillan.

Bergson, H. (1997). *The creative mind: An introduction to metaphysics*. Sacramento: Citadel Press.

Brake, M. (1985). *Comparative youth culture: The sociology of youth cultures and youth subcultures in America, Britain, and Canada*. New York: Routledge.

Brewster, B. (1994). *A place at the table*. New York: Simon and Schuster.

Bordo, S. (1993). *Unbearable weight: Feminism, Western culture, and the body.* Berkeley: University of California Press.

Burston, D. (1988). *The wing of madness: The life and work of R.D. Laing.* Cambridge, MA: Harvard University Press.

Butler, J. (1990). *Gender trouble: Feminism and the subversion of identity.* New York: Routledge.

Casarino, C. (2002). *Modernity at sea: Melville, Marx, Conrad in crisis.* Minneapolis: University of Minnesota Press.

Casarino, C. (2003). Time matters: Marx, Negri, Agamben, and the corporeal. *Strategies: Journal of Theory, Culture and Politics 16*(2), 185–206.

Castaneda, C. (1991). *Tales of Power.* New York: Washington Square Press.

Chambers, I. (1990). *Border dialogues: Journeys in postmodernity.* New York: Routledge.

Clark, J. (1975). Style. In Hall & Jefferson (1975), (pp. 175–191).

Clech Lam, M. (1996). A resistance role for Marxism in the belly of the beast. In Makdisi, Casarino, & Karl (1996), (pp. 255–64).

Comstock, D.E. (1982). A method for critical research. In E. Bredo & W. Feinberg (Eds.), *Knowledge and values in social and educational research* (pp. 370–90). Philadelphia: Temple University Press.

Damasio, A. (2003). *Looking for Spinoza: Joy, sorrow, and the feeling brain.* Orlando: Harcourt.

de la Haye, A., & Dingwall, C. (1996). *Surfers, soulies, skinheads, and skaters: Subcultural style from the forties to the nineties.* Woodstock: Overlook.

Debord, G. (1967/1994). *The society of the spectacle* (D. Nicholson-Smith, Trans.). New York: Zone.

Deleuze, G. (1986/1988). *Foucault* (S. Hand, Trans.). Minneapolis: University of Minnesota Press.

Deleuze, G. (1988). *Spinoza: Practical philosophy* (R. Hurley, Trans.). San Francisco: City Lights.

Deleuze, G. (1992). *Expressionism in philosophy: Spinoza* (M. Joughin, Trans.). New York: Zone.

Deleuze, G. (1993). *The fold: Leibniz and the baroque* (T. Conley, Trans.). Minneapolis: University of Minnesota Press.

Deleuze, G. (1995). Control and becoming. In *Negotiations 1972–1990* (M. Joughin, Trans.) (pp. 169–76). New York: Columbia University Press.

Deleuze, G. (1997a). Desire and pleasure (D.W. Smith, Trans.). In A.I. Davidson (Ed.), *Foucault and his interlocutors* (pp. 183–94). Chicago: University of Chicago Press.

Deleuze, G. (1997b). *Essays critical and clinical* (D.W. Smith & M. Greco, Trans.). Minneapolis: University of Minnesota Press.

Deleuze, G. (2006). *Nietzsche and philosophy* (H. Tomlinson, Trans.). New York: Columbia University Press.

Deleuze, G., & Guattari, F. (1987). *A thousand plateaus: Capitalism and schizophrenia* (B. Massumi, Trans.). Minneapolis: University of Minnesota Press.

Deleuze, G., & Guattari, F. (1994). *What is philosophy?* (H. Tomlinson & G. Burchell, Trans.). New York: Columbia University Press.

Derrida, J. (1980). *Writing and difference* (A. Bass, Trans.). Chicago: University of Chicago Press.

Derrida, J. (1988). *Limited Inc.* (G. Graff, Ed., S. Weber, Trans.). Evanston, IL: Northwestern University Press.

de Toro, F. & de Toro, A. (Eds.). (1995). *Borders and margins: Post-colonialism and post-modernism.* Madrid: Iberoamericana.

Durrant, M. (1983). *Competency based residential treatment.* New York: Norton.

Engels, F. (1972). *The origin of the family, private property, and the state.* Harmondsworth, Middlesex: Penguin.

Evans, N. (2006). *State of the evidence: What's the connection between the environment and breast cancer?* Breast Cancer Fund.

Fabian, J. (1983). *Time and the other: How anthropology makes its object.* New York: Columbia University Press.

Foucault, M. (1972). *The archaeology of knowledge and the discourse on language* (A.M. Sheridan Smith, Trans.). New York: Pantheon.

Foucault, M. (1975). *Discipline and punish: The birth of the prison* (A.M. Sheridan Smith, Trans.). New York: Random House/Vintage.

Foucault, M. (1976). Two lectures (C. Gordon et al., Trans.). In C. Gordon (Ed.), *Power and knowledge: Selected interviews and other writings 1972–1977* (pp. 78–108). New York: Pantheon.

Foucault, M. (1978/1990). *The history of sexuality: Vol. 1. An introduction* (R. Hurley, Trans.). New York: Vintage.

Foucault, M. (1982). The subject and power. In H. Dreyfus & P. Rabinow (Eds.), *Michel_Foucault: Beyond structuralism and hermeneutics* (pp. 208–28). Chicago: University of Chicago Press.

Foucault, M. (1986). Of other spaces. *Diacritics 16*(Spring), 22–7.

Freud, S. (1963). *General psychological theory* (P. Rieff, Ed.). New York: Scribner.

Garland, E.J. (2004). Facing the evidence: Anti-depressive treatment in children and adolescents. *Canadian Medical Association Journal 170*(4), 489.

Genosko, G. (Ed.). (1996). *The Guattari reader: Collected essays and interviews.* London: Blackwell.

Genosko, G. (Ed.). (2002). *Felix Guattari: An aberrant introduction.* New York: Continuum.

Gershowitz, M., & MacFarlane, A. (1990). The therapeutic potential of emergency shelters. *Child and Youth Services 13*(1), 95–106.

Giroux, H.A. (1996). White panic and the racial coding of violence. In *Fugitive cultures: race, violence, and youth* (pp. 27–54). New York: Routledge.

Giroux, H.A. (2000). *Stealing innocence*. New York: St Martin's.

Giroux, H.A., & McLaren, P. (1986). Teacher education and the politics of engagement: The case for democratic schooling. *Harvard Educational Review 56*(3), 213–38.

Gramsci, A. 1971. *Selections from the prison notebooks of Antonio Gramsci* (Q. Hoare & G.N. Smith, Eds. & Trans). New York: International Publishers.

Gray, J. (2000). *False dawn: The delusion of global capitalism*. New York: New Press.

Guattari, F. (2000). *Three ecologies*. London: Athlone.

Guevara, C. (2003). *Che Guevara reader: Writings by Ernesto Che Guevara on guerrilla strategy, politics, and revolution* (D. Deutschmann, Ed.). St Paul, MN: Ocean Press.

Hall, G.S. (1904). *Adolescence: Vols. 1 & 2*. New York: Appleton.

Hall, S. (1986). The problem with ideology: Marxism without guarantees. *Journal of Communication Inquiry 10*(2), 28–44.

Hall, S., & Jefferson, T. (1975). *Resistance through rituals: Youth sub-cultures in post-war Britain*. London: Unwin Hyman.

Hamm, M.S. (1993). *American skinheads: The criminology and control of hate crime*. Wesport: Oraeger.

Hardt, M., & Negri, A. (2000). *Empire*. Cambridge, MA: Harvard University Press.

Hardt, M., & Negri, A. (2004). *Multitude: War and democracy in the age of empire*. New York: Penguin.

Haug, W.F. (1987). *Commodity aesthetics, ideology, and culture*. New York: International General.

Hebidge, D. (1979). *Subculture: The meaning of style*. New York: Routledge.

Hills, M. (2002). *Fan cultures*. New York: Routledge.

Ignatiev, N., & Garvey, J. (1996). *Race traitor*. New York: Routledge.

Jameson, F. (1991). *Postmodernism, Or, the cultural logic of late capitalism*. Durham, NC: Duke University Press.

Jameson, F. (1996). Actually existing Marxism. In Makdisi, Casarino, & Karl (1996), (pp. 14–54).

Klein, G. (2003). Image, body, and performativity: The constitution of subcultural practice in the globalized world of pop. In Muggleton & Weinzierl (2003), (pp. 41–50).

Klein, N. (2004, September). Pillaging Iraq in pursuit of a neocon utopia. *Harpers 309*, 43–54.

Knight, K. (1997). *Skinhead*. New York: Omnibus.

Korzybsky, A. (1941). *Science and sanity: An introduction to non-Aristotelian systems and general semantics*. Lancaster, PA: International Non-Aristotelian Library Science Press.

Leblanc, L. (1999). *Pretty in punk: Girls' gender resistance in a boys' subculture*. New Brunswick, NJ: Rutgers University Press.

Lewis, S. (2005). *Race against time*. Toronto: Anansi.

Lorde, A. (1984). *Sister outsider*. Berkeley: Crossing Press.

Luhmann, N. (1995). *Social systems*. Stanford: Stanford University Press.

Luzatto, L. (1997). Young rebels and revolutionaries. In G. Levi & J.C. Schmitt (Eds.), *A history of young people in the west: Vol. 2. Stormy evolution to modern times* (C. Volk, Trans.) (pp. 174–231). Cambridge, MA: Harvard University Press/Belknap Press.

Lydon, J., with Zimmerman, K., & Zimmerman, K. (1995). *Rotten: No Irish, no blacks, no dogs: The authorized autobiography, Johnny Rotten of the Sex Pistols*. New York: Picador.

Maffesoli, M. (1996). *The time of the tribes: The decline of individualism in mass society*. London: Sage.

Makdisi, S., Casarino, C., & Karl, R.E. (Eds.). (1996). *Marxism beyond Marxism*. New York: Routledge.

Males, M. (1996). Disowning the future. *New designs for youth development* 12(4), 12–15.

Marcus, G. (1989). *Lipstick traces: A secret history of the twentieth century*. Cambridge, MA: Harvard University Press.

Marshall, G. (1994). *Spirit of 69: A skinhead bible*. Dunoon, Scotland: Author.

Marx, K. (1978/1992). *The Marx Engels reader* (R.C. Tucker, Ed.). New York: Norton.

Marx, K. (1993). *Grundrisse*. New York: Penguin Classics.

Massumi, B. (1996). The autonomy of affect. In P. Patton (Ed.), *Deleuze: A critical reader* (pp. 217–39). Cambridge: Blackwell.

Miller, G. (2005). *R.D. Laing*. Edinburgh: Edinburgh University Press.

Mitterauer, M. (1986). *A history of youth*. Cambridge: Blackwell.

Moore, J.B. (1993). *Skinheads shaved for battle: A cultural history of American skinheads*. Bowling Green, OH: Bowling Green University Popular Press.

Muggleton, D. (2000). *Inside subculture: The postmodern meaning of style*. New York: Berg.

Muggleton, D., & Weinzierl, R. (Eds.). (2003). *The post-subcultures reader.* New York: Berg.

Nealon, J.T. (1998). *Alterity politics: Ethics and performative subjectivity.* Durham, NC: Duke University Press.

Negri, A. (1991). *Marx beyond Marx.* New York: Autonomedia.

Negri, A. (1996a). Constituent republic. In M. Hardt & P. Virno (Eds.), *Radical thought in Italy: A potential politics* (pp. 213–24). Minneapolis: University of Minnesota Press.

Negri, A. (1996b). Twenty theses on Marx: Interpretation of the class situation today. In Makdisi, Casarino, & Karl (1996), (pp. 149–80).

Negri, A. (2003). *Negri on Negri.* New York: Routledge.

Negri, A., & Guattari, F. (1990). *Communists like us: New spaces of liberty, new lives of alliance.* New York: Semiotext(e).

Oliviera, T.C. (1995). Being with street children: Political, romantic, and professional lived experiences in youth work. (Doctoral dissertation, University of Minnestota, 1995). *Dissertation Abstracts International: The Humanities and Social Sciences 56*(4), 1528A.

Perrot, M. (1997). Worker youth: From the workshop to the factory. In G. Levi & J.C. Schmitt (Eds.), *A history of young people in the west: Vol. 2. Stormy evolution to modern times* (C. Volk, Trans.) (pp. 66–116). Cambridge, MA: Harvard University Press/Belknap Press.

Quart, A. (2003). *Branded: The buying and selling of teenagers.* Cambridge, MA: Perseus.

Rabinow, P. (1986). Representations are social facts: Modernity and post-modernity in anthropology. In J. & G.E. Marcus (Eds.), *Writing culture: The poetics and politics of ethnography* (pp. 234–62). Berkeley: University of California Press.

Roediger, D.R. (1991). *The wages of whiteness: Race and the making of the American working class.* New York: Verso.

Sabin, R. (1999). *Punk rock: So what? The cultural legacy of punk.* New York: Routledge.

Said, E.W. (1979). *Orientalism.* New York: Vintage.

Scheper-Hughes, N. (1992). *Death without weeping: The violence of everyday life in Brazil.* Berkeley: University of California Press.

Skott-Myhre, H.A., & Gretzinger, M. (2006). Radical youth work: Creating mutual liberation for youth and adults, Part II. *Journal of Child and Youth Work, 20,* 110–27.

Spinoza, B. (2000). *Ethics* (G.H.R. Parkinson, Ed. & Trans.). Oxford: Oxford University Press.

Spivak, G. (1988). Can the subaltern speak? In C. Nelson & L. Grossberg (Eds.), *Marxism and the interpretation of culture* (pp. 271–313). Basingstoke: Macmillan.

Stahl, G. (2003). Tastefully renovating subculture theory: Making space for a new model. In Muggleton & Weinzierl (2003), (pp. 27–40).

St John, G. (2003). Post-rave technotribalism and the carnival of protest. In Muggleton & Weinzierl (2003), (pp. 65–82).

Stoler, A.L. (1995). *Race and the education of desire: Foucault's* History of sexuality *and the colonial order of things*. Durham, NC: Duke University Press.

St Pierre, E.A. (1997). Nomadic inquiry in the smooth spaces of the field: A preface. *International Journal of Qualitative Studies in Education 10*(3), 265–84.

Surin, K. (1996). The continued relevance of Marxism as a question: Some propositions. In Makdisi, Casarino, & Karl (1996), (pp. 181–213).

Szasz, T.S. (1984). *The myth of mental illness: Foundations of a theory of personal conduct*. New York: Harper Paperbacks.

Tarulli, D., & Skott-Myhre, H.A. (2006). The immanent rights of the multitude: An ontological framework for conceptualizing the issue of child and youth rights. *International Journal of Children's Rights 14*(2), 187–201.

Thompson, S. (2004). *Punk productions: Unfinished business*. Albany: SUNY Press.

Tyler, S.A. (1986). Postmodern ethnography: From document of the occult to occult document. In J. Clifford & G. Marcus (Eds.), *Writing culture: The poetics and politics of ethnography* (pp. 122–40). Berkeley: University of California Press.

Virno, P. (1996). Virtuosity and revolution: The political theory of exodus. In M. Hardt & P. Virno (Eds.), *Radical thought in Italy: A potential politics* (pp. 189–209). Minneapolis: University of Minnesota Press.

Weinzierl, R., & Muggleton, D. (2003). What is 'post-subculture studies' anyway? In Muggleton & Weinzierl (2003), (pp. 3–26).

Wells, P.S. (1999). *The barbarians speak: How the conquered people shaped Roman Europe*. Princeton, NJ: Princeton University Press.

White, M., & Epston, D. (1990). *Narrative means to therapeutic ends*. New York: Norton.

Whittaker, C.R. (1994). *Frontiers of the Roman Empire: A social and economic study*. Baltimore: Johns Hopkins University Press.

Wilder-Mott, C., & Weaklund, J.H. (Eds.). (1981). *Rigor and imagination: Essays from the legacy of Gregory Bateson*. New York: Praeger.

Williams, C. (2005). Althusser and the persistence of the subject: Caroline

Williams speaks with David McInerney. *Borderlands* 4(2). Available at http://www.borderlandsejournal.adelaide.edu.au/

Willis, P.E. (1977). *Learning to labour: How working class kids get working class jobs.* Farnborough: Saxon House.

Wood, R.T. (1999). The indigenous, nonracist origins of the American skinhead subculture. *Youth and Society* 31(2), 131–51.

Žižek, S. (1989). *The sublime object of ideology.* London: Verso.

Zourabichvili, F. (1996). Six notes on the percept (On the relation between the critical and the clinical). In P. Patton (Ed.), *Deleuze: A critical reader* (pp. 188–216). Oxford: Blackwell.

Index

models of time and development (and the science of the body), 42–7; postmodern capitalism and, 52; self-production in unmeasured time, 54; subjects of, 55; teleological time, 42; the time of authentic revolution, 56; time outside of capital, 56; two types of, 54

terrorist (also referred to as the non-state-affiliated combatant; the stateless subject), 77

total subsumption, 105; and the appropriation of resistance, 129; and margins as sites of alternative production, 106; punk and skin subcultures within, 115. *See also under* Hardt and Negri; Marx

Tyler, Steven: the poetic as a vehicle to the discovery of pass-words, 41; postmodern ethnography and evocation, 36–7; two types of 'fantasy' text, 94–5

undocumented bodies: and refugees, 76–7

use value: the concept of (*see under* Marx); as related to ideology and the revolutionary potential of youth work, 158–9

'war on terror': the U.S. termed, 77

Wells, Peter: the native peoples of Europe, 135

'whiteness': and the American revolution, 169–70; as a colonial construction, 167–8; the concept of, 167–74; the purchase of, 170. *See also under* Stoler; Roediger; Said

Whittaker, C.R.: the frontier as an area inviting entrance, 136, 140; Roman and 'barbarian' relations as paradoxical, 135

'working class youth,' 25–6

youth work (occasionally referred to in a broader context as youth-adult relations): accommodation, exploitation, and resistance, 125; administrative and agency structures, 159–60; appropriation of revolutionary impetus and the production of the consuming (bourgeois) subjects, 149, 152; the exploitation of youth and youth workers, 152–3, 154; and becoming-youth, 93; boundaries between youth workers and youth, 152–3, 155, 157; and the capacity to modify material/lived conditions, 156, 158; captured by capital as exchange value, 160; colonial youth work, 142–3; conceptualizations of youth and corresponding approaches of youth workers, 125; communication and conversation within youth work, 131–2; —, in the society of control, 149; —, in the society of discipline, 148–9; differing roles and intentions of youth workers, 124; and democratic practices, 155, 156; Euro-American capitalism (and European modernity) as a framework of, 125–6; the fragmented adolescent, 149; innovation and the appropriation of the revolutionary impetus of youth, 122; managing the pain of, 165–6;